ARISTOTLE ON RELIGION

Aristotle is a severe critic of traditional religion, believing it to be false, yet he also holds that traditional religion and its institutions are necessary if any city, including the ideal city he describes in the *Politics*, is to exist and flourish. This book provides, for the first time, a coherent account of the sociopolitical role that Aristotle attributes to traditional religion despite his rejection of its content. Mor Segev argues that Aristotle thinks traditional religion is politically necessary because it prepares the ground for what he considers the pinnacle of human endeavor: attaining the knowledge of first philosophy, whose objects are real beings worthy of being called gods. Developing this interpretation, Segev goes on to analyze Aristotle's references to the myths of traditional Greek religion and to assess his influence on medieval Jewish and Christian theology and philosophy of religion.

MOR SEGEV is Assistant Professor of Philosophy at the University of South Florida. His work includes articles published or forthcoming in *Oxford Studies in Ancient Philosophy*, the *British Journal for the History of Philosophy, Polis, History of Philosophy Quarterly*, and *Classical World*.

T0381620

ARISTOTLE ON RELIGION

MOR SEGEV

University of South Florida

CAMBRIDGE
UNIVERSITY PRESS

CAMBRIDGE
UNIVERSITY PRESS

University Printing House, Cambridge CB2 8BS, United Kingdom

One Liberty Plaza, 20th Floor, New York, NY 10006, USA

477 Williamstown Road, Port Melbourne, VIC 3207, Australia

314-321, 3rd Floor, Plot 3, Splendor Forum, Jasola District Centre, New Delhi - 110025, India

79 Anson Road, #06-04/06, Singapore 079906

Cambridge University Press is part of the University of Cambridge.

It furthers the University's mission by disseminating knowledge in the pursuit of education, learning and research at the highest international levels of excellence.

www.cambridge.org
Information on this title: www.cambridge.org/9781108401012
DOI: 10.1017/9781108231756

First published 2017
First paperback edition 2019

A catalogue record for this publication is available from the British Library

ISBN 978-1-108-41525-5 Hardback
ISBN 978-1-108-40101-2 Paperback

Contents

v

Figures and Tables

Figures

Tables

Acknowledgments

Many people contributed to the project over several years. Above all, I am indebted to John M. Cooper and Alexander Nehamas, my former dissertation advisers at Princeton University, for many conversations and detailed comments. My project simply could not have taken the shape that it has without their dedication and guidance.

I am grateful to Benjamin Morison, Christian Wildberg, Jonathan Beere, Agnes Callard, Charles Kahn, Stephen Menn, Philip van der Eijk, Eric Hansen, Sukaina Hirji, Brad Inwood, David Kaufman, Michaela McSweeney, Arie Finkelberg, Robert Bolton, Edward Halper, Owen Goldin, Victor Caston, Ronald Polansky, and my anonymous referees for their helpful comments and suggestions, and to Hilary Gaskin of Cambridge University Press for helping me prepare the book for publication.

I wish to thank the Philosophy Department at Princeton University for their support during my graduate studies, and the Graduate School at Princeton University for granting me the Charlotte Elizabeth Procter Honorific Fellowship for the 2013–14 academic year. Thanks are also due to the Graduate School of Ancient Philosophy at the Humboldt Universität zu Berlin for hosting me as a visiting graduate student during the winter semester of 2012. I am also grateful to Roger Ariew, Eric Winsberg, and my other colleagues at the department of philosophy at the University of South Florida.

Finally, I would like to express my deep gratitude to my family and friends for all their help and support over the years.

A shorter version of Chapter 2, also incorporating some discussions from Chapter 1, is forthcoming as a paper titled "Traditional Religion and Its Natural Function in Aristotle" in *Classical World: A Quarterly Journal on Antiquity* 111.3 (Johns Hopkins University Press).

Introduction

In the fourth century BC, the ubiquitous presence of religion in every civilization known to the Greek world was an observable fact. Greek *poleis*, in particular, invariably administered a wealth of religious practices, permeating virtually every facet of their citizens' lives. Festivals, sacrifices, libations, prayers, hymns, and statues in honor of the gods, as well as temples and altars operated by priests, civic and Panhellenic cults, divination, and oracles, were routine. Moreover, the divinities associated with these rituals and institutions had a central place in standard education (essentially covering epic poetry), cultural life (including the recitation of epic poems by rhapsodes and the performance of tragedies in a religious context and usually with plots involving myths about the gods), the visual arts, law, and politics. Judging by the words of the Athenian in Plato's *Laws*, depictions of the traditional gods, through storytelling and live shows, were in fact presented to (prospective) citizens already in infancy (X. 887d; cf. *Republic* 377a).

As such a regular and prominent political phenomenon, traditional religion does not, indeed could not, escape Aristotle's notice. Since he views the *polis* as existing "by nature" (φύσει: *Pol.* I. 2, 1252b30; 1253a2), and since, in his day, religion is embedded in the very fabric of the *polis*, without exception, Aristotle must account for the regular appearance of religion in political organization, either as a predictable, though in principle dispensable, concomitant, or else as serving some natural sociopolitical purpose. He seems to think that proper consideration of the natural functioning of the *polis* requires the second option, and describes the "supervision of religious matters" as a necessary task without which the *polis* simply cannot exist as such (VI. 8, 1322b18–22; VII. 8, 1328b2–13).

The attribution of a naturally necessary function to the institutions of traditional religion is striking given Aristotle's explicit criticisms of the purported uses of traditional religious practices. Divination by dreams is discredited so long as the gods are taken to be involved in it (*Div.* 462b20–2).

Prayers and offerings are deemed ineffective so long as they are expected to make a meaningful contribution to a god's life (*NE* VIII. 14, 1163b15–18). Even if such a contribution were possible, the nature of the gods that Aristotle argues are the only ones that exist denies them any interaction with human beings. These gods are incapable of returning a favor or loving anything or anyone (*MM* II. 11, 1208b26–31). They are denied all "bountiful deeds," and in fact any action whatsoever, save theoretical contemplation on the basis of metaphysical knowledge and understanding (*NE* X. 8, 1178b7–23).

In the absence of any "care for human affairs by the gods" (*NE* X. 8, 1179a24–5), traditional religion seems futile, and it is not at all obvious why Aristotle describes it as necessary, and whether he can in fact be committed to this description. It is no wonder, then, that no comprehensive account of the role of traditional religion in Aristotle's theory has been offered so far, except one that disregards Aristotle's criticisms of traditional religious ideas and practices already noted and ascribes to him the belief in the traditional Greek gods and their benevolent concern for human beings.[1]

Nevertheless, I claim, it is possible for Aristotle to consistently hold that traditional religion and its institutions have a positive role, and a necessary one, in the *polis*, while maintaining that the traditional gods, those that one worships with the hope of pleasing and gaining something in return, do not at all exist. The main aim of the present work is to provide, for the first time, a coherent account of the sociopolitical role Aristotle attributes to traditional religion despite his rejection of the existence of its gods. Ultimately, I shall argue that Aristotle views traditional religion as necessary in order for the *polis* to exist as such because an acquaintance with its (false) conceptions of divinity is a necessary condition for arriving at the knowledge of first philosophy, which must be provided for in any *polis* that

---

[1] R. Bodéüs, *Aristotle and the Theology of the Living Immortals*, trans. J. E. Garrett (Albany, 2000). In addition, two unpublished doctoral theses are devoted to related topics. H. S. Price, *The Philosophies of Religion of Plato and Aristotle* (PhD Dissertation, Swansea University, 1962), compares Aristotle to Plato on theological and religious issues, though he adopts the view that "Aristotle is not seriously concerned with religion as such, and is only interested in it so far as it seems to corroborate his philosophical views" (pp. 187–8). J. B. Rowland, *The Religion of Aristotle* (PhD Dissertation, Temple University, 1953), systematically compiles the relevant evidence for a thorough investigation of Aristotle's view of religion and helpfully points out the basic tension with which my project deals, namely that "Aristotle [a] was somewhat skeptical of [traditional religion] ... [b] was conservative regarding its rites and practices ... [c] had a high estimate of the utility and importance of religion to the state" (p. 191). Shorter works on related topics include W. J. Verdenius, "Traditional and Personal Elements in Aristotle's Religion," *Phronesis* 5.1 (1960), pp. 56–70 and J. K. Feibleman, "Aristotle's Religion," in ed. H. Cairns *The Two-Story World* (New York, 1966), pp. 126–34.

exists according to human nature and is hence directed at the flourishing lives of its individual citizens, in keeping with their potential.

However, a few preliminaries are in order. First, one may wonder whether we are entitled to attribute to Aristotle a criticism of the "traditional" conception of gods, as if there were such a unified entity as "traditional religion." It is precisely the salience of religion in every part and aspect of classical Greek culture that makes it difficult to demarcate it as an independent phenomenon. Indeed, it has been conjectured that it is because religion was "such an integrated part of Greek life that the Greeks lacked a separate word for [it]."[2] Scholars have gone as far as postulating a distinction between different types of Greek religion and Greek *gods*, based on the various cultural contexts in which gods are dealt with and represented, e.g., mythological poetry and cult rituals. Mikalson famously and forthrightly puts forth this view as follows:[3]

> The gods of cult and poetry shared names, and this of course suggests some identification, but, to put it simply, they shared first names only. We do not know whether an Athenian, as he made his morning offering at the little shrine of Zeus Ktesios in his house, thought of Homer's thunder-bearing, cloud-gathering Zeus. There is no evidence that he did, and the two deities, both named Zeus, are very different in both appearance and function.

There is an ongoing controversy among classicists, one that we need not go into in detail, about whether or not this way of viewing the relation between Greek poetry and practiced religion is the correct one.[4] For our present purposes it suffices to say that, even if we allow for the radical differentiation between these systems and the gods they refer to, they share enough in common in order to evaluate them under one heading.

The common denominator between the various forms of (what I shall henceforth call) traditional Greek religion is the anthropomorphic depiction of gods, and Aristotle's criticism applies to all such forms insofar as it is directed at this feature. Let us grant, à la Mikalson, that when Aristotle criticizes the depiction of Zeus as king (or lord, or father) of the gods for its obvious underlying anthropomorphism (*Pol.* I. 2, 1252b24–7), he has the Homeric or Hesiodic Zeus exclusively in mind. Still, the same argument is just as effective, and on the same grounds, considered as mounted against

---

[2] J. N. Bremmer, *Greek Religion* (Cambridge, 1999), p. 2.
[3] J. D. Mikalson, *Honor Thy Gods* (Chapel Hill, 1991), p. 4.
[4] However, see C. Sourvinou-Inwood, "Tragedy and Religion: Constructs and Readings," in C. B. R. Pelling (ed.), *Greek Tragedy and the Historian* (Oxford, 1997), pp. 161–86, for a persuasive rebuttal of Mikalson's theory.

the many manifestations and epithets of Zeus in cult practices. To take the example already used, Zeus Ktēsios ("Zeus [the protector] of property"), worshipped in domestic settings and symbolized by the kadiskos, a small urn, was prayed to with anticipation of being granted "good health and good property" by him (Isaeus, *De cirone*, 16. 3–8).

But, as we shall see in detail in Chapter 1, the divine beneficence or providence underlying that anticipation is strictly rejected by Aristotle, as it rests, again, on the attribution to divinity of specifically human features, such as the ability to perform altruistic deeds or to form friendly or reciprocal relationships with human beings. Thus, even if the gods possessing such features need not be literally man-shaped, or even bring to mind such man-shaped gods (implausible though this may be), Aristotle still would, and does, charge them with obvious and unjustified anthropomorphism, to be contrasted with his own conception of divinity, lacking all properties attributable to human beings, with the exception of the intellect.[5]

Hence, it is the anthropomorphizing of divinity, broadly construed, that separates Aristotle's own view of (what he takes to be) the true gods from the content of what we have termed "traditional religion," a content whose truth Aristotle rejects, whether it appears in Homer, Euripides, Plato, in a public sanctuary, or in the privacy of a household shrine. That anthropomorphic gods are to be reliably found in popular religions, perhaps as an essential component, is supported by modern research in anthropology, psychology, sociology, and classics, *inter alia*.[6] Aristotle's recognition, and systematic criticism, of the anthropomorphism underlying all traditional religion, though preceded by the remarks of earlier thinkers such as Xenophanes, should in itself be viewed as a major contribution to post-Greek culture and thought, especially if one takes into account the extent to which Aristotelian philosophy helped shape (say) medieval Jewish and Muslim theology, with their emphasis and insistence on the entirely non-anthropomorphic nature of God. However, Aristotle goes further. As mentioned earlier, he argues that the same traditional religion whose content he rejects is useful, indeed necessary, for completely

---

[5] And perhaps sense perception in the case of some gods, viz. the celestial bodies, as we shall see in Chapter 3, pp. 98 ff.
[6] S. E. Guthrie refers to a long list of relevant scholars on this point, from Edward Tylor, Robin Horton, Franz Boas, Claude Lévi-Strauss, and Gilbert Murray to Sigmund Freud: *Faces in the Clouds* (Oxford, 1993), pp. 178–9. Guthrie himself argues, more radically, that religion just is (a species of) anthropomorphism, ibid. p. 185.

legitimate political purposes.[7] It is this view, primarily, that the present work aims to elucidate.

As a second preliminary, then, we might do well to explain what a natural, necessary political function is, in Aristotle's theory, so that we would know what to expect him to mean by attributing such a thing to the institutions and practices of traditional religion. Every *polis*, in Aristotle's theory, comes to be (gradually and naturally, out of more basic forms of community [κοινωνία] including the household and the village) "for the sake of living," but remains in existence for the sake of "living well" (*Politics* I. 2, 1252b29–30). Political organization, if it is to function correctly and naturally, must not simply secure the continued existence of its citizens, or even merely their safety or decent living conditions, but must, in addition, ensure that they are capable of leading flourishing lives, in accordance with their individual potentials.[8]

If that were not the case – that is to say, if a community could count as a *polis*, in the full sense of the word just explicated, simply by making sure that its members are healthy and secure – then, Aristotle says, we could have equally talked about "a *polis* of slaves or of the other animals; but, now, such a thing does not exist, because these share neither in flourishing (*eudaimonia*) nor in a life determined by rational choice" (III. 9, 1280a32–4). Since a community that is "slavish" cannot even be *called* a *polis* (IV. 4, 1291a8–10), every institution in the *polis* that is necessary for enabling the citizens to escape "slavishness" by realizing their potential and living self-sufficiently or flourishingly must count as serving a necessary function in the *polis*, and every *polis* must have such institutions as natural parts.

As I alluded to at the beginning, Aristotle views traditional religion, along with its practices, institutions, and the class of citizens maintaining them, as such indispensable natural parts of any correctly organized *polis*. Based on what we have just seen, this does not commit Aristotle to viewing traditional religion as necessary for maintaining the lives of the citizens in the *polis*. Traditional religion may be necessary for any *polis* to exist as such, in his view, because it has some crucial contribution to make to the *flourishing* lives of the citizens without the ability to enable which no *polis*

---

[7] In this, too, he is followed by some prominent medieval philosophers and theologians, as we shall see when we compare Aristotle to Maimonides in Chapter 2, pp. 83 ff. and later on in Chapter 5.

[8] "Living-well" (εὖ ζῆν) and "flourishing" or "happiness" (εὐδαιμονία), in this context, are closely connected and perhaps interchangeable. Aristotle uses them as such, e.g., in VII. 2, 1324a5–13. In III. 9, during a discussion echoing the one surrounding I. 2, 1252b29–30, he again closely associates both terms, this time along with "self-sufficiency" (αὐτάρκεια) (1280b29–1281a2).

can be truly deserving of the title. Now, *eudaimonia*, or human flourishing or happiness, as we learn from the concluding book of the *Nicomachean Ethics* (*NE*), consists primarily in a life of theoretical contemplation based on knowledge or understanding of the first principles of being as such (8, 1178b7–ff.). And so, Aristotle's account of the *polis*, whose staying in existence is for the sake of the flourishing lives of its citizens, "must," in the words of J. M. Cooper, "include the provision that among [its people] will be a group of citizens who live the contemplative life (and so are provided an education that will enable them to live that way)."[9]

It is precisely in the educational program that would enable those citizens who are intellectually capable of it to live contemplative lives of the highest achievable kind that I locate, in what follows, the necessary natural political function of traditional religion in Aristotle's theory. Specifically, I shall argue that traditional religion is necessary for any *polis* to exist as such because it secures the existence in the *polis* of the practice of "first philosophy," the science dealing with the gods of Aristotle's metaphysics (primarily the unmoved movers of the heavenly bodies and spheres, which are of course quite different from the gods of traditional religion). Aristotle considers these gods the most honorable and best beings, and knowing or understanding them is therefore, in his view, the topmost intellectual achievement, and *ipso facto* the top human good, which, to repeat, is precisely what any correctly organized *polis* is naturally aimed at achieving for its citizens.

Apart from the obvious advantage of providing, for the first time, a unified, comprehensive, and hopefully correct account of the role of traditional religion in Aristotle's theory, this book has several additional benefits to offer. First, the function that Aristotle attributes to traditional religion, in my interpretation, makes it clear that his project in the *Politics* is intimately connected to his projects in the *Ethics* and the *Metaphysics*. In particular, the place of traditional religion in Aristotle's political theory sheds light on the fact that he views the primary goal of political organizations (ones that function correctly and naturally, at least) as being theoretical contemplation on the basis of full metaphysical knowledge and understanding, in the manner of the explication of *eudaimonia* in book X of the *NE* and the descriptions of "first philosophy" in the *Metaphysics*. This is not always taken for granted, as scholars often take the (admittedly

---

[9] J. M. Cooper, "Political Community and the Highest Good," in *Being, Nature and Life in Aristotle* (eds. J. G. Lennox and R. Bolton) (Cambridge, 2010), p. 241, n. 40.

few) explicit references to "philosophy" in the *Politics* to signify a broader notion of musical education, which would be the "political analogue of and substitute for contemplation proper, which they presume to be politically inaccessible, even in a best regime."[10] But the role of traditional religion in Aristotle as I present it in what follows should count as evidence against these views, since it shows that *poleis*, if they are to count as such, in Aristotle's view, must make use of traditional religion precisely for the sake of enabling their citizens to engage in theoretical contemplation "proper," as far as they are able.

Second, the role of traditional religion in Aristotle, as I interpret it, shows that Aristotle prefigures and sometimes directly influences theories of theologians and philosophers of religion prevalent from the Middle Ages onward. As we shall see in Chapter 5, the criticism of anthropomorphisms with regard to the gods, with the apprehension that such depictions might nevertheless be useful for arriving at knowledge of *the true* God or gods (whatever their nature might be and however adequately we may be able to grasp it), can be found in the writings of Moses Maimonides and Albertus Magnus, with Aristotle as the clear origin. Through these figures these ideas have had a lasting influence.

Third, Aristotle's view of traditional religion may be of interest to a general audience as well. It exemplifies the possibility of learning certain truths even, and in some cases perhaps exclusively, on the basis of falsehoods, a possibility that is both intriguing and easily ignored. We may also learn from this view, quite generally, to look attentively for the usefulness in regularities, as Aristotle does. Even when the prospect does not seem promising, we may stumble, again as Aristotle often does, on fascinating and surprising results.[11]

There is no extant treatise by Aristotle dedicated to a systematic discussion of traditional religion. The list of Aristotle's works in Diogenes Laertius' *Lives of the Philosophers* includes titles of works on relevant topics, including *On Prayer, Concerning the Mythological Animals,* and *Homeric Puzzles*. Hesychius' list adds to these a work on *Hesiodic Puzzles* and, perhaps most relevant of all, a work on *Puzzles Pertaining to Divine Things*

---

[10] D. J. DePew, "Politics, Music and Education in Aristotle's Best State," *A Companion to Aristotle's Politics*, ed. D. Keyt and F. D. Miller (London, 1991), pp. 346–80, at n. 2. DePew rejects this position. We shall return to this controversy in Section 6.2.

[11] One example is Aristotle's theory of dreams, which I have dealt with *in extenso* elsewhere, see M. Segev, "The Teleological Significance of Dreaming in Aristotle," *Oxford Studies in Ancient Philosophy* 43 (2012), pp. 107–41.

(ἀπορημάτων θείων). Quite clearly, based on surviving fragments, the lost dialogue *De philosophia*, though of course primarily dealing with philosophy, was also imbued with discussions comparing and contrasting philosophical traditions with religious ones. Of the work *On Prayer* we have one surviving fragment, quoted directly and referred to by name in Simplicius' commentary on *De caelo* (485.19–22=*On Prayer*, Fr. 1, Ross). The fragment states, rather cryptically, only that "God either is intellect (νοῦς) or is something beyond." The task of reconstructing Aristotle's view of traditional religion, therefore, largely depends on examining his various remarks on the phenomenon in the context of discussing other matters.

In Chapter 1, I show that Aristotle does not – and, given his philosophical commitments, cannot – countenance the existence of traditional, anthropomorphic gods. Indeed, Aristotle does not object merely to the depiction of gods as having human shapes or living in political communities. He rejects in principle any characterization of the gods as capable of intention, deliberation, communication, or providence. It is true that Aristotle speaks (in the *NE* and *Topics*) of the importance of honoring the gods, and compares our relation to the gods to our relation to our parents (in the *Ethics*). But honoring the gods may well be important without there being any gods capable of acknowledging the honor. As for our friendship (*philia*) toward the gods, Aristotle in fact thinks it remains unreciprocated. Accordingly, we see that Aristotle wishes to replace existing traditional explanations of phenomena such as divination through dreams (in *Div.*) or good luck (in *EE*), normally appealing to divine intervention, with naturalistic accounts.

In addition to criticizing the belief in anthropomorphic and providential gods, Aristotle also provides a critical account of a major line of reasoning leading to such a belief. In his version of Plato's Allegory of the Cave (Cicero *N.D.* II. 37. 95–6=*De phil.* Fr. 13a Ross), Aristotle presents a double criticism of Plato's theory of Forms and the teleological argument (or "argument from design") for the existence of god(s). Aristotle thinks Plato illegitimately infers the existence of separable Forms from mathematical objects similar but inferior to them and from perceptible objects similar but inferior to both. Aristotle thinks there is an analogy to be made between Plato's fallacy and the "teleological argument," which infers the existence of intelligent benevolent gods from the natural world presumed to be created by them and from artifacts created by human artisans.

Despite explicitly rejecting the content of traditional religion, Aristotle allows for the possibility that traditional religion employing just that content might nevertheless be useful. In fact, his view is that traditional religion is not only useful but politically necessary. I deal with that view in Chapter 2. In the *Politics*, Aristotle is committed to viewing the "supervision of matters pertaining to divinity" and the class of citizens maintaining it, namely priests, as necessary in order for any city to exist as such, including the ideal *polis* of books VII–VIII. The religion that Aristotle retains even in the "city of our prayers" is clearly an unrevised form of the traditional religion of his day, whose content, involving the anthropomorphic and mythical depictions of gods, he rejects. Traditional religion is kept, I argue, because it serves a necessary function. As I have said, it prepares the ground for what Aristotle considers the pinnacle of human endeavor: attaining the knowledge that constitutes first philosophy. Religion performs this function by exposing citizens to the traditional depictions of divinity. These, in turn, generate in the citizens with the right potential the sense of "wonder" (*thaumazein*) at the gods that guides them from such mythological conceptions to an inquiry into the nature of the true god(s) of Aristotle's *Metaphysics*. The content of traditional religion, then, is naturally used by the *polis* via its religious institutions for the attainment of a beneficial (albeit rare) outcome, even though that content is conventional and unnatural (not to mention false). There are parallels to that phenomenon. Aristotle views money, for instance, as having an integral role in a natural (albeit rare) sociopolitical process, namely natural wealth acquisition, though it is an unnatural and intrinsically valueless convention. Finally, though Aristotle does view traditional religion as useful for maintaining social stability, and possibly also for basic moral education, these uses cannot exhaust the natural function of the phenomenon in his theory.

The true gods of Aristotle's metaphysics, i.e., the unmoved movers, share something significant in common with humans, insofar as the latter may engage in, and the former in fact consist of, intellectual contemplative activity. Thus, gods are not merely the objects of the highest science; they are also the paradigms for human action. Reflecting on them is simultaneously both the topmost intellectual achievement and an assimilation of their very condition. Chapter 3 aims to elucidate both of these facts, and to explain why the gods of traditional religion are the proper tools for motivating people to learn them. Traditional gods are the appropriate type of thing to lead one toward an inquiry into the nature of true gods because they are easy to identify with and in fact share in the definition of "god" along with true gods such as the unmoved mover(s) of the heavens and the celestial bodies. Since traditional gods also share in the definition of "human being," and since, though powerful and everlasting, they also lead political and social lives and are therefore not, strictly speaking, self-sufficient, as true gods should be, they are effective in raising the question of how and to what extent, being human, one might imitate the activity characteristic of gods – that is to say, theoretical contemplation on the basis of knowledge and understanding (preferably with the gods as its objects).

Aristotle thinks that we may imitate the divine activity in question only by coming to know ourselves. This may appear paradoxical, until we take into consideration the fact that human beings, in his theory, essentially consist in intellect, which is divine. By learning of our own selves (which requires friendship), first by becoming aware of our particular personality and characteristics, we gradually progress toward the apprehension of our true nature – our intellect. Fully knowing this true nature, namely the intellect, involves knowing its best possible application, and that is in turn tantamount to knowing the nature of the gods. By *activating* this knowledge, finally, we approximate the condition of these gods, albeit necessarily only temporarily and imperfectly.

In Chapter 4, I go on to survey and analyze Aristotle's discussions of particular religious myths. Aristotle's various references to the myths of traditional Greek religion, especially as related in Homer and Hesiod, permeate his writings. They appear in his discussions of topics as diverse as metaphysics, ethics, politics, and music. Aristotle is as likely to use such myths as evidence for his own theories as he is to rebut the accounts they seem to express. Hence, it is sometimes said that the only criterion by which Aristotle decides to "approve of one of these ancient accounts and reject the other ... appears to be simply that underlying one account he detects a view in agreement with his own, while underlying the other he discerns a view that he wants to reject."[12]

However, the uses that Aristotle himself ascribes to myths in general, as analyzed in Chapters 1–3, shed light on his positive reasons for dismissing the content of certain myths. Aristotle thinks that myths are useful for social stability and moral habituation. In addition, he thinks that some myths usefully reflect the norms and practices of the past. I argue that when Aristotle is willing to consider the content of myths, he generally has these uses in mind. Some myths are too unclear to be taken seriously,[13] and others are merely coincidental results from other myths. Nevertheless, whenever a myth is both independent and intelligible, but turns out not

---

[12] Palmer, J., "Aristotle on the Ancient Theologians," *Apeiron* 33.3 (2000), pp. 181–205, at p. 201.
[13] Ibid., pp. 182–91.

to be indicative of any truth, Aristotle can (and often does) still explain its usefulness by appealing to at least one of the normal uses of the content of traditional religion. Importantly, since *all* traditional myths concerning the gods are useful toward the fulfillment of the necessary function of traditional religion, namely the initiation of philosophical inquiry, it is specifically the non-necessary uses of the content of traditional religion that distinguish particular myths from one another.

In Chapter 5, I assess the influence of Aristotle's view of religion on Maimonides and, through him, though with some significant differences, on Albertus Magnus.

Aristotle's view of religion has had a tremendous and lasting influence on subsequent philosophy of religion, especially through the mediation of medieval Jewish, Christian, and Muslim thinkers. Maimonides – a self-proclaimed Aristotelian – makes conscious use of Aristotle's writings in his effort to delineate the various aims of the Torah. In the *Guide of the Perplexed*, Maimonides comes very close to Aristotle's view of the usefulness of anthropomorphic depictions of divinity (as presented in Chapters 1–3). Similarly to Aristotle's threefold distinction between the uses of the false anthropomorphic depictions of the gods, Maimonides says that the Law and its commandments, with their various anthropomorphisms and parables, which intellectuals should not interpret literally, are intended to (1) develop true opinions on the way toward philosophical apprehension, (2) deter people from wrongdoing, and (3) promote moral excellence (*Guide* III. 26–8).

Specifically on the issue of the use of traditional anthropomorphic depictions of divinity for reaching philosophical knowledge, Maimonides' reliance on Aristotle is perhaps most clearly brought up in his analysis of the story and character of Abraham (*Guide* III. 29). Maimonides thinks that Abraham's philosophical apprehension resulted from a rejection of the various dicta of the star-religion prevalent in his day. Examining these erroneous views, according to Maimonides, is still necessary in order to understand the meaning and aim of Jewish Law. Like Aristotle, then, Maimonides views the exposure to erroneous depictions of divinity as a crucial step toward full philosophical knowledge, which, in his opinion, cannot be properly attained at just any stage of intellectual development, just as no infant could survive "being fed wheaten bread, meat and wine" (*Guide* I. 33; trans. following Friedländer).

Maimonides' reading and use of Aristotle's view of traditional religion and its uses is valuable for understanding the influence that view has had on the rest of theology and philosophy in the Abrahamic traditions. Immediately influenced by Maimonides' interpretation is Albertus Magnus, through whose influence (together with his immediate pupil Thomas Aquinas) Aristotle's view has continued to influence Christian thought for centuries.

CHAPTER I

Aristotle's Rejection of the Content of Traditional Religion

The only gods whose existence Aristotle acknowledges are radically different from those depicted in traditional Greek religion. The true gods, he thinks, include first and foremost the ultimate causes of reality, i.e., the unmoved movers of the heavenly bodies and spheres, described in the *Metaphysics* as each consisting of an instance of the best, most pleasant, eternal intellectual activity (Λ. 7, 1072b14–30). As mentioned in the Introduction, he also makes it clear in the *Ethics* that the intellectual activity of which these gods consist is the only one available to them (*NE* X. 8, 1178b7–23; cf. *MM* II. 11, 1208b26–31). The activities traditionally attributed to the gods, such as intervening in human affairs or interacting with human beings in ways familiar to us from cases of interpersonal exchanges in humans, are in Aristotle's view all completely inaccessible to these true gods.[1]

It is appropriate to ask, since these eternal substances are considerably different from the gods as depicted in traditional religion, what motivated Aristotle to designate them as gods at all. We shall return to this question, and to the commonality between Aristotle's gods and the gods of traditional religion, to the extent that it exists, in Chapters 2 and 3. The purpose of this chapter is to establish the point that, in Aristotle's view, whatever it is that these two types of being may share in common, they must also differ in at least two crucially important respects. First, for him, unlike the traditional gods, the unmoved movers of the heavenly bodies in fact exist. Second, unlike the gods of traditional religion, the true gods of Aristotle's system lack not only humanlike appearance, but also any humanlike intentional behavior. They are completely unresponsive to us and oblivious to our needs. For Aristotle, then, there can be no divine providence or supervision.

---

[1] As we shall see, Aristotle also seems to accept the divinity of the heavenly bodies themselves. But these, in Aristotle's view, are not capable of performing the activities traditionally ascribed to the gods any more than the unmoved movers can. The activities available to the heavenly bodies, according to Aristotle, include, apart from eternal theoretical contemplation, only eternal physical motion in a fixed circle, and possibly eternal, unchanging sense perception, most likely restricted to self-perception. See Chapter 3.

Indeed, scholars widely agree both that Aristotle rejects the existence of anthropomorphic gods and that beings whose existence and divinity he does accept, primarily the prime mover, cannot be conceived of as providential gods in any way.[2] However, it is in principle possible that Aristotle, though both rejecting (certain aspects of) the anthropomorphic depictions of divinity and upholding the existence of completely non-providential gods such as the unmoved movers of the heavens, nonetheless does countenance a form of divine providence. This possibility must be given due consideration. Consider an equivalent case. Xenophanes of Colophon, whose criticism of anthropomorphic conceptions of the gods in fact supplies the model for Aristotle's rejection of the gods of traditional religion (see Section 1.1), posits a "greatest" deity whom he quite clearly describes as non-providential (DK B23–6). And yet, though Xenophanes is sometimes interpreted as a monotheist, his fragments do not seem to exclude the possibility of other gods existing alongside that supreme deity.[3] Such additional gods, if Xenophanes thinks they exist, would surely not resemble us in appearance and would not be morally imperfect. Otherwise, Xenophanes would be exposing his view to the same criticisms he mounts against the Homeric and Hesiodic depictions of divinity, which he finds morally reprehensible (B11). However, such gods may nevertheless be in some sense providential.[4]

Similarly, Aristotle can in principle be committed to the existence of divine providence conferred by certain (comparatively) non-anthropomorphic gods different from his true gods. Such a view has indeed been attributed to him. R. Bodéüs has argued that Aristotle is committed to the existence of providential and benevolent gods – the same ones, in fact, as those worshipped in traditional Greek religion – even though he renounces the

---

[2] See, for example, G. R. Lear, *Happy Lives and the Highest Good: An Essay on Aristotle's* Nicomachean Ethics (Princeton, 2004), p. 195; S. Menn, "Aristotle's Theology," in C. Shields (ed.), *The Oxford Handbook of Aristotle* (Oxford, 2012), pp. 422–64 at pp. 423–4; M. R. Johnson, *Aristotle on Teleology* (New York, 2005), p. 262 and p. 275, discussed further later on in this chapter.

[3] For a defense of this view and a survey of the controversy on the issue of whether or not Xenophanes should be interpreted as a monotheist, see J. Lesher, "Xenophanes," in *The History of Western Philosophy of Religion* v. 1 ed. G. Oppy and N. Trakakis (Oxon, 2014), pp. 41–52 at pp. 41–5. Lesher concludes that "we must acknowledge that the case for viewing Xenophanes as an exclusive monotheist, based on the fragments of his poetry that have come down to us, is more suggestive than definitive" (ibid., p. 44).

[4] Lesher brings up this possibility, too (ibid., p. 47): "[Xenophanes] may consistently think of the divine as possessing a body of some (extremely unusual) sort, or a mind of some (extraordinary) kind, as well as a will of some (superlative degree of) goodness." Lesher, though, is not committed as

mythological depictions of them.[5] Thus, according to Bodéüs, though Aristotle would agree that it is baseless and misleading to say that "Zeus is a king, Ares an amorous warrior[,] Leto becomes a she-wolf, etc.," we should entertain the possibility that for him "Zeus, Ares, and Leto may be perfectly real beings."[6] For Bodéüs, this is "our best hypothesis" concerning Aristotle's position, "[u]ntil the contrary is proven."[7]

In order to "prove the contrary," and show that Aristotle leaves no room for divine providence in his philosophical system, we shall first delineate his explicit rejection of anthropomorphic depictions of divinity. We shall see that the type of anthropomorphism of the divine that Aristotle rejects extends not only to descriptions of the gods as wearing human clothes or throwing spears in battle, but indeed to any intentional conduct whatsoever, including any action that could plausibly be described as providential or beneficent. Then, we shall survey the presumed evidence for divine providence in Aristotle's view. As we shall see, even though Aristotle speaks of the importance of honoring the gods, and occasionally compares the relation between gods and humans to relations between different groups of humans (e.g., parents and children), these remarks are not meant to attribute beneficence or intentionality to divinity. Again, though Aristotle discusses such phenomena as good luck and divination through dreams, he explains them naturalistically, without resorting either to popular conceptions of the divine or to religious doctrine. As we shall see in the final section of this chapter, Aristotle occasionally even indicates his positive reasons for mistrusting the content of traditional religion, including the idea of divine providence. A fragment from *De philosophia*, in which Aristotle expounds his own version of Plato's Allegory of the Cave, presents a detailed criticism of the "teleological argument" for the existence of god(s), representative of the type of reasoning leading to the belief in divine providence. Having established these conclusions, we would face the task, undertaken in Chapter 2, of explaining how Aristotle could ascribe a necessary political function to traditional religion while rejecting its content.

to whether such features would in Xenophanes' view pertain to the "greatest" deity, to the subsidiary deities (if they exist), or to both.

[5] R. Bodéüs, *Aristotle and the Theology of the Living Immortals*, trans. J. E. Garrett (Albany, 2000), pp. 81–6.

[6] R. Bodéüs, ibid., p. 85. Bodéüs makes it clear that the gods of traditional religion in which Aristotle believes are not to be confused with the eternal substances of his metaphysics, like the prime mover, which are only called gods "by analogy" (ibid., pp. 26–9). Cf. p. 17, n. 10.

[7] Ibid., p. 85.

1.1 Aristotle's Rejection of Anthropomorphic Depictions of Divinity

The most explicit criticism of the content of traditional religion in ancient Greek philosophy is found in the fragments of Xenophanes, who rejects the anthropomorphic depictions of divinity at the basis of traditional religion in general (DK B14–16), with special emphasis on the attribution of morally reprehensible behavior to the Olympian gods in Homer and Hesiod (B11). Aristotle explicitly aligns himself with that view. In the *Poetics*, he tells us that Xenophanes may have been right in thinking that "the things [said] concerning the gods," though of course widely believed, are "neither what is better to say nor true" (1460b35–1461a1). In *Politics* I. 2, Aristotle more specifically echoes Xenophanes' critique of the anthropomorphic depictions of divinity (though without mentioning Xenophanes by name), this time actively endorsing it.[8] He says:

> All people say that the gods are ruled by a king for this reason, namely that some of them to this day are, and others in the distant past were, themselves ruled by a king. Just as human beings make the shapes [of the gods] similar to their own, thus [they] also [do this in the case of] the gods' ways of life. (*Politics* I. 2, 1252b24–7)

Here, Aristotle applies his criticism to a particular conviction at the center of popular Greek religion. The designation of Zeus as the king of the gods is of course found in Hesiod (e.g., *Theog.* 886: Ζεὺς δὲ θεῶν βασιλεύς), as well as in other ancient Greek epic poems.[9] Aristotle himself attributes the description of Zeus as "ruling as king and governing" (βασιλεύειν καὶ ἄρχειν) to "the poets" (οἱ ποιηταί) (*Metaph.* N. 4, 1091b4–6), and, by undermining its legitimacy, he repudiates the contents of the religious tradition associated with, and to a large extent informed or even constituted by, the works of such people.

---

[8] G. Boys-Stones argues that Xenophanes' fragments (B14–16) do not in fact criticize traditional religion, but rather "merely point out that other people do, and other species might, depict their gods in other ways"; see "Introduction," in *The History of Western Philosophy of Religion* v. 1, edited by G. Oppy and N. Trakakis (Oxon, 2014), pp. 1–22 at pp. 4–5. But, whatever may be said of Xenophanes' intent, Aristotle certainly does interpret him as criticizing traditional conceptions of the gods, as is clear from the *Poetics* passage described here. Aristotle also clearly follows that critical line himself, as is clear from *Politics* I. 2; see also J. Lesher, "Xenophanes," p. 46.

[9] Hesiod: *Theog.* 71, 923; *Works* 668. *Cycle*: *Thebaid*, fr. 3 [Kinkel]; *Cypria*, fr. 6 [Kinkel]. *Hymn to Demeter*, 335. A similar point may be made about Homer, though, as G. M. Calhoun notices, Homer, in contrast to these other texts, consistently designates Zeus as ἄναξ rather than βασιλεύς ("Zeus the Father in Homer," *Transactions and Proceedings of the American Philological Association* 66 [1935], pp. 1–17).

Now, it has been argued that Aristotle's criticism of the anthropomorphic nature of Greek religion is *restricted* to the works of the ancient poets and theologians, which leaves room for Aristotle to view *some* traditional religious views concerning the divine, i.e., "those that everyone shares and those of highly regarded minds" (corresponding to the two types of *endoxa* discussed in *Topics* I. 14), as a respectable source of truths on such matters.[10] One immediate problem with this proposal is that we simply have no means of distinguishing the (false) "theological" views of the ancient poets concerning the gods from the (supposedly true) "consensus" of the many or of the wise. When Aristotle says, as we have already mentioned, that the portrayal of gods as ruled by kings is due to a projection onto them of people's personal experience with being ruled thus (*Pol.* I. 2, 1252b24–7), he clearly criticizes this belief for its underlying anthropomorphism (i.e., the idea that gods are of such a nature as to be capable of living in a monarchical political system, similarly to humans), which is present in the portrayal of these gods in practically every extant epic poem. However, Aristotle attributes this belief to "all people" (πάντες). This formulation indicates that the belief in question is universal.[11]

Furthermore, far from accepting the consensus view about gods, Aristotle directly criticizes the opinions of "the many" concerning the gods. Aristotle follows his statement in the *Poetics* passage quoted earlier (1460b35–1461a1), i.e., that things said concerning the gods (τὰ περὶ θεῶν) may be "neither what is better to say nor true," as Xenophanes thinks, by saying that these things are "nevertheless certainly in accordance with opinion" (ἀλλ᾽ οὖν φασι). The context of this remark is a discussion of the descriptions found in poetry, and so this passage makes it clear (as does the one from *Pol.* I. 2 about Zeus as King of the gods) not only that Aristotle does not accept as authoritative the beliefs of the many or of the wise concerning religious matters, but that he thinks of these beliefs as closely connected, if not identical, to the religious content found in the ancient poets.

---

[10] R. Bodéüs, *Aristotle*, pp. 113–14. In fact, Bodéüs thinks of the traditional views in question as "the primary basis for all knowledge about the gods' nature" (ibid., p. 113). He argues that the *endoxa* Aristotle accepts as truths regarding matters of religion are not even affected by (if anything, they themselves affect) his own metaphysical theory (which, for Bodéüs, does not deal with gods at all, but rather only with beings that are in some way *analogous* to gods; see ibid., pp. 26–9), giving them a privileged status as sources of true information concerning the gods over both theology (understood as the practice of poets) and "theoretical philosophy" (ibid., pp. 185–7). For a recent criticism of Bodéüs on these points see Blyth, "Heavenly Soul in Aristotle," *Apeiron* 48.4 (2015), pp. 427–65 at p. 457 n. 59 and p. 458 and n. 62; Blyth, "The Role of Aristotle's *Metaphysics* 12.9," *Methexis* 28 (2016), pp. 76–92 at p. 86 n. 34.

[11] As Bodéüs himself says, *Aristotle*, pp. 113 and 255 n. 22.

Aristotle does not distinguish between different classes of contents in traditional religion, let alone does he recognize a hierarchy of such classes, and he ought not to have done so, given the obvious overlaps and mutual influence (indeed, possible identity) there must have been between the ideas presented in poetry and theology and those making up the "consensus" view. When we discuss Aristotle's views of traditional religion, then, we must understand this term as including the entirety of these ideas. And, as we have seen so far, Aristotle decisively dismisses and rejects these ideas.

This critical outlook is further attested in a key passage from *Metaphysics* Λ. 8, to which we shall return in the following chapters:

> It has been transmitted to us through the ancients and very-old ones, and has been passed on to future generations, in the form of a myth, that these [sc. the highest substances, acting as primary movers of the heavenly bodies][12] are gods, and that the divine encloses the whole of nature. The rest has been added, mythically, with a view to persuading the masses and for its usefulness in supporting the laws and bringing about the general advantage. For they say that they [sc. the gods] are man-shaped or resemble certain other animals, and [they add] other things, which are consequent on or similar to those already said. If one were to take the first point by itself, separately from those [additions], namely that they think the first substances are gods, they would be thought to have spoken excellently (lit. divinely), and though every art/science (τέχνη) and philosophy have probably been discovered as far as possible and destroyed again and again, these opinions of theirs have been preserved like remains up until now. The ancestral opinion, that we have obtained through the first ones, is clear to us only to this extent (ἐπὶ τοσοῦτον). (1074a38-b14)

Here Aristotle says that one needs to strip the tenets of popular Greek religion[13] of all their anthropomorphic and mythical features in order to uncover the basic, true, and philosophically significant theses that they conceal – in this case, that there necessarily are eternal unmoved movers of the heavenly bodies, which are substances, and that these beings are gods, i.e., eternally existing tremendously powerful beings, exactly as Aristotle's philosophical analysis in Λ. 7 and the prior part of Λ. 8 has established.

---

[12] Taking οὗτοι at 1074b3 to refer to the unmoved movers of heavenly bodies, as opposed to the heavenly bodies themselves, with J. Palmer, "Aristotle on the Ancient Theologians", *Apeiron* 33.3 (2000), pp. 181–205 at pp. 198–200. See p. 59.

[13] Whether or not Palmer is correct in attributing the tradition in question, not to Aristotle's immediate predecessors, but rather to those living "in the period before the most recent cataclysm" (ibid., p. 198), Aristotle must have thought of this tradition as being at least mediated by popular Greek religion and its particular (say, mythical) modes of presentation, which is the main object of the criticism here.

Such philosophical truths, then, for Aristotle, are independent of the content of traditional religion (though our learning of them might depend on the exposure to such content, or even on religious belief, to some extent, e.g., given our particular cognitive mechanism). Moreover, it is not just that the content of traditional religion, constituted by anthropomorphic, mythical depictions of divinity, is *separable* from philosophical truth. For Aristotle, there is simply *nothing* true in mythical stories about the gods or in religious beliefs, even though there *is* truth in the ancient wisdom on which some of them are based.

Even though the explicit object of criticism in the texts discussed earlier is the attribution to gods of such features as human appearance or human ways of life, the scope of Aristotle's criticism of traditional religion and its anthropomorphic depiction of divinity is arguably much broader. In the Λ. 8 passage quoted earlier, he says that the mythical additions to the true ancestral opinion he describes include, apart from the human or animal shape of gods, also "other things, which are consequent on or similar to those already said." Those "other things" would plausibly include the features standardly attributed to gods in myths that portray the gods as humanlike, most importantly for our purposes intentional behavior as well as interactions and communication with humans. If so, then Aristotle rejects a fundamental belief at the heart of traditional religion. It is easy enough to envisage a version of traditional religion that excludes, perhaps even bars as a matter of principle, any depiction of divinity as having human (or any) shapes or as engaging in political action (the Abrahamic religions generally exclude such features, for instance). It is much more difficult to imagine traditional religion, particularly Greek traditional religion, being sustained without belief in divine intention or intentional action (indeed, the rejection of such a belief would deviate from many prominent versions of Abrahamic monotheism as well).

And Aristotle gives us more reasons, and more explicit ones, for thinking that his rejection of the content of traditional religion does extend to divine will. In *EE* VIII. 3, he says that human beings should live according to their own "ruling principle" (ἀρχή) (1249b11). He goes on to speak of this ruling principle as "the theoretical faculty" (τὸ θεωρητικόν), which he then seems to assimilate to God (1249b13–14). "God" here, then, corresponds to the use of the word in the *Metaphysics* to designate the eternal, theoretical, intellectual activity of which we humans may partake, albeit only in a deficient, discontinuous, and temporary way (Λ. 7, 1072b14–18). The use of the singular noun "God" should not make us think that it is only a single deity, say the prime mover, that is appealed to here. As S. Menn notes, Aristotle "often uses 'god' as a collective singular, like 'man,'"[14] and he seems to be doing so both in Λ. 7, 1072b28–30 and here (in *EE* VIII. 3, 1249b13–14). The class "God," which Aristotle in *EE* VIII. 3 assimilates to "the theoretical faculty," then, would include all gods whose existence Aristotle acknowledges, all of which essentially have (or even consist of) eternal theoretical activity. This reading is supported by the immediately preceding chapter of *EE* (VIII. 2), according to which we may know that *God* initiates movement in the soul *because* "the divine [element] within us in a way moves everything" (1248a25–7). The divine element within us, as Aristotle states using almost identical language in *NE* X. 7, is theoretical *nous* (1177b26–1178a8).[15]

According to *EE* VIII. 3, then, one should lead one's life accepting the intellect, or more specifically "God" who essentially has or *is* an intellect, as one's governing principle. But one should do so only in one crucially specific sense. Such a governing principle, that is, should not determine our actions in the way in which, for example, the principles of medical science guide a doctor treating a patient. Rather, humans should perform their actions having (the imitation or knowledge of) God as their target, similarly to the way in which a doctor operates on patients for the sake of producing health in them. God, as Aristotle puts it there, is not a "ruler that gives commands" (ἐπιτακτικῶς ἄρχων: 1249b13–14). M. R. Johnson appropriately appeals to this text to show that Aristotle's suggested analogy between God or the first unmoved mover and an army general in *Met.* Λ. 10, 1075a13–15 cannot possibly be taken to imply that this being acts "in the way a providential or creator god might."[16] He also concludes, based on this text, more generally, that "Aristotle explicitly repudiates the anthropomorphic conception of the gods, which ought to include the picture of gods as craftsmen."[17] Indeed, if Aristotle in *EE* VIII. 3 uses "God" as a collective singular, as he seems to, this idea should be taken to apply more generally to the gods, or to those of them that Aristotle thinks exist.

---

[14] S. Menn, "Aristotle's Theology," p. 422.

[15] The reference to *nous* in Aristotle's question at 1248a28–9 ("what would be greater than knowledge <and *nous*> except for God?") is due to an addition by Spengel based on the Latin version (*De bona fortuna*), which reads: "*scientia et intellectu*." Even if this is a part of the original text, which is very doubtful, Aristotle's point may simply be that God, namely pure and eternal intellectual activity, is superior to other instances of such an activity and the capacity for such an activity, e.g., in humans. P. Van der Eijk, for example, reads this line as indicating that God is superior to the human intellect, though he doubts that God refers here to the gods of Aristotle's *Metaphysics*, see "Divine Movement and Human Nature in *Eudemian Ethics* 8, 2," *Hermes* 117 (1989), pp. 24–42.

[16] M. R. Johnson, *Aristotle on Teleology* (New York, 2005), p. 275.

[17] Ibid., p. 262.

In Aristotle's view, divinity exists, and is indeed responsible for the initiation of all movement both in our souls and in the universe at large. Nevertheless, divinity is denied, not only any specifically human action, but any intentional behavior whatsoever.[18]

1.2 Aristotle's Rejection of Divine Providence

Since Aristotle's criticism of anthropomorphic depictions of divinity extends to depicting divinity as exhibiting intentional behavior in general, as we have seen, it is difficult to imagine in what way divine providence might still figure in his theory. However, several texts in the extant *Corpus Aristotelicum* may at first sight seem to suggest that Aristotle accepts the existence of providential and beneficent gods.[19] It is worthwhile to consider these texts carefully, and to see whether they can really support such a view. In what follows in this section we shall see that they cannot, and that some of these texts are in fact quite revealing of Aristotle's dismissal of the idea of divine providence.

Aristotle's presentation of traditional ideas concerning divine providence is sometimes glaringly noncommittal. Two prominent examples are given in the *NE*:

> If anything (else) is (also) a gift of the gods to humans, it is reasonable that *eudaimonia* should be god-given ... (εἰ μὲν οὖν καὶ ἄλλο τί ἐστι θεῶν δώρημα ἀνθρώποις, εὔλογον καὶ τὴν εὐδαιμονίαν θεόσδοτον εἶναι . . .). (I. 9, 1099b11–18)
> ... For if there comes to be any care for human affairs by the gods, as people think, it would in fact be reasonable for them to be pleased by what is best and most akin to them ... (... εἰ γάρ τις ἐπιμέλεια τῶν ἀνθρωπίνων ὑπὸ θεῶν γίνεται, ὥσπερ δοκεῖ, καὶ εἴη ἂν εὔλογον χαίρειν τε αὐτοὺς τῷ ἀρίστῳ καὶ συγγενεστάτῳ . . .). (X. 8, 1179a22–32)

We shall return to these texts in Chapter 3, and provide positive reasons for thinking that they are not meant to support divine providence, based on the language employed in them, the context in which they are presented, and Aristotle's philosophical commitments in the *NE*. For now, it suffices to

---

[18] In *GC* II. 10, 336b31–2, Aristotle says that "the god completely filled the universe" (συνεπλήρωσε τὸ ὅλον ὁ θεός) by making generation continuous. Scholars commonly agree that he is speaking figuratively (see, e.g., Menn, "Aristotle's Theology," p. 439 and p. 456 n. 26). This even includes Bodéüs, who thinks Aristotle countenances divine providence, and nevertheless reads "God" in 336b31–2 as a metaphor for "nature" (Bodéüs, *Aristotle*, p. 162).

[19] Bodéüs, *Aristotle*, pp. 7–8 and chapter 5.

note that the very fact that these remarks are presented as conditionals leaves open the question of whether Aristotle means to endorse or reject the ideas they allude to, i.e., that there is some "gift of the gods to humans" or "care for human affairs by the gods."

Aristotle occasionally speaks of honoring the gods, and of the importance of doing so. At *NE* IV. 3, 1123b17–20, he says that honor is the greatest external good, and that the greatest honor is the one we bestow on the gods. In *Topics* I. 11, 105a5–7, he says that, whereas those who cannot tell whether snow is white or not are in need of perception, those who wonder whether or not gods should be honored and parents loved must be punished: "one must not inquire into every problem or every thesis" (105a3–4). Now, that "we" – meaning Greeks or more generally people of Aristotle's day – assign (ἀπονέμομεν) the greatest honor to the gods (*NE* IV. 3 1123b18), e.g., through sacrifices and prayers, is simply an observable fact. Noting that fact does not commit Aristotle to upholding the existence of the gods worshiped in this way, i.e., the gods of traditional religion standardly conceived of as capable of responding to such human gestures. That Aristotle uses the first-person plural in making that statement may be taken to suggest that he at least views such religious practices as legitimate. Indeed, the *Topics* passage mentioned, if it reflects Aristotle's own view, does indicate that he thinks of honoring the gods as an unquestionable duty, and of violating that duty as a punishable offense. But these views do not commit him to upholding the existence of the traditional gods either. Maintaining traditional religious practices and attitudes toward divinity may be important, even necessary, for reasons that do not presuppose the truth of the content of traditional religion. Indeed, as we shall see in Chapter 2, Aristotle thinks that traditional religion has a *necessary* sociopolitical role, which is perfectly consistent with the falsity of its content. People honor the gods, presumably generally with the expectation of pleasing them and possibly gaining something in return, and they *should* do so. But that need not mean that divine providence actually exists.

In *NE* VIII. 12, 1162a4–7, Aristotle again discusses gods alongside parents, as he does in *Topics* I. 11, this time saying that our *philia* (love, friendship)[20] toward both is of the same kind, namely *philia* toward what is "good and excellent" (ἀγαθὸν καὶ ὑπερέχον). One might think that this comparison, and indeed the very description of the relation of humans to gods as *philia*, must mean that Aristotle thinks there exist providential gods who actively participate in a loving or friendly relationship with such

---

[20] On the difficulties involved in translating the term *philia* see A. Nehamas, "Aristotelian *Philia*: Modern Friendship?," *Oxford Studies in Ancient Philosophy* 39 (2010), pp. 213–48.

human beings. After all, Aristotle notes that parents seem to naturally have *philia* toward their offspring and vice versa (indeed, not only in humans) (*NE* VIII. 1, 1155a16–19), and that *philia* differs from mere goodwill (εὔνοια) precisely in that it includes reciprocity (2, 1155b32–4). However, though reciprocity is a precondition for the type of *philia* Aristotle discusses in *NE* VIII. 3–6, i.e., that which holds between equals, *philia* "according to superiority" (καθ᾽ ὑπεροχήν) constitutes an entirely "different form" of *philia* (VIII. 7, 1158b11–12). It is worth examining the extent to which reciprocity is expected in the case of that type of *philia*, to which both the *philia* of humans toward their gods and that of children toward their parents belong.

Philia based on superiority holds between people unequal in "worth" (ἀξία), and so, Aristotle says, the "loving" (φίλησις) involved in it must be "proportionate" (ἀνάλογον), i.e., the superior must be loved more than the inferior, and more so the larger the distance between the two, so that equality is obtained "in a way" (*NE* VIII. 7, 1158b23–8). Though parents are superior to their children, the gap between the two is narrow enough for them to have *philia*, involving a mutual exchange (21–3). When the gap (διάστημα) between the two parties widens, however, as it does in the case of rulers and subjects, and even more so in the case of gods and human beings, we can no longer say that the two parties are each other's *philoi* (1158b33–1159a3). What Aristotle goes on to say at 1159a3–5 has been taken to mean that *philia*, in such cases, evaporates.[21] Read thus, Aristotle would be contradicting his explicit remark in *NE* VIII. 12, 1162a4–7, which implies that humans *do* have *philia* toward the gods. But, in fact, *philia* is not explicitly mentioned in 1159a3–5, which is better translated as follows:

> Therefore, there is no exact definition in the case of people of this kind, up to what point the friends [remain such].[22] For with many things being taken away, it nevertheless remains, but with one being much removed, for instance the god, [it remains] no longer.

I suggest that the subject of μένει in 1159a5 is not ἡ φιλία. Aristotle's idea is that there is a point, difficult to locate, at which one party is so far removed

---

[21] See the following translations ad loc.: T. Irwin (trans. and comm.), *Aristotle: Nicomachean Ethics* (Indianapolis, 1999); R. Crisp (trans. and ed.), *Aristotle: Nicomachean Ethics* (Cambridge, 2000); W. D. Ross (trans.), *Nicomachean Ethics* in J. Barnes (ed.), *The Complete Works of Aristotle* (Princeton, 1991); H. Rackham (trans.), *Aristotle: Nicomachean Ethics* (Cambridge, Mass., 1934).

[22] Ross' critical apparatus indicates that οἱ φίλοι at 1159a4 may instead be ἡ φιλία, in which case the latter could function as the subject of the following sentence. But that option is unavailable (e.g.)

from and superior to the other party that it no longer accepts, needs, or regards the latter as its *philos*. But since such a case is just an extreme case of superiority *philia*, the relation of the *inferior* party to the superior is itself appropriately called an instance of *philia*, even though it is unreciprocated.

Unlike the cases described in *NE* VIII. 2 of one's goodwill toward an equal who chooses not to return it, or of the goodwill between two equals unaware of each other's feelings, the superiority *philia* involving human beings and their gods achieves "equality" through proportionate loving based on their worth.[23] And so, as to be expected, the only loving involved in such a relation would be on the part of the immeasurably inferior party, i.e., human beings. Indeed, in *EE* VII. 3, Aristotle explicitly says that in *philia* based on superiority "loving in return" (ἀντιφιλεῖσθαι) either does not exist or exists in a different way, since it would be absurd (γελοῖον) to blame god for not loving in return to the extent that he is loved (1238b18–30). In fact, as Aristotle says elsewhere in the same book, since god has no need for a *philos*, he would have none (VII. 12, 1244b7–10). And in *MM* II. 11 the point is made that *philia* toward god is receptive "neither of loving in return, nor of loving in general" (*MM* II. 11, 1208b26–31).[24]

The outcome of this discussion of *philia* as it extends to humans and their gods is that the standard conception of the gods who care about us and respond to our requests is entirely misguided. We may form a loving or friendly relation to gods, but we may not expect anything to be given to us in return. Those gods that are thought to be in a reciprocal relationship

---

to Irwin, who obviously retains οἱ φίλοι in his translation of 1159a3–4 (as "Now in these cases there is no exact definition of how long people are friends").

[23] Or at least such a *philia* approximates equality (cf. *NE* VIII. 7, 1158b27–8: τότε γίνεταί πως ἰσότης). In fact, as Aristotle says more than once, one should not expect to be able to honor or love one's superiors (be they gods or parents) according to their true worth (*NE* VIII. 14, 1163b15–18; IX. 1, 1164b2–6).

[24] It is true that in this passage Aristotle also makes the point that those who assume that there is *philia* toward the god are incorrect, since *philia* requires "loving in return" (ἀντιφιλεῖσθαι). But this statement occurs during the introductory discussion of friendship, equivalent to the initial discussion cited earlier from *NE* VIII. 2. And, as in the *NE*, later on in the *MM* Aristotle goes on to introduce superiority-*philia* as a special type, which he again says is "proportionate" (κατὰ λόγον), since no one would afford an equal good to both the better person and the worse (II. 11, 1211b12–15). Toward the end of what remains of the *MM*, Aristotle promises to go on to discuss the proper treatment of a *philos*, especially among equals, stating that between unequals (e.g., fathers and sons, husbands and wives, and rulers and subjects) equality is not to be expected (II. 17). Perhaps in that discussion Aristotle would have discussed superiority-friendship in more detail, and would have alluded to the case of gods, toward whom we may have that type of *philia*, though we may not expect it to be reciprocated. Finally, though 1208b30–1 is often translated so as to preclude the very possibility of human beings loving gods, it need not be read thus: "ἄτοπον γὰρ ἂν εἴη εἴ τις φαίη φιλεῖν τὸν Δία" could, and probably does, refer to the absurdity in supposing that Zeus loves, rather than that one loves Zeus (contra the Oxford translation by St. G. Stock ad loc.).

with human beings do not exist, and those gods that exist are not responsive to us in any way.[25]

1.3 Rejection of Explanations of Phenomena Based on Divine Providence

If those gods that actually exist are in general incapable of loving, then *a fortiori* one should not expect particular phenomena to be explained in terms of divine love. Aristotle rejects explanations of this kind on a number of occasions. In *EE* VIII. 2, for instance, he criticizes the view, rooted in tradition, according to which "the lucky" individual (ὁ εὐτυχῶν) is lucky due to being loved by a god functioning as his "good captain" (1247a23–7). Such an explanation of good luck cannot work, according to Aristotle, because it is absurd to suppose that a god or a daemon would love such a person, rather than "the best and the wisest" (1247a28–9). Importantly, Aristotle's subsequent discussion in *EE* VIII. 2, 1248a25-b7 of (one form of) "good luck" (εὐτυχία) as being "divine" (θεία) and as occurring "through god" (διὰ θεόν) does not imply divine providence either. For the god mentioned there is the "principle of [all] movement in the soul," responsible, in the words of P. van der Eijk, for "a psycho-physiological mechanism" as opposed to "incidental and momentaneous inspiration" (as is sometimes assumed).[26] It is, specifically, as we have seen previously, theoretical *nous* that Aristotle's gods possess (or consist of) and that we, too, share.[27]

---

[25] Similarly, R. Parker stresses the nonreciprocal nature of the superiority *philia* between humans and gods as Aristotle conceives of it; see "Pleasing Thighs: Reciprocity in Greek Religion" in C. Gill, N. Postlethwaite, and R. Seaford, *Reciprocity in Ancient Greece* (Oxford, 1998), pp. 105–25 at pp. 122–4. But note that Parker goes as far as doubting the possibility of human beings "loving" gods, in Aristotle's view (ibid., p. 123). This would make it difficult to understand how there could be any *philia* (even superiority *philia*) applicable to the case of humans and gods, which Aristotle expressly says there is. J. D. Mikalson notes that Parker fails to acknowledge places where Aristotle, contrary to his other discussions, does seem to support the existence of reciprocity between humans and gods; see *Greek Popular Religion in Greek Philosophy* (Oxford, 2010), p. 182 n. 111. But these texts (*EE* VII. 3, 1238b26–30 and *NE* X. 8, 1179a23–32), as we have seen (and as we shall see in more detail in Chapter 3 with regard to the *NE* X passage), do not in fact support that idea. F. Dirlmeier, surveying the evidence, also concludes that Aristotle consistently rejects a reciprocal relationship between humans and gods; see *Aristoteles Nikomachische Ethik* (Berlin, 1999), p. 521. See also J. Owens, "The Relation of God to World in the *Metaphysics*," *Études sur la Métaphysique d'Aristote* (*Symposium Aristotelicum VI*) (Paris, 1979), pp. 207–22 at n. 26.

[26] P. Van der Eijk, "Divine Movement," at pp. 30–1.

[27] See pp. 19–20. As noted at p. 20, n. 15, though, P. Van der Eijk, "Divine Movement," pp. 30–1, n. 17, raises doubts about identifying "god" in this chapter with the god(s) of Aristotle's *Metaphysics*. For a recently proposed mechanism by which Aristotle thinks God, understood as the prime mover, causes good luck, see P. T. Struck, *Divination and Human Nature* (Princeton, 2016), pp. 130–56.

Another phenomenon traditionally explained by appealing to divine providence and love is dreaming. Indeed, one lost fragment of Aristotle's *De philosophia*, taken from Sextus Empiricus, lists as one of the two chief sources (ἀρχαί) of the conception of gods (ἔννοια θεῶν) in humans, alongside astronomical phenomena, "the occurrences surrounding the soul," and especially "the divination coming into being in sleep" (*Adversus mathematicos*, 9. 20–23=*De phil.* Fr. 12a, Ross). Aristotle himself, however, would not be inclined to uphold a belief springing from such a source. In his *De divinatione per somnum*, he explicitly rejects prophetic dreams as god-sent, saying that such dreams would then have to be sent equally to commonplace people and even to nonrational animals, which is absurd (462b20–2; 463b12–13).[28] Building on principles laid out in *De anima* and certain parts of the *Parva Naturalia* (most prominently *De somno* and *De insomniis*), he provides an alternative justification for the claim that some dreams can be prophetic, by constructing a naturalistic account of the use of dreams for preparatory purposes, namely for predicting impending physiological conditions and for resolving actual conflicts in the dreamer's daytime life.[29]

Aristotle's idea in Sextus' report must be, then, that people tend to derive their conception of gods based on *what they take* to be, and in actuality *is not*, divination based on dreams. Indeed, the rejection of a truly divine source of dreams and divination through dreams is compatible with the surviving evidence not only from *De philosophia*, but also from other lost Aristotelian dialogues. Take, for example, Cicero's portrayal in *De divinatione ad Brutum* I.25.53 of Eudemus' dream, usually attributed to Aristotle's dialogue *Eudemus* (Fr. 1, Ross). In the dream, Eudemus is told that (1) he would recover from the illness he had at the time, (2) the tyrant Alexander would die, and (3) Eudemus himself would return home. Aristotle is reported to have said that whereas (1) and (2) were fulfilled, (3) was not, or at least not literally, because

---

[28] Recent discussions of *De divinatione* include F. Radovic, "Aristotle on Prevision through Dreams," *Ancient Philosophy* 36 (2016), pp. 383–407, and P. T. Struck, *Divination*, pp. 91–170. Both agree that Aristotle rejects divine providence as a source of divination through dreams, though Struck, accounting for Aristotle's reference to dreams as "demonic" (463b), concludes that Aristotle views divination in dreams as owing to humans being "steered by a divine impulse toward actualizing potential toward the good, beneath our self-conscious awareness" (Struck, *Divination*, p. 163).

[29] For a detailed discussion of this account see M. Segev, "The Teleological Significance of Dreaming in Aristotle," *Oxford Studies in Ancient Philosophy* 43 (2012), pp. 107–41. For an early attempt to reconcile *De divinatione per somnum* with the fragments from Aristotle's *De philosophia*, see A. H. Chroust, "Aristotle's *Protrepticus* versus Aristotle's *On Philosophy*: A Controversy Over the Nature of Dreams," *Theta-Pi* (1974), pp. 169–78.

Eudemus ended up dying in battle at Syracuse. To make (3) fit in with the rest, then, it was interpreted as meaning that Eudemus' soul had returned to its home after leaving his body. Aristotle does not seem to "indicate here his belief that the messages which Eudemus received in his dreams . . . are bound to occur in the future,"[30] nor "to show that by [the] fulfillment [of the dream] the deity itself confirmed the truth of Plato's doctrine of the heavenly origin of the soul and its future return thither."[31] Rather, Aristotle's report here is fully congruent with his theory in *De divinatione per somnum*. Contents (1) through (3) of Eudemus' dream in fact correlate with the three types of dream content discussed by Aristotle in that treatise. Item (1) has to do with the dreamer's own bodily condition, a domain in which Aristotle explains that prediction using dreams is in fact possible, since certain dreams function as natural signs (σημεῖα πέφυκε) of physiological occurrences (463b30–1). The fact that Eudemus succeeded in predicting his own recovery, then, is not unbelievable on Aristotelian grounds. Item (2) has to do with an external event, of which Aristotle regards the prediction using dreams as entirely coincidental (463a30–b1). Eudemus' prediction of Alexander's death is equivalent to any other dreamer's prediction of a sea battle (463a31–b11), and both are equivalent to a game of dice (463b12–22). Item (3) has to do with an action to be carried out by the dreamer herself, of which a dream, according to Aristotle, may not only be a sign, but also a partial *cause* (463a21–3). Eudemus may have gone back home, on the basis of his dream, thus fulfilling it fully, if it were not for an intervening factor (death in battle). In this context, Aristotle himself says that many actions, though well planned (βουλευθέντα καλῶς), are prevented by stronger circumstances (*Div. Somn.*, 463b26–8).[32]

This view of the usefulness of dreams is quite far from the popular Greek notion of dreaming as facilitating "'illuminations,' 'inspirations' or 'revelations,'"[33] a notion which, in my view, Aristotle rejects both in *Div.* and in *De phil.* Aristotle's view is also fully congruent with his remarks in the *Protrepticus*, despite appearances.[34] There (Iambl. *Protr.* 8 [45.25–46.7 Pistelli], in Fr. 9, Ross), Aristotle says that sleep is not

---

[30] A. H. Chroust, "Eudemus or on the Soul: A Lost Dialogue of Aristotle on the Immortality of the Soul," *Mnemosyne* (1966), pp. 17–30 at 20.
[31] W. J. Jaeger, *Aristotle: Fundamentals of the History of His Philosophy*, trans. R. Robinson (Oxford, 1948), pp. 39–40.
[32] Cf. Segev, "Teleological Significance," 132 ff.
[33] Chroust, "Aristotle's *Prostrepticus*," p. 174.
[34] See ibid., for the opposite view.

"choice-worthy" (αἱρετόν), because it involves the experience of "false *phantasmata*." It may seem that in saying this Aristotle means to reject the natural usefulness of dreams, but, in context, this turns out not to be the case. Aristotle mentions sleeping in this text as a fourth example of things that, though pleasant, are not choice-worthy for their own sake. The other examples are being insane, being drunk, and being a child. Although being insane, drunk, or a child throughout one's life is potentially pleasurable, it is not choice-worthy, Aristotle says, because all three possibilities go against having wisdom, and so does being permanently asleep.

This, however, does not mean that sleep is valueless or not choice-worthy *at all*. We may concede that uninterrupted sleep is an undesirable state and still acknowledge the usefulness of sleep for the state that interrupts it, namely waking, and the best activities that take place in this state, namely, in the human case, rational activities (just as we acknowledge, on any reasonable view, the usefulness of childhood for human development although we may think that being a child is not to be chosen as the endpoint of the process, or as a permanent state). In fact, sleep may turn out to be necessary for such activities to occur, or even to be conditionally necessary for the percipient living being in which it occurs to exist as such, and in fact for Aristotle it *is* (cf. *De somno*, 455b16–28). Dreams can be similarly naturally useful for waking life (though they are not conditionally necessary for it).[35] It is true that Aristotle thinks dreams are generally false, just as the *Protrepticus* passage suggests, and even misleading, insofar as they are taken to be real, but this does not go against their natural usefulness.[36] And it is only such a natural usefulness, and not any benefit incurred due to anything like divine intervention, that Aristotle attributes to dreams.

---

[35] See Segev, "Teleological Significance," p. 128 ff.

[36] Ibid., pp. 121–4. I am thankful to Monte R. Johnson for a helpful correspondence on the *Protrepticus* fragment. For more discussion of it, see D. S. Hutchinson and M. R. Johnson, "4: Iamblichus: Chapter VIII, Commentary (28.8.2013)," in *Protrepticus: A Reconstruction of Aristotle's Lost Dialogue*, <http://protrepticus.info/evidence.html>. B. Effe, too, takes Aristotle's dialogues to be generally compatible with his rejection in *Div.* of the view that dreams are god-sent or can be used for divination in any other way that cannot be explained naturalistically. Effe, however, argues for this position by taking the description of Eudemus' dream (Fr. 1, Ross) to be a literary device, and by ascribing the view of dreams presented in Sextus' report (*De phil.* Fr. 12a, Ross) (which, Effe says, directly contradicts the view of the *Protrepticus* and has nothing to do with that of *Div.*) to certain non-Aristotelian philosophers or philosophical schools appearing in the *De philosophia* (possibly Pythagoreanism); see B. Effe, *Studien zur Kosmologie und Theologie der Aristoelischen Schrift* "Über die Philosophie" (Munich, 1970), pp. 78–87, esp. at pp. 80, 82, and 85.

1.4 An Argument against Divine Providence: Aristotle's Version of the Allegory of the Cave

In *De natura deorum* II. 37. 95–96 (=*De phil.* Fr. 13a, Ross), Cicero has his Quintus Lucilius Balbus quote Aristotle in support of his defense of Stoic theology:

> "If," [Aristotle] says, "there were people who had always lived under the earth in good and well-lighted houses, which were decorated with figures and paintings and furnished with all the things of which those who are deemed happy have an abundance, but they had never gone above ground, but rather had learned by rumor/tradition [*fama*] and report [*auditio*] that there was a power/will [*numen*] and force [*vis*] of gods, and then at some time when the jaws of the earth opened up they could exit and escape from their hidden dwelling-places into these places which we inhabit: then when they had suddenly seen the earth and seas and the sky, when they had become acquainted with the greatness of clouds and the force of winds and had beheld the sun and had become acquainted not only with its greatness and beauty but also with its efficient power [*efficientia*], by which it produced day, pouring forth light through the whole sky, and when night darkened the lands they perceived the whole sky adorned and decorated with stars, and the variation of the moonlight as [the moon] waxes and wanes, and the risings and settings of all these objects and their courses which in all eternity are settled and immutable – when they saw these things, of course they would suppose both that there are gods and that these things, being so great, are the works of gods."

Scholars tend to agree that this passage is genuinely Aristotelian (transmitted by Cicero either in literal translation or in paraphrase), and to ascribe it, based mainly on its content, to (usually the third book of) his *De philosophia*.[37] In the passage, Aristotle describes people confined to a cave throughout their lives and having exposure only to the content of traditional religion and to human-made artifacts. Upon exiting their cave and witnessing natural phenomena for the first time, these people conclude that there are gods, these phenomena being their creation. Two things are not immediately clear from the text, however. First, it is not explicitly said what the line of reasoning leading to the cave dwellers' conclusion is.

---

[37] There are also exceptions to this consensus. As has been helpfully pointed out to me by an anonymous referee, W. Jaeger, in one place, assigns the fragment to Aristotle's *Eudemus*, which for him is supposed to belong to an early, Platonic period in Aristotle's philosophical development; see W. Jaeger, *Aristotle*, p. 30. See also A. P. Bos, *Cosmic and Meta-Cosmic Theology in Aristotle's Lost Dialogues* (Leiden, 1989), p. 184.

Second, Aristotle does not state whether he means to criticize, or rather commend, the cave dwellers for reasoning thus, and why.

Clarifying these interpretive issues is surely relevant to understanding Aristotle's view of traditional religious ideas, especially divine providence. As is explicitly stated in the passage, it is only traditional ideas concerning the gods that the cave dwellers are exposed to and entertain while still underground. Determining what might be concluded from the passage concerning such gods and people's conceptions of and reasoning about them would be invaluable toward understanding Aristotle's own position on these matters. In what follows I shall examine and compare three possible readings of this passage. I shall conclude that in the passage Aristotle means to attribute to his cave dwellers a version of the "teleological argument" for the existence of god(s), or the "argument from design." The cave dwellers conclude on the basis of their knowledge of artifacts and their new experience of natural phenomena that nature as a whole must have been created by an intelligent, intentional deity, just as artifacts are made, intentionally, by intelligent human beings. I shall further argue that Aristotle in fact criticizes the cave dwellers for adhering to that line of reasoning. If so, then Aristotle's fragment supports the interpretation offered so far in this chapter, on which Aristotle consistently rejects the existence of anthropomorphic or providential gods. As we shall see, the fragment in fact does more than that. Through an instructive comparison between traditional religion and Plato's theory of Forms, the text shows us what Aristotle thinks is misguided about a process of reasoning, dominant to this day, that leads to the belief in anthropomorphic, providential gods.

In order to interpret Aristotle's version of the cave allegory, we shall make use of the following two criteria. First, many different sources unanimously attribute to Aristotle's *De philosophia*, and to his dialogues more generally, a recurring attack on Plato, and in particular on his theory of Forms.[38] In the passage with which we are presently concerned Aristotle is obviously responding to Plato's Allegory of the Cave in *Republic* VII.[39] Given the central role that the theory of Forms

---

[38] Cicero, *D.N.* I. 13. 33=*De phil.* Fr. 26, Ross; Plutarch, *Adversus Colotem*, 1115B-C=*De phil.* Fr. 10b, Ross; Proclus, Apud Philoponus, *De aeternitate mundi*, p. 31. 17 (Rabe)=*De phil.* Fr. 10a, Ross; Syrianus, *Commentarius in Metaphysica* 159.33–160.5=*De phil.* Fr. 11a, Ross; etc. Notice, though, that Aristotle is also reported to have agreed with Plato on several points in the *De philosophia*, e.g., on the unchangeability of the divine (as well as on the argument to be used for showing it), see Simplicius *in De caelo* 289. 1–15=*De phil.* Fr. 16, Ross; cf. *De caelo* 279a12-b3, *Republic* II, 381b-c.

[39] There are also considerable differences between Plato's and Aristotle's versions of the allegory, which we shall deal with later (see pp. 33 ff.).

plays in Plato's text, as well as the fact that Aristotle's *De philosophia* is known to have included a criticism of that theory, one would expect Aristotle's version of the cave allegory to embody that criticism.[40] Any successful interpretation of the fragment, then, should show how our fragment can be used as a criticism of Plato's theory of Forms (henceforth, criterion *a*).

Second, we should aspire, as far as possible, to avoid reading the passage as being inconsistent with Aristotle's overall theory. It is sometimes assumed that the *De philosophia* belongs (along with other dialogues) to an early period in Aristotle's philosophical development.[41] Whatever the actual chronology is, there is no evidence that Aristotle's views in this work should be incongruent with those of the extant corpus. If anything, the critique of the Forms just mentioned suggests that in the *De philosophia* Aristotle took an approach characteristic of his views in the extant corpus rather than an allegedly early pro-Platonic stance. Furthermore, there is a direct reference to *De philosophia* in the *Physics* (II.2, 194a35–6), on the issue of the (double) meaning of the term "that for the sake of which," which is crucial for the purposes of Aristotle's theories in the extant corpus. Thus, we would expect our fragment (and the *De philosophia* as a whole) to be consistent with Aristotle's extant writings. We may posit the requirement that Aristotle's fragment be interpreted as being consistent with his corpus as a second criterion for an adequate interpretation of that text (henceforth, criterion *b*). I shall evaluate three possible readings of Aristotle's version of the cave allegory in the *De philosophia* based on the two criteria, i.e., criterion *a*, the inclusion of a criticism of Plato, and criterion *b*, consistency with the corpus of Aristotle's writings.

1.4.1 The Acceptance of the "Teleological Argument" for the Existence of God(s)

As we have seen, the context in which Cicero quotes Aristotle's version of the cave allegory is his character Balbus' defense of Stoic theology,

---

[40] It has also been suggested that Aristotle presents his cave allegory as an "opposition to the Platonic doctrine of the createdness of the cosmos, in a polemic against the cosmogony of the *Timaeus*" (A. P. Bos *Cosmic and Meta-Cosmic Theology in Aristotle's Lost Dialogues* (Leiden, 1989), pp. 175–6). Although this is possible, such a criticism could not have plausibly appeared independently of a criticism of Plato's theory of Forms in the context, since Aristotle's fragment clearly responds directly to *Republic* VII, not the *Timaeus*.

[41] W. Jaeger's developmentalist position in fact rejects the assumption that the *De philosophia* is as early as the rest of Aristotle's dialogues, and identifies it as a *transitional* work, written in a period

adhering to the "teleological argument" for the existence of gods, according to which the utility (*usus*) or beauty of the world's structure shows that it must come about, not by chance, but rather by intelligence and divine providence (*sensu . . . divinaque providentia*) (*ND* II, 34.87). This, of course, need not confine us to any particular interpretation of Aristotle's original text. Though we may have no reason to question the reliability of Cicero's quotations, we have every reason to doubt the context in which they appear as an accurate representation of the philosophical views of their original authors.[42] Nevertheless, it has been widely agreed, or rather presupposed, that the use of Aristotle's cave allegory by Cicero (or Balbus) for a standard (say, Stoic) proof of the existence of gods follows Aristotle's original intention in writing it.[43]

---

following Plato's death and probably overlapping with the composition of the criticism of the theory of Forms in *Metaphysics* A (Jaeger, *Aristotle*, pp. 125–8).

[42] T. B. De Graff, by examining Cicero's references to surviving works (i.e., Plato's dialogues), concludes that he "should be praised for having preserved to us the material of so many of the philosophical treatises extant in his day, but unhappily long since lost" ("Plato in Cicero," *Classical Philology* 35.2 [1940], pp. 143–53 at p. 143). In light of this achievement, she holds that Cicero must not be censured for "his failure to treat more of the abstract passages [in Plato]" (ibid., p. 153). According to De Graff, when the circumstances in which Cicero mentions a Platonic text indicate an incomplete grasp of Plato's ideas, this "is due, in part at least, to the fact that [Cicero] is much more concerned with adapting [Plato's ideas, here specifically the theory of Forms] to his own uses than in translating or interpreting Plato" (ibid., p. 148). For a recent discussion of a related case, in which Cicero paraphrases Plato in order to validate a point in Stoic theory, as well as a general account of Cicero's use of Plato, see I. Gildenhard, "Of Cicero's Plato: fictions, Forms, foundations," in M. Schofield (ed.), *Plato, Aristotle and Pythagoreanism in the First Century BC: New Directions for Philosophy* (Cambridge, 2013), pp. 225–75 especially at pp. 270–1. Indeed, Cicero is quite capable of presenting a text in a partial manner even when he is concerned with translating or interpreting it. Recently, D. Sedley showed how, in his translation of Plato's *Timaeus* (in particular, 28b4-5), Cicero, though not *distorting* the original text, nevertheless "is not unreflectively assuming a literal reading . . . but is quite consciously choosing the appropriate language to favour" one reading over the other ("Cicero and the *Timaeus*," in M. Schofield (ed.), *Plato, Aristotle and Pythagoreanism in the First Century BC: New Directions for Philosophy* (Cambridge, 2013), pp. 187–205 at p. 198). Given such shortcomings, we may assume further that Cicero is quite capable of using our *De philosophia* passage, which for all we know he translates or paraphrases reliably, in order to support certain philosophical points that go against the views advanced in Aristotle's original dialogue.

[43] "Die dem platonischen Gleichnis innewohnende Spannung von Schatten – und Lichtsymbolik ist verpufft und zu einem Gottesbeweis nach dem *argumentum e gradibus* abgewandelt" (H. Flashar, "Aristoteles, *Über die Philosophie*," in A. Bierl, A. Schmitt, and A. Willie (eds.), *Antike Literatur in neuer Deutung* ["*Über die Philosophie*"] (Munich/Leipzig, 2004), pp. 257–73 at p. 271), cf. H. Flashar and E. Grumach (ed.), *Aristoteles Werke Bd. 20, 1: Fragmente I* [*Fragmente*] (Berlin, 2004), p. 140; "In one passage Philo describes how a man viewing with awe the works of the cosmos comes to the conclusion that these are the works of god (. . .) Cicero, *N.D.* II. 95–6 (=fr. 13) assigns such a proof for God's existence to Aristotle" (D. E. Hahm, "The Fifth Element in Aristotle's *De Philosophia*: A Critical Examination," *Journal of Hellenic Studies* 102 [1982], 60–74 at 70); "This passage has been preserved by Cicero, and certainly belongs to the proof of God's existence in the third book *On Philosophy* (. . .) What [Aristotle] gives us instead of [Plato's] Ideas is the contemplation of the wonderful shapes and arrangements of the cosmos, a contemplation which, intensified

Unlike the inhabitants of Plato's cave, whom Glaucon initially (understandably) calls "strange" (ἄτοποι), before Socrates explains to him in what way they "resemble us" (ὁμοίους ἡμῖν: *Rep.* VII. 515a4–5), the subjects of Aristotle's narrative are designed to resemble his readers in many respects even on a first, pre-allegorical reading. Proper lighting provides these people with standard vision, which would require no significant period of transition or repair when they arrive above ground. They occupy houses, and have access to art, culture, and even religion (based, as the Greek one was, on "reports" in poets and other oral traditions passed on from generation to generation by priests to parents and parents to children). According to the interpretation proposed, Aristotle expects his cave dwellers, once freed from their underground dwelling, to combine their prior knowledge of houses and decorative artifacts and the stories they have heard about gods as artisans with the natural phenomena to which they are now exposed for the very first time, and to infer that these phenomena must have been created by the gods they have heard of, in a similar fashion (i.e., intentionally, and for a particular beneficial purpose) to the artifacts they have previously known.[44] As far as this goes, this reading is quite plausible, as we shall further see in Section 1.4.3.

However, it is difficult to see why Aristotle should be taken to approve of the inference that, according to this interpretation, he attributes to his cave dwellers. First, this inference is compatible with Plato's theory of Forms, which (according to the *Timaeus*) are (imperfectly) instantiated in matter by a divine demiurge, and it is therefore unclear how the former could be used for criticizing the latter, as our criterion *a* requires. Accordingly, scholars who take Aristotle to accept the "teleological argument" for the existence of gods formed by his cave dwellers often assign the *De philosophia* to a period in which Aristotle "was still a young acolyte of Plato."[45] But this would make no sense in a dialogue that included a serious critique of the Forms. Second, as we have seen in the previous sections

---

until it becomes religion, leads up to the intuition of the divine director of it all" (W. Jaeger [n. 2], pp. 163–4). See also I. Bywater, "Aristotle's Dialogue On Philosophy," *Journal of Philology* 7.13 (1876), pp. 64–87 at pp. 82–7; A. H. Chroust, "Aristotle's *on Philosophy*," *Laval Théologique et Philosophique* 29 (1973), pp. 19–22.

44 I. Bywater, for instance, suggests attributing to Aristotle also the two lines in Cicero immediately preceding the fragment, in which an analogy is established between man-made artifacts and the universe as a whole (Bywater, "On Philosophy," p. 83).

45 R. J. Hankinson, *Cause and Explanation in Ancient Greek Thought* (New York, 1998), p. 125. For an earlier, influential version of this developmentalist approach see Jaeger, *Aristotle*, pp. 24–38. Though notice that Jaeger himself does not place *De philosophia* along with Aristotle's earliest writings (cf. pp. 31–32, n. 41).

of this chapter, the notion of divine providence and the anthropocentric and anthropomorphic aspects of traditional Greek religion in general are not only foreign to, but are also explicitly rejected by, Aristotle's view in the extant corpus (and so this reading of the fragment does not meet our criterion *b*).

1.4.2 Aristotle's Cave Dwellers as Ascending Toward Philosophical Apprehension

A second (more plausible) reading would take the cave dwellers' advancement from knowledge of artifacts, through knowledge of natural phenomena, to knowledge concerning divine beings, to represent Aristotle's views of the way in which philosophical knowledge of what he takes to be divine beings (e.g., the first unmoved mover) is acquired (thus meeting our criterion *b* – consistency with Aristotle's extant corpus).[46] According to this reading, Aristotle's cave allegory, much like Plato's, would be concerned with philosophical education, albeit one that would follow Aristotelian, rather than Platonic, philosophy as a model. In this way, it would be possible to view Aristotle's version as a refinement of and reaction to Plato's (thus satisfying criterion *a*). Aristotle's cave dwellers are said to deduce the existence of gods as the efficient causes of natural phenomena, by extrapolating from the efficient causes of objects they are already familiar with, i.e., the artifacts within their cave. Since the prime mover, for Aristotle, apart from being a final cause in the sense of an object of desire (*Metaph.* Λ.7, 1072a21–7), seems also to be the efficient cause of all natural beings (*Phys.* VIII. 6, 258b10–12), he may intend his cave dwellers to infer the existence of just this type of being, an inference which he would then of course endorse himself.

However, it is not clear in what way artifacts can function as the paradigm on the basis of which scientific knowledge of a first unmoved mover is supposed to be achieved, for Aristotle. First, his proof of the existence of this being, as it is presented in both *Physics* VIII and *Metaphysics* Λ, proceeds from a consideration of (only) natural motion. Since animals are incapable of initiating their own motion and rest (*Phys.* VIII. 2, 253a11–19), though they are thought of as the most obvious case of self-motion in nature, Aristotle says, there is no self-motion in nature, which shows the eternity of motion (VIII. 1, 252b5–6), and, finally, in order to avoid an

---

[46] The interpretation dealt with in this subsection has been helpfully suggested to me by Benjamin Morison.

infinite regress, the existence of a first unmoved mover (VIII. 6, 258b10–12). Second, not only does the argument for this unmoved mover not *require* an appeal to artifacts, but it also seems to work *only* when using *natural* beings as a paradigm. For Aristotle, as we have just said, the unmoved mover is not merely an efficient, but is also a final, cause. However, these two types of cause, Aristotle explicitly says in *Physics* II.7, only coincide in the natural realm ("for man begets man – and, generally speaking, [this is the case with things] in as much as, being moved, they move [something else] (and in as much as they do not [do so in this way], they no longer fall under 'natural philosophy'" [οὐκέτι φυσικῆς: 198a26–8]). According to the account given in the *Physics*, then, it is only a consideration of natural beings, as opposed to unnatural ones such as artifacts, that may properly lead us to infer the existence of god(s), i.e., the unmoved mover(s). But in *De philosophia* Aristotle's cave dwellers are said to infer the existence of god(s) specifically on the basis of their knowledge of unnatural things, i.e., the artifacts within their cave. Reading 2, which puts on a par the cave dwellers' and Aristotle's own arguments for the existence of divine beings, then, seems not to meet our criterion of consistency with the corpus (criterion *b*) after all. If Aristotle meant to attribute to his cave dwellers his own argument for the existence of a first unmoved mover as he expounds it in *Physics* VIII, he could have easily done so by specifying a number of *natural* things within the cave on whose basis these people would be expected to derive the existence of divine living beings. Moreover, since Aristotle's own formulation of the argument for the existence of the unmoved mover (in *Physics* VIII) uses as its basic (in fact, its sole) evidence, as we have just seen, the movement of living things, arrival at this argument does not seem to require Aristotle's cave dwellers to go above ground at all. Observing *themselves* as such moving things, they could have concluded, in the way Aristotle does, that such a mover necessarily exists, even prior to leaving their cave.

Finally, we have more reasons to think that it is the "teleological argument" for the existence of a divine craftsman (or divine craftsmen), rather than a sophisticated argument designed to arrive at the conclusion of the existence of an Aristotelian unmoved mover, that Aristotle is concerned with in the fragment from the *De philosophia*. If Philoponus' report of the ten books of Aristocles' "περὶ φιλοσοφίας" indeed refers back to Aristotle's *De philosophia*,[47] then Aristotle described in that work people's tendency

---

47 See I. Bywater, "On Philosophy," pp. 64–70. For a different opinion see Flashar and Grumach, *Aristoteles Werke*, p. 136.

to ascribe their own achievements, including the discovery of arts (τέχναι) aimed at "beauty and elegance" (τοῦ καλοῦ καὶ ἀστείου), to (a) god (εἰς θεόν), whom they conceive of as a "wise craftsman" (σοφὸς τέκτων) (*in Nicom. Isagogen* I. I=*De phil.* Fr. 8b, Ross). The same is implied by Sextus Empiricus' discussion in *Adversus Mathematicos* 9 of the identification by the observers of celestial phenomena of God with "the craftsman" (ὁ δημιουργός) of these phenomena, and by Philo's discussion in *Leg. Alleg.* 3.32.97–9 of the apprehension through an investigation of nature of "the craftsman of the universe – God" (ὁ . . . τοῦ παντὸς δημιουργός – ὁ θεός), grasping him "through his shadow, coming to knowing the artisan (τὸν τεχνίτην) through his works." Both texts are included as fragments of Aristotle's *De philosophia* by most editors (and in Ross, as Fr. 12b and Fr. 13b, respectively).[48] For all we know, the cave dwellers in Aristotle's version of the cave allegory represent those people who would reach, under the envisaged circumstances, the same conclusions alluded to by Philoponus (or Aristocles), Sextus, and Philo. He gives us no reason to think of his cave dwellers as intellectually privileged or philosophically gifted.

These considerations point in the direction of the "teleological argument" for the existence of god(s), as opposed to an argument for the existence of an unmoved mover. And there is further evidence to this effect. Alexander of Aphrodisias, we are told by Elias in his commentary on the *Categories* (115. 3–5), claims that Aristotle's dialogues differ from his "acroamatic" works (the works such as *Physics* and *Metaphysics*) in that Aristotle expresses (λέγει) his own positive views in the latter and the false views of others (τὰ ἄλλοις δοκοῦντα, τὰ ψευδῆ) in the former. Now, since the treatises of the extant corpus obviously contain discussions of Aristotle's predecessors and contemporaries, it seems plausible that Alexander does not mean to exclude all discussion of positive Aristotelian doctrines from the dialogues. The point seems to be rather that, just as the main objective of the acroamatic works is to establish Aristotle's own theories as truths using criticisms of or comparisons with previous theories when necessary, so too the primary aim of the dialogues was to establish the falsity of some of the theories of Aristotle's contemporaries and predecessors, again using, whenever necessary, positive ideas from his own theories for that purpose.

---

[48] I. Bywater thinks of Philo's argument not only as taken directly from Aristotle's *De philosophia*, but also as referring back to the very passage with which we are dealing (i.e., Aristotle's version of the cave allegory) (Bywater, "On Philosophy," pp. 83–4). For a more cautious assessment see Flashar and Grumach, *Aristoteles Werke*, p. 140 (and p. 141 for Fr. 12b).

This, of course, gives us no basis to infer the impossibility of a *reference to* Aristotle's own idea of the unmoved mover in the *De philosophia*, or in any other dialogue. Indeed, it is quite likely, based on one fragment in particular (i.e., Cicero, *DN* I. 13. 33=*De phil.* Fr. 26 Ross) that Aristotle *did* refer to the unmoved mover in the *De philosophia*.[49] However, it does seem improbable, at least if we accept Elias' report of Alexander, and if we accept in addition Alexander's own assessment of the differences between Aristotle's dialogues and his acroamatic works, that Aristotle would have introduced an entire simile in a dialogue with the intention of arguing for the existence of the prime mover philosophically.[50] Now, the interpretation we have been considering in this section assumes that, by introducing his version of the Allegory of the Cave, Aristotle was interested in establishing

[49] In this fragment, Aristotle is said to have created much confusion in book 3 of *De philosophia* by dissenting from Plato: "At times he attributes all divinity to mind (*mens*), at times he says the world itself is a god, at times he appoints another [god] (*alius quidam*) in command of the world, and assigns to it parts so that it rules and maintains the world's movement by a kind of backward turning (*replicatio*). Then he says the heat of the heavens (*caeli ardor*) is a god, not grasping that the heavens are part of the world, which he has himself elsewhere designated as a god." It is quite possible that upon laying out these various candidates for being a god Aristotle in fact intended to embark on a process of elimination, at the end of which something like his "unmoved mover" would have remained as the most promising candidate. Notice that, in order to do so, Aristotle would not have needed to offer a detailed account of such an entity, a project which would have been postponed until an acroamatic work suitable for that purpose (e.g., the *Metaphysics*). At any rate, it is a highly contested issue whether the "*alius quidam*" in *De phil.* Fr. 26, Ross is meant to refer to Aristotle's notion of the unmoved mover, as (e.g.) Jaeger maintains (Jaeger, *Aristotle*, pp. 138–9). A. P. Bos surveys the controversy. According to him (A. P. Bos, *Cosmic and Meta-Cosmic Theology in Aristotle's Lost Dialogues* (Leiden, 1989), pp. 186–90): H. von Arnim, "Die Entstehung der Gotteslehre des Aristoteles", *SB. Akad. W. Wien*, 212.5 (1931), pp. 3–80; repr. as "Die Entwicklung der Aristotelischen Gotteslehre" in F. P. Hager, *Metaphysik und Theologie des Aristoteles* (Darmstadt, 1969), pp. 1–74; W. K. C. Guthrie, "The Development of Aristotle's Theology," *The Classical Quarterly* 27 (1933), pp. 162–71; J. Moreau, *L' âme du monde de Platon aux Stoïciens* (Paris, 1939; repr. Hildesheim, 1965), p. 118; H. Cherniss, *Aristotle's Criticism of Plato and the Academy* (Baltimore, 1944); J. Pépin, *Théologie cosmique et théologie chrétienne* (Paris, 1964), pp. 135–72 and 216 ff., for example, all reject, for different reasons, Jaeger's identification of *alius quidam* in the fragment with the unmoved mover. B. Effe, *Studien*, p. 161 and B. Dumoulin, *Recherches sur le premier Aristote* (Eudème, de la Philosophie, Protreptique) (Paris, 1981), pp. 44–52 return to Jaeger's position on this question.

[50] A. P. Bos argues that, in our fragment, "*quae in quae cum viderent* refers to the sun, the moon and the stars and . . . these celestial beings are concluded to be divine beings on account of their *efficientia* and . . . *haec tanta*, i.e. the natural things 'in our world' . . . are products of . . . the celestial gods mentioned earlier on" (*Cosmic and Meta-Cosmic Theology in Aristotle's Lost Dialogues* (Leiden, 1989), pp. 177–8, n. 8). If so, then the only gods mentioned in the fragment would seem to be the heavenly bodies, even though Bos says that these would have been presented, presumably in other parts of Aristotle's dialogue(s) (he mentions *De phil.* Fr. 12a-b, 13b-c Ross in this respect, ibid.), as "subordinate . . . to a higher, purely metaphysical deity" (ibid., p. 184). However, even if Aristotle intended his version of the cave allegory to establish his positive view, not of the prime mover, but of the heavenly bodies as gods, he would still deviate in doing so from his standard practice in the dialogues (as reported by Alexander) of arguing negatively against other people's views rather than propounding his own.

his own model of philosophical education. Such a project would have required an elaborate account of the first unmoved mover as the highest object of human inquiry. But, since we suppose that the *De philosophia* did not contain any such account, the interpretation at hand turns out to be insufficient.[51]

1.4.3 *The Rejection of the Teleological Argument*

A further reason against the interpretation of our fragment (*De phil.* Fr. 13a, Ross) presented in the previous section (1.4.2), according to which Aristotle wrote his version of the cave allegory as an illustration of what he takes to be the correct way of arriving at metaphysical knowledge, is the close affinity between Aristotle's exposition of the experience and reasoning of his cave dwellers and the presentation of the teleological argument for the existence of god(s) by authors in his immediate intellectual environment. Aristotle's readers would have recognized the traditional argument

---

[51] B. Effe's position does not quite fit in with either of the interpretations presented in this section and the previous one, although it shares an essential feature with both of them. Effe takes Aristotle's version of the cave allegory to be an argument, most probably mounted against the Atomists, against the view that the ordered cosmos and the regularities within it are due to chance. The argument, according to Effe, is reminiscent of the arguments Cicero gives in the discussions surrounding his quotation of Aristotle's text (Effe, *Studien*, p. 91): People, like the Atomists, are all too used to witnessing natural phenomena, and thus overlook the beauty and magnificence of the universe (ibid., p. 93). Had they, like Aristotle's cave dwellers, been exposed to nature for the first time only as adults, they surely would have arrived immediately at the certainty (*Gewissheit*) concerning a divine force at work (ibid., p. 92). This "certainty," Effe maintains, is based solely on the experience or *pathos* generated by the encounter with the natural world, and this type of immediate knowledge is to be contrasted with the knowledge of God arrived at by discursive thinking (ibid., p. 101). Thus, Effe thinks that Aristotle endorses the conviction arrived at by his cave dwellers (similarly to the interpretations we have considered in Sections 1.4.1 and 1.4.2), but he also seems to think that the conviction in question is not based on any kind of argument, e.g., the "teleological argument" for the existence of god(s) or Aristotle's argument for the existence of a first unmoved mover (by contrast to the interpretations considered thus far). The ample evidence just given for the treatment in the *De philosophia* of the traditional teleological argument points against Effe's proposal. Moreover, since Effe himself thinks the context of the quotation in Cicero would reveal Aristotle's original intent (ibid., p. 89), it is curious that he bypasses Cicero's (or rather, Balbus') intention of proving the existence, not simply of a *göttliche Kraft*, but of providential, beneficent gods (cf. e.g., *ND* II, 34.87), whose existence Aristotle rejects out of hand. Generally speaking, it is difficult to see how the transition from the experience of natural phenomena to the "certainty" regarding the existence of a divine being could be characterized as anything but an inference, especially since, as Effe recognizes, the cave dwellers' conviction is based on their prior possession of a concept of "god" and on their knowledge of human artifacts (ibid., p. 92). Surely, the cave dwellers come to be "certain" of the existence of god(s) by comparing natural phenomena to human artifacts and human artisans to divine craftsmen, and this quite obviously relies on more than a *pathos* generated by the witnessing of nature and leading "immediately to the certainty of an active divine force" (ibid., p. 101).

W. Blum, by contrast, seems to combine the interpretations presented in Sections 1.4.1 and 1.4.2, as he reads Aristotle's version of the cave allegory as possibly constituting a teleological argument for the existence of gods, while also associating it with Aristotle's notion of the unmoved mover; see *Höhlengleichnisse: Thema mit Variationen* (Bielefeld, 2004), pp. 58–9.

in the text as quoted by Cicero, for instance from Xenophon's Socrates' presentation of it to Euthydemus, which uses remarkably similar imagery (*Mem.* IV. 3. 3–5):

> "Tell me, Euthydemus," [Socrates] said, "have you ever had the occasion to ponder how attentively the gods have afforded humans those things which they need? (. . .) Don't you know that what we primarily need is light, a thing which is provided for us by the gods? (. . .) And, since we need rest as well, the gods offer us night, the fairest time for rest (. . .) And, since the sun, being bright, illuminates the hours of the day and all other things for us, and night, due to its darkness, is indistinct, have they not kindled stars at night, which make visible for us the hours of the night, and through this we do many of the things we need to do? (. . .) The moon, furthermore, shows us not only the parts of the night, but also of the month. And since we need nourishment, do they not give it out of the earth and produce regulated seasons for this purpose, which prepare many and all sorts of things – not just things we need, but also things in which we rejoice?" "No doubt," [Euthydemus] said, "these things too show a love for mankind."

In this version of the "teleological argument," Socrates' list of natural regularities matches that given by Aristotle in our fragment. The earth, moon, stars, and the sun, with its power of bestowing light and creating day, are all listed as things an exposure to which causes both the cave dwellers and Euthydemus to conclude that there are gods. The only thing that Aristotle's version seems to lack is an explicit reference to that common feature by which these phenomena are taken to be associated with providential gods, i.e., the usefulness of these phenomena for man, which must be due to a certain "φιλανθρωπία" of the gods.

But Aristotle could hardly expect his cave dwellers *not* to reason similarly to thinkers in his immediate environment, on the basis of such similar data, especially given their prior knowledge of man-made artifacts and exposure to religion. Indeed, there is evidence that the "teleological argument" for the existence of god(s) was both more prevalent and more traditional than its occurrences in fourth-century philosophy. As R. Parker notes, the "teleological argument" for the existence of god(s), apart from making an appearance elsewhere in Xenophon (*Mem.* I. 4) and in Plato (*Laws* 886a, and to some extent in the *Timaeus*), also has several "5th c. precursors," including passages in Herodotus, Euripides, and Aristophanes (though not explicit formulations of the argument).[52] After suggesting, and

---

[52] R. Parker, "The Origins of Pronoia: A Mystery," in *Apodosis: Essays Presented to Dr. W. W. Cruickshank to Mark His Eightieth Birthday"* (London, 1992), pp. 84–94 at pp. 89–9. cf. Herodotus III. 108; Euripides, *Supplices* 195–215; Aristophanes, *Thesmophoriazusae* 13–18, Antiphon, *Tetralogy* III.α2. See also J. D. Mikalson, *Greek Popular Religion*, pp. 215–19.

then doubting, pre-Socratic philosophical theories (i.e., Anaxagoras' and Diogenes') as the origins of the argument, Parker considers the possibility that "the Greek argument from design, in its 'creationist' and anthropocentric aspects, derives not from any formal system but from a popular, sub-philosophical tradition of teleological explanation."[53] Though Parker ends his study of the origin of the teleological argument "in uncertainty,"[54] the data he surveys at the very least show that educated fourth-century Greeks would have been familiar both with the "teleological argument" itself and with a related set of ideas, rooted in their culture and tradition, that give rise to that argument.

This lends support to reading 1 in attributing to Aristotle's *cave dwellers* the teleological argument. We have already seen that the attribution of this argument to Aristotle *himself* fails to meet either of our criteria. It therefore remains to be seen whether these criteria might be satisfied by reading Aristotle's cave allegory, contra Cicero's (or his character Balbus') *use* of it, as attributing to his *cave dwellers* the argument in question, for the purpose of *rejecting* it.

In effect, criterion *b* is already met by this reading (henceforth, reading 3) if we bear in mind Aristotle's insistent criticism, in various places in his corpus (discussed previously), of the anthropomorphic conception of gods in traditional Greek religion. It gains special support when one attends to other fragments attributed to the *De philosophia*, which, as Monte Johnson argues, suggest that, in that dialogue, Aristotle was not interested in defending the "teleological argument" as much as in explaining what leads people to be attracted to it, and "what might cause people to think that there are gods in the first place".[55] These include Sextus Empiricus' report, according to which Aristotle in *De philosophia* considers people's conceptions of the gods as based either on divination through dreams or on astronomical phenomena (*Adversus mathematicos*, 9. 20–23=*De phil.* Fr. 12a, Ross). We have already seen that Aristotle rejects divination as a genuine source of truth. And as for astronomical phenomena, though Aristotle thinks *they are* divine,[56] he also seems to denounce the standard belief in divinity to which they tend to give rise, as he is reported to have "charged with great godlessness (ἀθεότητα)" those who have

---

[53] Parker, "Origins of Pronoia," p. 92.

[54] Ibid., p. 94.

[55] M. R. Johnson, *Aristotle on Teleology*, p. 261. Cf. Sextus Empiricus, *Adversus mathematicos*, 9. 20–23=*De phil.* Fr. 12a, Ross; Philo of Alexandria, *De allegoriis legum*, 3.32.97–9=*De phil.* Fr. 13b, Ross.

[56] Cf. *De caelo* 292a18–21; Cicero, *De natura deorum* II. 15. 42, II. 16. 44=*De philosophia*, Fr. 21(a-b), Ross.

supposed that the sun, moon, and the planets "do not differ from artifacts" (τῶν χειροκμήτων οὐδὲν . . . διαφέρειν: Philo, *De aeternitate mundi*, III.10–11=*De phil.* Fr. 18, Ross).

Thus, I concur with Johnson that "there is no good evidence, direct or indirect, that Aristotle supported a 'teleological proof for the existence of god,' whether in the lost work *On Philosophy*, or anywhere else," and that he was more plausibly interested in it in "correct[ing] the traditional views,"[57] which would mean that reading 3 enjoys the benefit of meeting our criterion *b*. In presenting his cave allegory in particular, Aristotle's point seems to be similar to Spinoza's criticism of the "teleological argument" in the appendix to part I of his *Ethics*: people are predisposed to infer the existence of gods, erroneously, from witnessing natural regularities that aid their own survival and well-being by supposing that this aid must have been conferred upon them by intentional agents acting specifically for the benefit of human beings. Though divinity might (indeed, for both Aristotle and Spinoza, must) be found, one must seek it (again, according to both) in a different way from this very particular kind of *a posteriori* reasoning. Aristotle takes issue with the tendencies to anthropomorphize the causes of natural phenomena, and to think that such phenomena are anthropocentrically oriented, tendencies which in his mind give rise to the erroneous notion of divine intervention or benevolence at the center of traditional religion.

The question remains of whether the interpretation of the fragment as a rejection of the traditional teleological argument for the existence of god(s) could be used to criticize Plato's theory of Forms (our criterion *a*). Importantly, Aristotle does link his criticisms of traditional religion and Platonic forms in the extant corpus. In *Metaphysics* B. 2 he gives the following explanation of why the basic proposition of Platonic metaphysics (namely that there are certain natures besides the perceptible objects that, though eternal, are the same as the latter in every other respect) is absurd (ἄτοπον):

> For they say there is a human-being-in-itself and a horse-in-itself and a health-in-itself, with no qualification besides, and in so doing they resemble those who said that there are gods, but in human shape. For the latter were positing nothing but eternal human beings (ἀνθρώπους ἀιδίους), nor are the former making the Forms anything but eternal perceptible things. (997b8–12)

[57] M. R. Johnson, *Aristotle on Teleology*, p. 262.

As S. Menn points out, a similar criticism of Plato is raised in *Met*. Z. 16, 1040b30–4, where Aristotle says that the Platonists, ignorant of the true nature of separable substances, assimilate them to perishable objects, and distinguish them from the latter simply by adding the word "itself" to designate them. But, Aristotle continues, "even had we not seen the stars, nonetheless, I think, there would be eternal substances beside those which we would know, so that also now if we do not have [knowledge of] what they are, still it is perhaps necessary that there are some [such things]" (1040b34–1041a3).[58]

If, then, as reading 3 maintains, Aristotle's version of the cave allegory is used to criticize the existence of the traditional gods, based on their suspicious likeness to human beings, there is reason to believe that such a criticism would go hand in hand, as it does in *Met*. B. 2 and Z. 16, with a criticism of Platonic Forms, based on their suspicious likeness to perceptible phenomena in general, including human beings. However, Aristotle's version of the cave allegory significantly advances over these criticisms. Specifically, the criticisms offered in B. 2 and Z. 16 focus only on perceptible phenomena as the basis for concluding the existence of Platonic Forms, and only on human beings as the basis for inferring the existence of anthropomorphic gods. However, Plato's envisaged freed prisoner in the Allegory of the Cave in *Republic* VII in fact sees the original animals and stars (i.e., the Forms) not only after seeing what is inside the cave,

---

[58] Menn connects these discussions in *Met*. B. 2 and Z. 16 to Aristotle's version of the Cave: "'If we had never seen the stars' [i.e., in Z. 16] means 'if we had spent our whole lives in a cave,' as in *De philosophia* Fr. 13 Ross, where 'those who had always lived under the earth,' even in pleasant and well-decorated subterranean dwellings, would be ignorant of the stars and thus of divinity" (*The Aim and the Argument of Aristotle's* Metaphysics [a work in progress], IIα3, p. 24; cf. IIβ2, pp. 54–5). Menn takes Aristotle's cave dwellers, while still underground, to correspond to the Platonists who "'have never seen the stars' and are still in the cave" (ibid., Iα4, p. 3). He assumes that once the cave dwellers leave their cave and witness natural phenomena including the stars, they would gain what Aristotle deems true knowledge of divinity. This amounts to a version of what earlier we have called reading 2 of the fragment. It is true that in *Met*. B. 2 and Z. 16 Aristotle confines his criticism of traditional religion to concluding that anthropomorphic gods exist based solely on human appearance and behavior, which the cave dwellers could do even while still in their cave. But, in fact, Aristotle's cave dwellers are not said to conclude anything until they leave their cave and witness nature for the first time. It is also true that if by the hypothetical scenario in Z. 16 of us never having "seen the stars" Aristotle directly refers to his version of the Cave, then he may well intend his freed cave dwellers to reach true knowledge upon seeing the stars. But the connection between the two images is quite loose. No other feature of his cave allegory, such as the other natural phenomena listed alongside the stars as influencing the cave dwellers' reasoning, is mentioned in Z. 16. As I shall now argue, there are good reasons for thinking that the cave allegory goes beyond the criticism of *Met*. B. 2 and Z. 16, and so that reading 3, on which Aristotle in fact criticizes the *entire* thought process he ascribes to his cave dwellers, along with the equivalent thought process in Platonism, is preferable.

but also after seeing the reflections outside the cave (we shall presently see what these objects stand for). And similarly, Aristotle's cave dwellers conclude that gods exist not only after seeing what is inside their cave (which includes human beings, on whom they later model their gods), but also after witnessing the natural world outside their cave. The reasoning behind both conclusions is more intricate than appears from such abbreviated criticisms as the ones offered in *Met.* B. 2 and Z.16, and therefore merits a more detailed criticism.

Here is how the double criticism of Plato's theory of Forms and of traditional religion might work in Aristotle's version of the cave allegory. In David Sedley's analysis of Plato's cave allegory, the shadows of puppets in the cave, constituting the whole of the prisoners' experience, symbolize (1) the "inadequate pretenses" of what the puppets themselves depict, namely (2) "whatever item outside the cave symbolizes the Form of [X]" or whatever mimics "the true nature of [X] with sufficient success to merit the predicate '[X].'"[59] The reflections and shadows of animals and other originals outside the cave stand for (3) "intelligible images of Forms," and the things whose images these are, are of course (4) the Forms themselves.[60] We may expect the transition relevant to Aristotle's criticism here to correspond to the transition relevant to his criticism of the teleological argument, i.e., the shift between the two first stages outside the cave (in Plato, from (3) to (4)), which depends on the experience gained already *inside* the cave (in Plato, stages (1) and (2)). To borrow the terminology of the analogy of the divided line,[61] Aristotle must be concerned here with the leap from the experience of objects of both εἰκασία ("imagination") and πίστις ("trust") (or, taken together, of δόξα ["opinion"], as represented in the Line), which is confined to the sensible world,[62] combined with the first class of objects of ἐπιστήμη (knowledge), i.e., those grasped by διάνοια (thought), to the recognition of the objects of νόησις (intellection), the Platonic Forms.

---

[59] D. Sedley, "Philosophy, the Forms, and the Art of Ruling," in G. R. F. Ferrari (ed.), *The Cambridge Companion to Plato's* Republic (Cambridge, 2007), pp. 256–83 at p. 264. I use X instead of Sedley's preferred example of "justice" to facilitate general application.

[60] Ibid., p. 265.

[61] I follow Sedley, and the traditional interpretation, in assigning stages (1) to (4) in the cave to εἰκασία, πίστις, διάνοια and νόησις, respectively. M. F. Burnyeat takes both stage (2) and (3) to correspond to the objects of διάνοια, and more specifically to "mathematical objects (perhaps conceived at different levels of abstraction)," see "Plato on Why Mathematics Is Good for the Soul," *Proceedings – British Academy* 103 (Oxford, 2000), pp. 1–82 at p. 43. Cf. M. F. Burnyeat, "Platonism and Mathematics: A Prelude to Discussion," in A. Graeser (ed.), *Mathematics and Metaphysics in Aristotle* (Berne, 1987), pp. 213–41.

[62] D. Sedley, "Philosophy, the Forms," p. 265.

Table 1.1. *The relation between Plato's Allegory of the Cave and Aristotle's version of it*

	Inside the cave	Outside	
Plato	Shadows (1) → Puppets (2) (objects of δόξα)	→ Reflections (3) → (objects of διάνοια)	→ Originals (4) → (objects of νόησις / Forms)
Aristotle	Artifacts + tradition	→ Nature	→ Gods
(*De an.*)	Perceptible objects	→ Intelligible objects	

The relation between Plato and Aristotle's versions of the cave allegory is represented in Table 1.1.

The distinction between stages (1) – (2) and stage (3) maps neatly onto Aristotle's discussion of perceptible objects (αἰσθητά) and intelligible ones (νοητά) in *De anima* III. 8. He says (431b20–3):

> Let us once again state that the soul is in a sense all things that are (τὰ ὄντα . . . πάντα). For things that are, are either perceptible or intelligible objects (αἰσθητὰ τὰ ὄντα ἢ νοητά), and knowledge is in a sense knowable objects, and perception perceptible objects.

Aristotle's statement here is predicated on his contention, explained in the previous sections of *DA* III, that thinking in fact necessitates previous acts of sense perceiving (and the mediation of these two activities through the operation of φαντασία, standardly translated as "imagination"). Accordingly, he goes on to say that there is nothing (in intelligible objects) besides (παρά), or separable (κεχωρισμένον) from, perceptible objects. Intelligible objects are merely abstractions (τά τε ἐν ἀφαιρέσει) from, or else states and affections (ἕξεις καὶ πάθη) of, perceptible ones, and they inhere in perceptible forms (ἐν τοῖς εἴδεσι τοῖς αἰσθητοῖς τὰ νοητά ἐστι) (8, 432a3–6).[63]

With the elimination of anything apart or separable from perceptible objects, the transition into (Plato's) step (4) is here explicitly rejected. Intelligible objects are, so to speak, the final stop of one's inquiry into

---

[63] That is, as R. Polansky notes, "apart from those divine things that are completely separate from matter and are their own essences (see 429b11–12)," *Aristotle's* De anima (Cambridge, 2007), p. 497. However, note that "though not presently discussed, and only alluded to, human theoretical understanding of gods must develop from first considering sensible substances and concluding from them the need for necessary and eternal beings. All human knowledge for Aristotle presupposes and derives from sense perception" (ibid., p. 498).

the epistemological and ontological lessons to be derived from one's perceptual experience, and they are adequately explained *on the basis* of that experience (i.e., as either abstractions from or affections of the objects given by sense perception). Here we may finally apply Aristotle's version of the cave allegory to his criticism of Plato. The inference to the existence of gods using the teleological argument is analogous to the inference to Forms. In Aristotle's version of the cave allegory, the cave dwellers previously familiar exclusively with artifacts and traditions about the gods, upon perceiving natural objects and recognizing the grandeur and order of the natural world, wrongly infer that nature must be explained as the product of external, eternal, intelligent, and providential beings, operating similarly to human artisans. Thus, they erroneously conclude that anthropomorphic gods exist. Plato, Aristotle would say, errs similarly when, upon considering our ability to grasp intelligible objects, such as the objects of mathematics, using perceptible objects and their various characteristics as models, he wrongly infers that both kinds of object must be explained as having their being due to their relation to certain further external, eternal, immutable, self-standing intelligible objects. Thus, he erroneously concludes that separable Forms exist.

Following the cave allegory in *Rep.* VII, Socrates proposes an educational program for potential philosophers, culminating in the study of Forms through dialectic (521c–ff.). Throughout the previous stages, the link between mathematics and the perceptible world is present, and it is emphasized in the penultimate educational stage, consisting of a study of astronomy and harmonics. The case of astronomy is instructive. Since the study of three-dimensional geometry, or "the inquiry of the dimension of depth," is currently practiced "laughably," Socrates says it should be supplanted with the next best thing, i.e., the study of astronomy (528d-e). Astronomy would do because its objects, the heavenly bodies, are "the most precise" among visible objects (529c7-d1). They approximate, and hence can be useful "models" (παραδείγματα) for studying, such things as the "true motions," which are "in true number and all true figures" (529d). Once we succeed in gaining knowledge of the relevant intelligible objects by means of astronomy, Socrates suggests, we should "let go of the things in the heavens" (530b7). At this point we will have grasped the objects of mathematics, and the perceptible phenomena approximating them, to an extent sufficient for us to grasp the existence and nature of the Forms.

It is this move to which Aristotle vehemently objects. He objects to it because he thinks the relation that it posits between perceptible objects, mathematical objects, and Forms is both analogous to and as unfounded as the relation posited in the "teleological argument" between artifacts, natural phenomena, and anthropomorphic gods. He thinks, in other words, that using perceptible objects as models for learning of mathematical objects and using those in turn to learn of the Forms, which are presumed to be imitated by mathematical objects just as those are imitated by perceptible ones, is as problematic as using artifacts as models for learning of natural phenomena and using those in turn in order to learn about the gods, which are presumed to cause natural phenomena just as some natural phenomena (i.e., human artisans) cause artifacts.[64]

In both cases, the error in reasoning results in a similar hierarchical structure, in which the objects arrived at last in the process of inquiry assume the highest explanatory status. For Aristotle's cave dwellers, the existence of gods explains nature, but it also explains their experience inside the cave. The reports they have heard of the gods' will and power are of course confirmed by their reasoning, and the artifacts (paintings, statues) they have enjoyed in their cave turn out to imitate things already present in nature thanks to precisely these gods. For Plato, the Forms ultimately explain not only the "intelligible images," but also the sensible objects, which also only have their being due to imitation. As alternatives, Aristotle proposes to explain the benefits humans find in their environment by reference to natural teleology alone, and to reduce the grasping of intelligible objects to a manipulation of sense data through a psychological operation. These alternatives render both the traditional Greek gods, and Plato's Forms, artificial.

1.4.4 Conclusion

In conclusion, reading 3, according to which Aristotle's version of the cave allegory is meant to reject the "teleological argument" for the existence of gods, seems to have the advantage of expounding a criticism of Plato's theory of Forms (criterion *a*) as well as being consistent with the rest of the

---

[64] Interestingly, in the very discussion just mentioned from *Republic* VII Socrates exemplifies the relation between astronomy and mathematics by saying that just as even exquisitely executed diagrams by Daedalus or another craftsperson should not be taken to convey the full truth about mathematical ratios, one should not expect astronomical phenomena to convey the whole truth about, e.g., the type of motions they exhibit, even though these phenomena have been constructed "by the craftsman of the heavens" in the "finest" way possible for such things (529e–530a).

Aristotelian corpus (criterion *b*). By contrast, reading 1, on which Aristotle means in the fragment to endorse the "teleological argument," does not meet either criterion, and reading 2, on which Aristotle intends in this text to endorse an argument of his own for the existence of gods whose existence he acknowledges (e.g., his unmoved mover), fails to meet criterion *b*.

The upshot of the criticism of traditional religion relevant for our purposes, as it emerges from our interpretation of the fragment, is that, at least insofar as it promotes the belief in anthropomorphic, providential gods on the basis of the "teleological argument," religion is quite problematic as a source of knowledge about reality. For Aristotle, there seem to be errors fundamental enough in the approach of traditional religion to questions about the origin of the natural world and its mode of existence for us to doubt its reliability as a source of knowledge and the truth of its content in general. Aristotle famously calls for the abandonment of Platonic Forms, though devised and held by people "dear to him," upon proving them (in his eyes) to be philosophically unsatisfactory (*NE* I. 6, 1096a11–17). By the same token, Aristotle must think of the "teleological argument" for the existence of gods, at the center of the belief in divine providence, and hence central to traditional religion, as being unreliable as a source of knowledge, since it has been shown to be unsatisfactory along with Platonic metaphysics and for analogous reasons.

1.5 Conclusion

Like Xenophanes, Aristotle rejects the anthropomorphism characterizing the depictions of the gods in traditional religion. Though no surviving text provides a fully detailed account of Aristotle's criticism of the content of traditional religion, we have enough evidence to conclude that it is directed at anthropomorphic depictions of divinity broadly conceived, from the attribution to the gods of human shapes and appearance to the expectation to establish communication or reciprocal relations with them. Such ideas, whether read in the words of the ancient poets or adhered to by popular or expert opinion, Aristotle thinks, are all baseless. Insofar as they give rise to fanciful explanations of observable phenomena, such as useful dreams or good luck, they must give way to adequate explanations by the relevant sciences.

But, although Aristotle rejects the truth of the content of traditional religion out of hand, he is interested in explaining the reasoning behind it. He focuses on one argument leading people to uphold traditional ideas concerning the existence of providential gods, namely the teleological argument, and argues that it is flawed, for reasons resembling the theoretical flaws he finds in Plato's theory of Forms. Flawed though it is, Aristotle also argues that it is to be expected that people would be led to it, consequently presenting, upholding, and propagating traditional religious ideas. As we shall see in the following chapter, Aristotle believes that recognizing how prevalent and useful these ideas are is as important as realizing that they are false. That is because he thinks that the false content of traditional religion, not only is useful, but is in fact politically necessary.

CHAPTER 2

Traditional Religion and Its Natural Function in Aristotle

2.1 The Problem: A Necessary Function for a False Religion

Aristotle is quite clear on the extent to which he thinks the content of traditional religion should be taken seriously by philosophers. As we saw in the previous chapter, he warns us not to model the shapes and lifestyles of the gods on our own, in the way that led to the popular belief that they are ruled by a king (1252b24–7). Clearly, Aristotle criticizes these types of belief in anthropomorphic gods because he thinks they are false. This is attested by the discussion in *Metaphysics* Λ. 8. There, Aristotle says that it is only insofar as traditional myths allude to the existence of divine "first substances" that they are intelligible to us (as philosophers), with the rest of their content, e.g., regarding "the human shape" of these substances, amounting to a fabrication added "with a view to persuading the masses and for its usefulness in supporting the laws and bringing about the general advantage" (1074a38-b14). Further, we have seen that Aristotle's rejection of the anthropomorphic content of traditional religion extends to the denial of divine providence.

When Aristotle goes on later in the *Politics* to describe his ideal *polis*, however, he makes it clear that traditional religion will have a large role to play in it. He reserves in the ideal city a place for a class of retired citizens who would function as priests (VII. 9, 1329a27–34), he allocates a fixed part of the city's budget to "costs related to the gods" (VII. 10, 1330a8–9), and he discusses the way in which buildings assigned to the gods should be erected (VII. 12, 1331a23–30; 1331b17–18). Indeed, even certain practices that are otherwise strictly prohibited in Aristotle's ideal *polis*, such as the display of statues or pictures representing unseemly acts, gain a special permission by him in the religious context (VII. 17, 1336b14–19). Thus, although Aristotle explicitly says that the content of the religion of his day is flawed, he, unlike Plato, does not seem to think that it needs to be revised in order to be accepted in a philosophically adequate state, even

49

in the one established under the most favorable political circumstances possible. One may wonder what good Aristotle thinks could come out of institutionalized rituals, sacrifices, and prayers dedicated to gods when he clearly thinks the only gods there are are not responsive to us and do not intervene in our individual daily lives in any conceivable way.[1]

This raises the question of whether and to what extent Aristotle is consistent in declaring traditional religious ideas false while also giving them and religious practices a positive place in his ideal *polis*.[2] The issue gets further complicated by the fact that Aristotle does not merely admit traditional religion into his ideal *polis*, but in fact does so because he views this religion and its institutions, or the "supervision concerned with religious affairs" and maintained by priests, as integral parts of political organization, conditionally necessary for any *polis* to exist as such (*Pol.* VI. 8, 1322b18–22; VII. 8, 1328b2–13).[3] In order for his view to be consistent, it turns out, Aristotle must supply a function for the performance of which traditional religion is absolutely necessary, so that we may see for just what reason the *polis* simply cannot do without it.

Discovering what the necessary natural function of religion in Aristotle's view should be proves challenging, since even the political usefulness that Aristotle explicitly ascribes to traditional religion cannot succeed in supplying such a function. In *Met.* Λ. 8, 1074b5, he states that traditional religion is politically useful for controlling certain people ("the many") by getting them to believe in its false content, with a view to supporting the laws and bringing about the general advantage. In the *Politics* Aristotle elaborates on the usefulness of traditional religion for securing social stability, and adopts it for himself, when he says, in the context of a discussion of the ideal *polis*, that it would be easy for the legislator

---

[1] See R. Mayhew, "Aristotle on Prayer," *Rhizai* 2 (2007), pp. 295–309 at p. 296.

[2] In order to eliminate the inconsistency, *inter alia*, S. Salkever goes as far as suggesting that the "*polis* of our prayers" discussed in book VII of the *Politics* is in fact the *polis*, not of Aristotle's own prayers, but rather of those of a "real [but unphilosophical] man . . . fully committed to political life," who "understands human virtue quite differently from Aristotle" ("Whose Prayer? The Best Regime of Book 7 and the Lessons of Aristotle's *Politics*," *Political Theory* 35.1 (2007), pp. 29–46 at p. 32, see pp. 36–38 for the discussion of religion). Unfortunately, this hypothesis rests on a thoroughly unnatural dichotomy between the discussion of chapters 4–12 of this book and that of the surrounding chapters (1–3, 13–15); Salkever interprets the book as a "dialogue between the prayer of the noble citizen . . . and the quite different voice of the theorist," respectively (ibid., p. 34).

[3] Hereafter, conditional (or "hypothetical") necessity is used to indicate the necessity of a certain thing in order for some goal or end to be accomplished (*PA* I. 1, 639b26–30). By sharp contrast, material necessity is the necessity, which Aristotle also finds to be regularly operative in nature, by which a certain thing invariably follows upon or is caused by a further thing or circumstance, without thereby implying the progression toward any end or goal (e.g., *GA* II. 4, 739b26–30).

to get pregnant women to exercise daily, which is required for their health, by "ordering them to take a daily walk to a place where they may worship the gods who are in charge of watching over birth," e.g., Artemis (VII. 16, 1335b12–16). Though Aristotle tells us that it would be easy (ῥᾴδιον) for the *polis* to make use of the false content of traditional religion in order to deceive the masses, thereby controlling their behavior and securing social stability, he does not say that traditional religion is necessary for that end. It may be equally possible to convince pregnant women to exercise daily by administering health education programs, or by propagating stories similar to, but other than, the myths about goddesses such as Artemis. In more difficult cases, say the prevention of criminal behavior, one might think that another task (ἔργον) in the *polis*, which Aristotle explicitly says is necessary for maintaining obedience (i.e., ὅπλα: 1328b7–10), could also be sufficient for that end. Punitive measures by the state, that is, may ensure adherence to the law, so that religion would not be required for that purpose.

Moreover, in Aristotle's *ideal polis*, the entire citizenry would consist, if not of actually wise people (*sophoi*), then at the very least of virtuous people of practical wisdom (*phronimoi*).[4] Aristotle expects such people to reject anthropomorphism with regard to divinity, as he makes clear by speaking openly to the audience of his *Ethics*, people of good upbringing who are now on their path to becoming *phronimoi*, about the vanity of speaking about gods as engaging in any action attributable to human beings, with the exception of theoretical contemplation (*NE* X. 8, 1178b7–23). Since such mature citizens, too, would be required to participate in traditional religion (oftentimes in settings excluding the presence of those noncitizens whom the city would control by getting them to believe in the content of that religion), one would expect Aristotle to find a direct benefit in traditional religion for the lives of those people – a benefit not confined to the advantage of living in a safe society as a result of the deception of some portions of its population.

In what follows I will argue that in order to locate the necessary natural function of traditional religion to which Aristotle's political theory is committed, we must uncover a usefulness for it in enabling the achievement for his citizens of what he considers the top human goal, the attainment of the knowledge of first philosophy, which, as he says, is the most worthy of being engaged in by god(s) and has god(s) as its object(s) (*Met.*

---

[4] See pp. 78 ff. Cf. *Politics* VII. 1, 1323b1–2; 2, 1324a24–5; 14, 1333a39-b5. See also C. D. C. Reeve (trans. comm.), *Aristotle: Politics* (Indianapolis/Cambridge, 1998), p. lxxii.

A. 2, 983a4–7). Roughly, my interpretation of the place of and need for traditional religion in any naturally constituted *polis*, on Aristotle's theory, is as follows. The *polis* is a community that has reached "the limit of complete self-sufficiency" and exists "for the sake of living well" (*Pol.* I. 2, 1252b27–30). It therefore aims at the flourishing lives of its members, and this includes, indeed as a top priority, the accommodation of philosophical pursuits, culminating in the contemplation of god(s).[5] Since Aristotle takes philosophical inquiry about X to commence from "wondering" at X (*Met.* A. 2, 982b12–17: θαυμάζειν – roughly, finding X wonderful or marvelous, but puzzling), he should think that in order to gain knowledge of "first philosophy," which is concerned with (the) god(s), one must first have a sense of "wonder" at god(s). Citizens (or future citizens) of the *polis*, then, must be made to "wonder" at divinity so that, in time, that sense of "wonder" would motivate those citizens with the appropriate intellectual ability to inquire philosophically into the true nature of divinity. Engendering this initial, pre-philosophical sense of "wonder" at the gods, in turn, should be carried out by the office concerned with "the supervision of matters relating to the gods," i.e., the priesthood maintaining religion. That it should be *traditional* religion in particular that is necessary for this end is explained by the fact that Aristotle thinks, quite reasonably, of humans, and in fact animals more generally, as being psychologically hardwired to take pleasure in (learning of) "things that are akin" to themselves (in this specific case, anthropomorphic gods) (*Rhet.* 1371b12–15). The function of traditional religion for learning, via the production in the learner of "wonder" (θαυμασία), though not mentioned explicitly by Aristotle, is strongly corroborated by later material directly engaging with and making use of his theory (in Strabo, as we shall see). Attributing it to Aristotle solves the problem of how he may think of traditional religion both as having a false content and as being a natural, conditionally necessary part of the *polis* as such.

In the next section, I shall show that, on Aristotle's theory, traditional religion, though its content is false, must have a *necessary* function in any naturally existing *polis*, such as the function I am proposing, despite possible and actual views to the contrary. Then, I will expound my positive proposal in Section 2.3, and support it in Section 2.4 with additional evidence from Aristotle's lost works. In Section 2.5, I consider a possible

---

[5] See J. M. Cooper, "Political Community and the Highest Good," in J. G. Lennox and R. Bolton (eds.), *Being, Nature and Life in Aristotle* (Cambridge, 2010), pp. 212–64 at p. 241 n. 40.

objection, according to which the content of traditional religion, being false, cannot have a natural use, let alone one whose result would not be regularly achieved, as for Aristotle it would not be. I reply by drawing attention to Aristotle's discussion of money (in the *Politics*), which, he thinks, is an unnatural convention, which nevertheless has a natural use in the not commonly encountered process of natural wealth acquisition. By analogy, Aristotle would be quite consistent in attributing to the content of traditional religion a natural role in a teleological process, even if that content is itself unnatural and false, and even if the goal of the process in question would only be seldom achieved. In Section 2.6, finally, I return to the use, mentioned previously, of religion for maintaining social stability, and introduce its possible use for moral education. I argue that these uses do not secure this phenomenon a necessary function, as, for Aristotle, it must be seen to have.

2.2 Avoiding the Problem: True Religion, Religious Reform, Unnecessary Religion

The initial problem we face arises because of the seeming inconsistency among Aristotle's apparent views that (*a*) the content of traditional religion is false; (*b*) traditional religion is to be kept *as is* (unreformed) in any naturally existing *polis*, even in the *ideal* city; and (*c*) traditional religion, and its institutions, are in fact conditionally necessary for the *polis* as such, that is, for any self-governing society that is politically organized according to nature. How could it be politically useful, let alone necessary, to preserve an unrevised version of a false religion in the city? Eliminating any one of these three items would enable us to avoid the problem. However, the strategy of arguing that Aristotle was in fact not actually committed to all three is doomed to fail. (1) As we have seen in Chapter 1, Aristotle generally rejects the content of traditional religion, which includes depictions of gods as anthropomorphic and providential, as false.

It has also been argued, and sometimes assumed, that, though Aristotle may view the traditional religion of his day as flawed and largely false, (2) the religion he envisages for his *ideal polis* would in fact be congruous with his own philosophy. The religion of *that* city, in other words, might either be a compromise with traditional religion, incorporating the worship of what both Aristotle and traditional religion agree are gods, say the "sun and moon,"[6] or even be limited to the worship of gods understood

---

[6] R. Kraut, *Aristotle: Political Philosophy* (Oxford, 2002), p. 204. Cf. R. Kraut (trans. comm.), *Aristotle: Politics Books VII and VIII* (Oxford, 1997), p. 102.

entirely in Aristotelian terms, such as the prime unmoved mover of the heavens.[7] On this proposal, we should deny (*b*), i.e., that Aristotle endorses the incorporation into *every* naturally constituted city of traditional religion as is, including his ideal city. But there is simply no good evidence for supposing that Aristotle recommends any such reform.[8] Indeed, the case discussed earlier of legislating a mandatory daily worship by pregnant women of "the gods who are in charge of watching over birth" (*Pol.* VII. 16, 1335b15–16), occurring in the context of the *ideal polis*, suggests that Aristotle wishes to retain even in that city the same old religious tradition along with its anthropomorphic ideas of the gods whose truth he denies. It is true that Aristotle does not mention the deities responsible for birth by name, but Eileithyia and Artemis, whom Aristotle's readers would have been reminded of, surely fit the bill better than "the most basic causes of [the] world"[9] or the prime mover of the heavens. It is also worth pointing out that within the context of discussing the program of music education in the ideal *polis* Aristotle brings up mythical depictions of two of the Olympians as examples, namely Zeus (*Pol.* VIII. 5, 1339b7–8) and Athena (VIII. 6, 1341b2–8). It seems that, in Aristotle's view, religious worship only makes sense within the framework of traditional religion whose content is false and whose gods are fictional. And yet, as we shall now see in detail, Aristotle also thinks this traditional religion and its institutions and practices must be kept in the *polis*.

Finally, then, (3) one cannot deny, or treat as a temporary aberration, Aristotle's quite explicit view that traditional religion is necessary for any *polis* to exist as such.[10] First, he includes in his list of "necessary supervisions" (ἀναγκαῖαι ἐπιμέλειαι) in a *polis*:

---

[7] D. Winthrop argues that Aristotle's intention in the *Politics* is "to suggest the desirability of reforming religion in such a way that the gods worshipped resemble as much as possible the Aristotelian *nous*," in "Aristotle's *Politics*, book I: A Reconsideration," *Perspectives on Political Science* 37 (2008), pp. 189–99 at n. 30.

[8] In support of his proposed reform of traditional religion in Aristotle's ideal *polis*, R. Kraut only cites *Met.* Λ. 8, 1074a38–b14, which he thinks discusses "a traditional part of religion that Aristotle treats with respect," namely the divinity of the "heavenly bodies" (*Aristotle: Political Philosophy*, p. 204 and n. 26; cf. *Aristotle: Politics Books VII and VIII* , p. 102). But, not only does this passage not recommend the abolition of traditional religious ideas in any political context, but it specifically introduces the traditional anthropomorphic depictions of divinity as useful for political purposes, as we shall further see in Section 2.3. Winthrop cites the same text, as well as *Pol.* III. 1286a9–1288a6 ("Aristotle's *Politics*," n. 30). It is unclear why the latter text would support religious reform.

[9] R. Kraut, *Aristotle: Political Philosophy*, p. 204.

[10] Thus, for instance, and despite Aristotle's explicit attribution to traditional religion of a conditionally necessary political role, R. Geiger, in a recent survey of the references to religion in the *Politics*, downplays the importance of religion in Aristotle's political theory, and concludes that "in seiner [sc. Aristoteles'] Systematik der politischen Analyse ist es [sc. die Religion] nur am Rande

The [supervision] that is concerned with the gods. For instance, priests, supervisors of matters concerning the holy places, the preservation of exist-ing, and the fixing of ruined, buildings, as well as those of the other [duties] inasmuch as they pertain to the gods. (*Pol.* VI. 8, 1322b18–22)

Later on, he elaborates on this idea by saying that "necessary supervisions" are those things that "a *polis* cannot exist without," again including among such things "the supervision relating to the divine (τὴν περὶ τὸ θεῖον ἐπιμέλειαν), which they call a 'priesthood' (ἱερατείαν)" (VII. 8, 1328b2–13). This elabo-ration makes it clear that the necessity Aristotle attributes to establishing religious offices in the city is conditional necessity,[11] i.e., that possessing these offices is necessary in order for any city to achieve its natural purpose of enabling its citizens to lead happy, naturally fulfilled lives. This explains why these offices are necessarily present in *any polis*, including Aristotle's ideal city, which is in fact the subject matter of the discussion in which the elaboration occurs. Evidently, for Aristotle, a *polis* simply cannot exist, as such, in the absence of institutionalized religion, which, based on our assessment of point (*b*), remains unreformed and thus includes anthropo-morphic and other mythical elements. In *Pol.* IV. 4, where Aristotle enu-merates the necessary parts (ἀναγκαῖα μέρη) of the *polis*, which he says are analogous to the things that are "necessary for every animal to have (e.g., some of the sense organs and the part that processes and receives food)" (1290b26–9), he skips from item [5] on the list to item [7], omitting item [6] (1290b39 ff.); see Table 2.1 and the following paragraph. C. D. C. Reeve contends that "the unidentified sixth part may be the class of priests (listed as an important part of any city at 1328b11–13),"[12] which seems correct if we compare the other items on the list to the list of necessary tasks (ἔργα) in the *polis* which Aristotle sets out at VII. 8, saying that among these the parts of the *polis* (as already set out in IV. 4) would necessarily be found. Following that suggestion, we may correlate the items on the two lists as shown in Table 2.1.

As we can see, the only item on Aristotle's list of necessary tasks in the *polis* missing a correlate on his list of the city's parts is the supervision of matters pertaining to the gods, whence we conclude that the missing item on the list of the necessary parts of the *polis* [6] is the class of priests. Thus, the institutions responsible for the maintenance of traditional religion, in

---

von Bedeutung" ("Aristoteles über Politik und Religion," in S. Herzbeg and R. Geiger (eds.), *Philosophie, Politik und Religion* [Berlin, 2013]).
[11] See p. 50, n. 3.
[12] C.D.C. Reeve, *Aristotle: Politics*, p. 108, n. 33.

Aristotle's view, are not merely beneficial for the *polis*; they are necessary for its proper functioning, and the people maintaining them (i.e., priests) are considered natural, and conditionally necessary, parts of the *polis*.

Now, Aristotle regards the art of warriors, as well as that of farmers and traders, all of which form natural parts of the *polis* on his list, as being "in accordance with nature" (even prior to becoming such parts, namely prior to the advent of the *polis*) (I. 8, 1256a29-b6; b23–6). There is every reason to assume, then, that Aristotle *generally* regards the (proper) practice of any natural part of the *polis* as being itself natural, and that this must apply to the maintenance of traditional religion by priests as well. Since Aristotle thinks that anthropomorphic depictions of divinity result from cognitive tendencies operative in all humans (*Pol.* I. 2, 1252b24–7), he may think that some forms of religion based on such false notions are naturally formed in any human association or community. However, a natural propensity to generate, propagate, and engage with religious ideas and practices is not sufficient to explain why traditional religion, with its false content in an unrevised form, constitutes a natural and conditionally necessary part of any *polis*, including the ideal one. A full explanation must, in addition, account for the necessary function to be fulfilled by religion in the city. Consider a comparable case. The most natural form of courage, Aristotle says, is courage "of passion," which explains why children "fight most excellently" (*EE* III. 1, 1229a27–8; *NE* III. 8, 1117a4). The *polis*

Table 2.1. *The correlation between the list of necessary parts of the* polis *(Pol. IV. 4, 1290b39–1291b2) and the list of necessary tasks in the* polis *(Pol. VII. 8, 1328b2–15)*

Necessary parts of the *polis*	Necessary tasks in a *polis*
[1] Farmers	[1] Food supply / [4] Supply of wealth
[2] Vulgar handicraftsmen (βάναυσοι)	[2] Crafts
[3] Traders	[1] Food supply / [4] Supply of wealth
[4] Hired workers (θῆτες)	[2] Crafts*a*
[5] Warriors	[3] The use of weapons
[6] ?	[5] Supervision of religious matters
[7] The rich	[4] Supply of wealth
[8] Public servants / statesmen	[6] Deliberative / judicial judgment

a Farmers, vulgar handicraftsmen, traders, and hired workers are the "four main parts of the multitude" (μέρη μάλιστα τοῦ πλήθους: VI. 7, 1321a5–6), and their tasks are closely associated (cf. III. 5, 1278a11–13; VI. 4, 1319a26–8).

employs this natural passionate propensity for fighting for its own purposes, in this case defense from both internal and external threats, ideally
through noble courageous action which Aristotle says is aided by passion
(*NE* III. 8, 1116b30–1). Now, it is this purpose for which the city utilizes the
passionate disposition of its members, rather than the dispositions themselves, that makes the class of warriors and their use of weapons a natural
and necessary part of the *polis*. Traditional religion and its institutions and
practices, then, must be seen to have a use for the *polis* in a similar way. It
remains to be seen just what such a religion could be politically necessary
for, in Aristotle's view.

2.3 The Necessary Function of Traditional Religion

In the following sections, I shall argue that the most promising candidate
for being the natural function of traditional religion in Aristotle's theory,
heeding the qualifications just mentioned, is the use of such a religion for
the process of learning first philosophy. The knowledge of first philosophy
is the central and most fundamental achievement in Aristotle's theory of
happiness, and any naturally existing *polis* must enable its citizens to attain
it. As we shall see, traditional religion contributes to this goal directly,
by generating in citizens a sense of "wonder" at gods, thereby prompting them to inquire philosophically into divinity. Since such an inquiry,
if carried out properly, ultimately leads to knowledge of first philosophy
(whose objects are the true gods of Aristotle's *Metaphysics*), and since the
sense of "wonder" at gods afforded by traditional religion is in fact necessary in order for that inquiry to begin, this use of traditional religion
should constitute its natural function in Aristotle's theory. (We shall also
see, in Section 2.5, why other possible uses of traditional religion fail as
alternatives.)

In order to see how such a function might fit in with Aristotle's theory, we need to look more closely at the passage of *Met.* Λ. 8 already discussed in Chapter 1, i.e., 1074a38-b14. It is worth quoting the passage in
full again here:

> It has been transmitted to us through the ancients and very-old ones, and
> has been passed on to future generations, in the form of a myth, that these
> [sc. the highest substances, acting as primary movers of the heavenly bodies]
> are gods, and that the divine encloses the whole of nature. The rest has been
> added, mythically, with a view to persuading the masses and for its useful-
> ness in supporting the laws and bringing about the general advantage. For
> they say that they [sc. the gods] are man-shaped or resemble certain other

animals, and [they add] other things, which are consequent on or similar to those already said. If one were to take the first point by itself, separately from those [additions], namely that they think the first substances are gods, they would be thought to have spoken excellently (lit. divinely), and though every art/science (τέχνη) and philosophy have probably been discovered as far as possible and destroyed again and again, these opinions of theirs have been preserved like remains up until now. The ancestral opinion, that we have obtained through the first ones, is clear to us only to this extent (ἐπὶ τοσοῦτον).

Here, Aristotle gives a conjectural history of the apprehension by certain very ancient persons of the fact that the unmoved movers of the heavens are gods, and the subsequent additions of anthropomorphic and mythical depictions of these gods for political purposes. At a first reading one might take this passage to make a general claim about the genesis of traditional religion, with its anthropomorphic and mythical conception of the gods, as being orchestrated by the "ancients and very-old ones" (ἀρχαῖοι καὶ παμπάλαιοι) that Aristotle refers to, or by the legislators subsequent to them, for the purpose of regulating "the many," namely the mass of little-educated workers. However, it is not said explicitly that either these "ancients" (by which Aristotle clearly means to refer only to a select group of thinkers in very ancient times) or (*a fortiori*) the statesmen making use of their teachings for their own political purposes are in fact responsible for the *invention* of either anthropomorphic or mythological depictions of divinity. Nor should we suppose that this is what Aristotle has in mind, since he seems to think (and quite plausibly) that such depictions are, most basically, a result of a human cognitive tendency. Thus he says, as we have seen, that it is *all people* (πάντες/οἱ ἄνθρωποι) that make the shapes and the lives of their gods similar to their own (ἑαυτοῖς ἀφομοιοῦσιν) (as opposed to simply believing the stories related to them about humanlike gods) (*Pol.* I. 2, 1252b24–7).[13] Hence, even though the passage from Λ. 8 implies that the traditional religions of the Greeks and other civilizations in Aristotle's day are based on the mythical interpretation of the statements made by the "ancients," anthropomorphic and mythical depictions of divinity should precede the advent of such traditions, on the account he means to be offering. Such conceptions and depictions, it appears, are in Aristotle's view primordially present in human communities. The very ancient thinkers and the legislators subsequent to them merely build upon those religious (or proto-religious) foundations.

[13] Cf. pp. 16–17; p. 56.

It is important to note, in this regard, that Aristotle attributes neither the idea that there are gods, nor the idea that gods are anthropomorphic (and in some cases zoomorphic), to his "ancients," but rather only the idea that there are entities of a specific kind that really are gods, and perhaps the propagation of the idea that *these* are anthropomorphic. If so, then it is quite possible for the opinion that there are gods, and that gods are anthropomorphic, to precede any original statement made, and any truth arrived at, by the particular "ancients" Aristotle is concerned with in the passage. Whether the "ancients" themselves believe in such traditional gods, or whether they are rather simply aware of their existence in the collective consciousness whose faults they already recognize, their philosophical endeavors lead them to recognize the existence of entities, of which neither they, nor presumably others in their environment, have previously been aware. For, as Palmer has argued, the entities with which "the ancients and very old ones" are concerned (οὗτοι: 1074b3) are the unmoved movers of the heavens, rather than the heavenly bodies, as has sometimes been supposed.[14] Apart from textual considerations in favor of this reading,[15] Palmer makes the point that the statements Aristotle attributes in the passage to his "ancients" represent, not the views of the "ancients of his own age," but rather the "developed wisdom of an earlier age preserved in myth," which Aristotle presumes includes knowledge of what he considers "the primary substances" (1074b9).[16] Palmer finds further support for this interpretation in Aristotle's commitment to the cyclical recurrence of cataclysms, wiping out fully developed civilizations whose wisdom nevertheless survives in tidbits, particularly in mythology (*Cael.* I. 3, 270b16–24; *Meteor.* I. 3, 339b16–30).[17] The ancients arrived at their metaphysical apprehension, in all likelihood, through rigorous philosophical reasoning later repeated by Aristotle and his school. Since Aristotle also tells us how these proto-philosophers interacted with and made use of the content of traditional religion, their case may shed light on the way Aristotle thinks (or should think) traditional religion is properly used, i.e., what its natural necessary function is.

Next, then, these "ancients" would have been in a position to make the statement that has subsequently been "passed on to future generations" (παραδέδοται . . . τοῖς ὕστερον), and that to Aristotle they seem to have

---

[14] J. Palmer, "Aristotle on Ancient Theologians"; cf. n. 25.
[15] Ibid., p. 198 n. 26; cf. W. K. C. Guthrie, "The Development of Aristotle's Theology – II," *Classical Quarterly* 38 (1934), pp. 90–8 at p. 95.
[16] Ibid., p. 199.
[17] Ibid.

uttered "excellently" (lit. divinely: θείως), namely that these things, of whose essence they have learned through philosophizing, are gods. In making this statement, to repeat, they are not introducing "god" as a new term, but rather they are showing, on philosophical grounds, that the subjects of their reasoning (the unmoved movers of the heavens) are worthy of being called "gods," the title itself being readily available and clear. This should not come as a surprise, as it is exactly what Aristotle has done himself in the preceding chapter in the *Metaphysics* (Λ. 7), where, *after* showing that the prime mover must be (1) eternal and (2) a living thing, he concludes that this being must be (a) god, using a readymade definition of "god" as "the best, eternal living thing" (ζῷον ἀίδιον ἄριστον: 1072b28–9).[18] Aristotle's proof of the existence of the unmoved mover(s) can stand without even using the term "god," as it indeed does in *Physics* VIII. Similarly, his characterization of the unmoved movers of the heavens as eternal, living things, as we have just seen, can in principle be made without appealing to the fact that possessing these properties is sufficient for these entities to count as gods given what we ordinarily mean by this word. These facts hold also for his "ancients," who seem to simply be precursors of Aristotelian philosophy.[19]

However, the basic statement made by the "ancients" (and by Aristotle), namely that the unmoved movers of the heavens are gods, is not insignificant. Though "god" means (according to the traditional definition adopted by Aristotle) "eternal living thing," by calling certain non-anthropomorphic entities "gods," as opposed to just saying that they are eternal living things, one immediately contrasts these beings with gods as ordinarily conceived. Why even retain, one might ask, the charged word "god," with its potentially misleading connotations of mythological and anthropomorphic fictions, in our philosophical account of eternal living things such as the unmoved movers of the heavens? One answer is that the "ancients," after arriving at their philosophical apprehension, need to preserve the link between mythological and metaphysical gods, since they then reapply the anthropomorphic portrayal of the gods to their newly discovered

---

[18] See Section 3.1. Cf. S. Menn, "Aristotle's Theology," in *The Oxford Handbook of Aristotle* edited by C. Shields (Oxford, 2012), pp. 422–64 at p. 423 and p. 452 n. 4; J. DeFilippo, "Aristotle's Identification of the Prime Mover as God," *The Classical Quarterly* 44.2 (1994), pp. 393–409 at p. 404. Furthermore, the addition of the predicate "best" (ἄριστον) in the definition is redundant, since Aristotle elsewhere defines "god" as an "eternal living thing," and clearly means for the predicate "best" to be subsumed under that definition (cf. *Topics* III. 1, 116b13–17; IV. 2, 122b12–17).

[19] See also T. K. Johansen, "Myth and Logos in Aristotle," in *From Myth to Reason? Studies in the Development of Greek Thought* edited by R. Buxton (Oxford, 1999), pp. 279–94 at p. 291.

substances, and do so "with a view to persuading the masses and for its usefulness in supporting the laws and bringing about the general advantage" (1074b3–5). However, since the "ancients" are not inventing, but only reintroducing, both the word "god" and the anthropomorphic ideas underlying it, for their political purposes (assuming that it is in fact they who, according to Aristotle's story, make such use of anthropomorphic depictions of divinity, and not instead people subsequent to their time, as may well be the case), it is possible that these ideas bear a previous advantage, which may have even benefitted the "ancients" themselves (as well as, later on, Aristotle himself), in encouraging and motivating their original inquiry into first causes, whereby they came to recognize the unmoved movers of the heavenly bodies and spheres as the ultimate causes and principles of being. It is true that these unmoved movers, for Aristotle, would exist as they are, and would be intelligible as such, regardless of there being myths depicting anthropomorphic deities. But, as we shall see presently, being exposed to gods in their ordinary, anthropomorphic form might still be helpful for arriving at the philosophical knowledge of such facts, just as it may also be helpful for controlling the masses. Indeed, it is possible that for human beings, given their particular psychological apparatus, arriving at the philosophical knowledge in question would be *conditioned* on being first exposed to traditional gods.

We find support for this last idea in Strabo's *Geographica*. There, Strabo discusses at length the use of anthropomorphic and mythical ideas of the gods for arriving at theoretical knowledge alongside their use for persuading "the many." His discussion evidently rests on Aristotle's texts, as we shall see, and so it might shed light on what Aristotle thinks, but does not explicitly state (in his surviving works), concerning the political function of traditional religion. Strabo writes (*Geographica*, 1.2.8):

> It was not only the poets who accepted the myths, but the *poleis* and the lawgivers also did so, and long beforehand, for the sake of their usefulness (τοῦ χρησίμου χάριν), having glimpsed into the natural condition of the rational animal. For man is a lover of knowledge (φιλειδήμων), and the beginning of this is being a lover of myths (φιλόμυθον). It is thence, then, that children begin to attend to, and to further partake themselves in, discourse. The reason is that the myth is a sort of a new language (καινολογία), telling [them] not of established facts but of other things besides. . . . And whenever you add the wonderful (τὸ θαυμαστόν) and the portentous, you increase the pleasure. . . . At the beginning, then, it is necessary (ἀνάγκη) to make use of such bait, and as [the children] come of age [one must] guide [them] toward learning of true facts, once the intelligence (τῆς διανοίας) develops and is no longer in need of "flatterers." But every ignorant and

uneducated man is in a sense a child, and is likewise a lover of myths. . . .
And since the portentous is not only pleasurable but also dreadful, there is a
use for both forms [of myth] with a view both to children and to adults. . . .
For, it is impossible for a philosopher to lead a crowd of women, or any vulgar multitude, toward reverence, piety and belief by using reason (λόγῳ),
but he must do so through religious fear (δεισιδαιμονία), and this in turn
cannot be achieved without myth-creation and talking marvels.

Scholars have acknowledged Strabo's reliance on Aristotle in this passage,
with regard to several points. His ascription to myths of usefulness for controlling the uneducated is similar to Aristotle's point about the persuasion
of the masses in our passage from Λ. 8.[20] The point about man being, owing
to its natural condition, a lover of knowing (φιλειδήμων) has been likened
to the famous opening statement of Aristotle's *Metaphysics*, according to
which all humans by nature desire to know (εἰδέναι: A. 1, 980a1).[21] The
reference to the "wonderful" (τὸ θαυμαστόν) for the initiation of learning
true facts, and the comparison in this context between the lover of knowledge and the lover of myths, has been rightly compared with an almost
identical formulation of these ideas in Aristotle's *Met.* A. 2, 982b12–19.[22] To
these we might add the similarity between Strabo's point about using fear,
as opposed to argumentation/reason (λόγος), to guide the behavior of "the
vulgar multitude," and Aristotle's similar point in *NE* X. 9 that whereas the
behavior of properly habituated people may be influenced by rational arguments (1179b20–6), "the many" are only responsive to fear (1179b10–13).

The conclusion to draw from the comparison between Strabo and
Aristotle is that Strabo's idea of the political use of mythology, not
only for persuasion of the masses to right behavior, but also for even-
tual learning of true facts by educated citizens, is also due to Aristotle.
Possibly, Strabo had access to a relevant lost work in which the point
was made.[23] Indeed, two other stretches of text in Strabo are standardly

---

[20] M. J. Hollerich, "Myth and History in Eusebius's "*De Vita Constantini*": "*Vit. Const.* 1.12" in its
Contemporary Setting," *The Harvard Theological Review* 82 (1989), pp. 421–45 at p. 428.

[21] R. Renehan, "The Private Aristotle: Two Clues," *Hermes* 123 (1995), pp. 281–92 at p. 289.

[22] D. Quinn, "*Me audiendi . . . stupentem*: The Restoration of Wonder in Boethius's *Consolation*,"
University of Toronto Quarterly 57 (1988), pp. 447–70. Aristotle and Strabo both use the same word
for "lover of myth" (φιλόμυθος), and use similar words for "wonder," "wonderful," "wondering," all
cognate with θαυμασία, to express their respective ideas.

[23] M. F. Burnyeat even argues, following F. Blass, that the passage we have been considering from
Met. Λ. 8 (1074a38-b12) was in fact copied by Aristotle from another, more polished, work: *A
Map of Metaphysics Zeta* (Pittsburgh, 2001), pp. 141–5; cf. F. Blass, "Aristotelisches," *Rheinisches
Museum* 30 (1875), pp. 481–505. Ross criticizes this view, drawing on W. Jaeger; see W. D. Ross,
Aristotle's Metaphysics: A Revised Text with Introduction and Commentary. Volume II (Oxford, 1924),
pp. 382, 384.

included in the editions of Aristotle's fragments, though neither of them mentions Aristotle by name.[24] It is important to note that Strabo's point builds on Aristotle's description (in Λ. 8) of the political use of mythical, anthropomorphic depictions of the gods, as opposed to "myth" generally speaking, so that it is not just any wonder aroused in children via myths, but specifically wonder at divinity aroused through making the gods seem humanlike, that would be relevant for the role of myths in the educational process, at the end of which, as I am proposing, the student is to learn not just any odd fact, but rather the facts of "first philosophy" dealing with the true nature of those existing entities that are worthy of being called "gods." Strabo omits this feature of Aristotle's account, since in writing his geography he is interested in the use of myths not for philosophical, but rather for historical and geographical, instruction, though his point about Homer's addition of false myths to actual occurrences for educational purposes (πρὸς τὸ παιδευτικόν) does presuppose that it is in order to learn of *those* facts that the myths are used, so that getting the audience to wonder at a different event, object, or subject matter would not be effective (or as effective) for that purpose (*Geographica*, 1.2.9).

Aristotle's own discussion of the relevance of "wonder" (θαυμάζειν) for philosophizing in *Met.* A. 2 corroborates this last point. For, as he says there, it is by wondering first at "the strange things ready to hand" (τὰ πρόχειρα τῶν ἀτόπων) that humans began, and still begin, to inquire, advancing gradually toward "raising puzzles about greater matters, e.g. about the conditions of the moon, and concerning the sun and the stars, and about the genesis of the whole world" (982b12–17).[25] It is wonder issuing from each particular issue, then, that prompts one to inquire into that issue, until one reaches a satisfactory account. The last issue just mentioned, the "genesis of the whole world," is linked to the ordinary conception of divinity, since Aristotle says that "god seems to all people to be among the causes and a kind of a first principle" (δοκεῖ . . . πᾶσιν: 983a8–9). Since, as he says in what immediately precedes (983a4–7), the most honorable science is that which both is fitting for god(s) to have and has god(s) as its object(s), Aristotle must deem the wonder aroused in a person at the god(s), which would then be a starting point for their inquiry into the nature of god(s), crucially important.

---

[24] Cf. Strabo 14.5.9=*Protrepticus* Fr. 16C Ross; 1.4.9=*Alexander* Fr. 2b Ross.
[25] Cf. Plato, *Theaetetus* 155d.

We should ask, though, whether traditional religion really is the appropriate means by which this sense of "wonder" at the divine could be reliably induced. After all, far from presenting anthropomorphic gods in order to puzzle an audience, mythology frequently seems to introduce such gods and their actions as *explanations* of puzzling facts.[26] Nevertheless, though a myth may be meant or at least taken to explain a particular phenomenon (say, the origin of crop cultivation) by presenting an action of a deity as its cause (say, Demeter's gift to Triptolemos of wheat and a flying chariot; cf. Apollod. I.V.2), this fact is quite compatible with the myth itself still having "wonderful" or puzzling features (say, Demeter's power and character). And Aristotle does insist that myths generally speaking, and hence also myths that may be given an etiological interpretation, are "composed of wonders" (*Met.* A. 2, 982b19). He also says that myths, such as those appearing in Homer, are fraught with "the wonderful" (τὸ θαυμαστόν), even more so than in tragic plays (*Poet.* 1460a11–14). Since he also thinks that (*a*) wondering at something implies the desire to learn (of that thing) (*Rhet.* 1371a30–2), and presumably therefore that the greater the wonder the stronger the desire would be, and that (*b*) one naturally enjoys more that which is akin to oneself ("e.g., a human being [is pleasant] to another human being, a horse to another horse, and a young person to another young person") (1371b12–15), it follows that the surest way of engendering a genuine enthusiasm about the gods, which would in turn be followed by a philosophical investigation of them, is through anthropomorphic, mythical depictions of divinity. It is not a far cry from this to suggest that it is at least partly for this reason that (1) Aristotle's "ancients" (or their heirs) made use of such depictions, and (2) traditional religion needs to be kept in every *polis*. Put in this light, Strabo's point that myths are used in the *polis*, not just for maintaining social stability, but also for the educational purposes of those citizens who are expected not to accept and hold traditional religious beliefs in adulthood, even if not directly borrowed, seems to provide us with a legitimate, and defensible, extension of Aristotle's view.[27]

---

[26] This point has been helpfully pointed out to me by an anonymous referee.

[27] J. Chuska touches briefly on the relation between the "wonder" in religion and in philosophy (*Aristotle's Best Regime: A reading of Aristotle's Politics VII. 1–10* [Lanham, 2000], p. 202). But, instead of considering the usefulness of the former for the latter, he emphasizes the "tension" between the two. He then proposes as reasons for keeping religion in Aristotle's ideal city several *ad hoc* uses, e.g., occupying retired citizens and enabling an economic reform. He also gives as such reasons the honoring of the *Aristotelian* god, and the use of such a god in supplying a model for contemplation (pp. 205–9). As Chuska himself recognizes, these last two uses would require "enrolling a new deity into the pantheon of the usual Greek gods" (p. 203). Thus, these are not uses of *traditional* religion, but of a reformed religion, which neither is indicated by, nor facilitates the understanding of, Aristotle's texts, as we saw in Section 2.2.

Moreover, not only is the role of traditional religion for the process of learning philosophical truths in line with Aristotle's theory, but there also seems to be every reason to accept this role as the natural function for which Aristotle deems traditional religion conditionally necessary in the *polis*. Persuading subjects to obey the laws of the city, though it might require instilling fear in them, does not in principle require that this fear be a fear *of the gods*. Though religion may facilitate such persuasion, then, it does not seem to be necessary for it (simple threat of punishment by the state might be enough). By contrast, ensuring that people learn about the gods *does* require instilling in them "wonder" *at the gods*. Since this requires anthropomorphic depictions of the gods (because people naturally take pleasure in what resembles them), and since such depictions constitute the content of traditional religion, this religion, with its institutions responsible for administering and distributing that content, turn out to have a key role in enabling people with the appropriate potential to gain philosophical knowledge about what for Aristotle are actually existing gods. Strabo, for his part, explicitly flags the necessity (ἀνάγκη) of using myths in order to get people to learn, and this idea seems at this point to fit in nicely with Aristotle's own theory.[28]

Finally, the aim of the process just described, namely the attainment of knowledge of first philosophy, is, for Aristotle, of crucial importance for both individual and civic flourishing. For the flourishing of a *polis* is determined by the flourishing of its citizens (*Pol.* VII. 2, 1324a5 ff.), and the most flourishing human life is that of a philosopher (*NE* X. 7), containing (and ideally dominated by) the highest or "most divine and most honorable" pursuit in existence, i.e., the exercise of the metaphysical knowledge of Aristotle's true gods, the unmoved movers of the outer sphere and the other movers of the individual heavenly bodies, the planets and the stars (*Met.* A. 2. 983a4–7). Indeed, according to Aristotle, the *polis exists* for the sake of the good life of its citizens (*Politics* I. 2, 1252b29–30), understood as their *eudaimonia* (cf. III. 9, 1280b29–1281a2; VII. 2, 1324a5–13), and an organized community with a government is not even worthy of being *called* a *polis* unless it is aimed at enabling its citizens to lead flourishing lives (III. 9, 1280a32–4; IV. 4, 1291a8–10), each according to his or her potential. Traditional religion, by enabling those citizens who are capable

---

[28] It is true that Strabo also says that one must use myths in dealing with "the vulgar multitude" (*Geographica*, 1.2.8). Crucially, however, he does not extend the use of myth in this context (as Aristotle does in Λ. 8) to maintaining social stability, but rather confines it to the maintenance of "reverence, piety and belief" through "religious fear" (δεισιδαιμονία).

of it to attain the highest kind of knowledge achievable, and thus the highest type of *eudaimonia*, is therefore necessary for the very existence of the *polis* as such.

2.4 The Usefulness of Traditional Religion in Aristotle's Lost Works

Further evidence for the interpretation of the natural function of traditional religion in Aristotle's view can be found in the various quotations from, and testimonies concerning, his lost works. Several of these fragments convey the idea that traditional religion, along with its practices and institutions, are valuable quite separately from any claim to providing truth. Let us begin with two fragments, usually attributed to the *De philosophia*. Synesius reports Aristotle as saying that

> those who are being initiated into the mysteries do not need to learn something, but rather need to be affected in some way (οὐ μαθεῖν τι δεῖν ἀλλὰ παθεῖν), and to gain a certain disposition (διατεθῆναι) – to become adapted for some purpose. (*Dio.* 10. 48a=*De phil.* Fr. 15a, Ross)

Similarly, in Michael Psellus' report, Aristotle discussed the Eleusinian rites, in which

> He who is initiated into the mysteries is being formed (τυπούμενος), but not taught. (*Schol. Ad Joh. Climacum* [*Cat. des Man. Alch. Grecs*, ed. Bidez, 1928], 6.171=*De phil.* Fr. 15b, Ross)

Traditionally, Aristotle's remarks in these fragments have been taken to indicate a contrast between public, civic religion and the secret practices of mystery cults in ancient Greece. Jaeger, for instance, takes Aristotle to be emphasizing (in Synesius' reported text) the "spiritual" value, as opposed to the "intellectual significance," of the contents of such cults. "The cults of the old gods," he writes, "lacked the personal relationship between the righteous man and his God, whereas the mysteries gave it the foremost place."[29]

However, as we have seen in Chapter 1, Aristotle, in several works including the *De philosophia*, rejects the content of traditional religion as false, and he could therefore not ascribe any genuine "intellectual significance" to it. The content of traditional religion, for Aristotle, has nothing whatsoever to teach us, though it is necessary in order to *get* us to learn first philosophy. At most, then, the contrast reflected in these fragments would

---

[29] W. Jaeger, *Aristotle*, p. 160. Cf. I. Bywater, "On Philosophy," p. 79.

be between the prevalent (but wrong) opinion regarding civic religion as conveying truth and the (presumably widely accepted) fact that mystery cults are not meant to convey true information, but are valuable because of something else. What we might expect Aristotle's point in these fragments to be, then, is to correct the misguided opinion concerning civic religion, and to argue that whatever value it might have would not lie in the truth it is presumed to provide. He does this by focusing on an example of a religious practice (initiation into the mysteries) whose force is uncontroversially *not* in the gathering of any knowledge or truth, but rather in the attainment of a certain state or condition that is thought to be somehow beneficial to whomever manages to reach it.[30]

Aristotle would have had a difficult time persuading his readers of the truth of his claim. Unlike mystery cults, civic religion in Greece did have an explicit claim to truth. Religious stories were a part of every citizen's education, and the heresy against the taught content and conventional wisdom on the subject was a punishable offense. Still, the point of Aristotle's criticism of traditional religion, as we have seen, remains that the truths it proclaims cannot constitute its true value. Its value must rather be found, similarly to that of mystery cults, in some other kind of benefit that it shows itself capable of bestowing upon its practicing members. This seems to be Aristotle's general view in the lost works, and it is supported by his attitude toward such religious festivities as the Olympic games and especially the performance of plays at the Dionysia. In the *Protrepticus*, Iamblichus reports, Aristotle says:

> Therefore it is not at all strange, if it [sc. understanding] would not appear useful or beneficial. For we say, not that it is beneficial, but rather that it is itself good, [and] it is befitting to choose it, not for the sake of some

---

[30] B. Effe thinks that the distinction between μαθεῖν and παθεῖν in the fragments (15a–b, Ross) corresponds to two kinds of knowledge of divinity, one arrived at by discursive thinking and the other arrived at immediately through experience (*Studien*, pp. 94–101). However, whereas Aristotle certainly distinguishes the experience of being initiated into the mysteries from knowledge arrived at through reasoning, there is no reason to think that he sees the mystical experience in question as itself involving, or leading immediately to, knowledge of divinity, or indeed of anything else. Effe bases his conjecture primarily on his reading of a passage in Dio Chrysostom (*Or.* 12. 33), which gives an initiation rite as an example of an experience (παθεῖν) leading to an apprehension of god. But Dio does not refer in this text either to Aristotle's dialogues (as he does in *Or.* 53. 1) or to his corpus, and does not even mention the distinction between μαθεῖν and παθεῖν. Effe attempts to establish a connection between Dio's text and the *De philosophia* by appealing to the presumed similarity between Dio's text and Aristotle's version of the cave allegory in Fr. 13, Ross, in which, Effe thinks, the cave dwellers arrive at an immediate knowledge of god through their experience of witnessing nature for the first time (ibid., p. 101). But we have already seen that Effe's interpretation of Aristotle's version of the cave allegory is itself unfounded (see p. 38, n. 51).

other thing, but rather because of itself. For just as we leave home to visit Olympia for the sake of the spectacle itself (αὐτῆς ἔνεκα τῆς θέας), even if nothing further is destined to result from it (for the viewing of the spectacle [θεωρία] is worth more than much money), and [just as] we view the Dionysia not in order to receive something from the performers, but rather *we* even give [them something, i.e. pay them] (. . .) thus also the viewing or contemplation [θεωρία] of the universe must be preferred over all those things that are considered useful. (from Iambl. *Protr.* 9 [52.16–54.5 Pistelli]=*Protr.* Fr. 12b, Ross)

The value of watching both the pan-Hellenic sports events and the staging of tragedies and comedies at the Dionysia is here contrasted with monetary profit, under the assumption that there is something to be gained directly from exposure to such spectacles, and by which alone their value should be measured.[31]

In another fragment, often attributed to *On Poets*, and discussing drama specifically, Aristotle clarifies just what he thinks makes such things as tragedy and comedy valuable. He says, as part of his criticism of Plato's *Republic*, that

> The rejection of tragedy and comedy is absurd, if indeed by means of them it is possible to moderately appease the affections (τὰ πάθη) and, in appeasing them, to have them working for educational purposes (πρὸς τὴν παιδείαν), once what was worn out in them has been treated. (Proclus, *in Remp.* I. 49. 13 [Kroll]=part of *De poet.* Fr. 5a, Ross)

Here, Aristotle finds the experience of attending a staging of a dramatic play at a religious festival (often on a religious theme) valuable, not due to any significance of its contents, but rather, as was the case for initiation rites, because of the (emotional) condition produced by it, a condition that is in turn capable of rendering the individual more suitable for a certain purpose, in this case learning. This is of course in line with Aristotle's view of tragedy in the *Poetics*, according to which myth as used by the poet is not meant to instruct, but to imitate action, thereby inciting the viewer's emotions (9. 1451b27–32; 1452a1–11).[32] In contrast to Plato, who thinks poetry should convey true information concerning divinity, and accordingly imposes restrictions on poets in his ideal *polis* (*Republic* II, 377b–383c), "for Aristotle," as Robert Parker puts it, "it really does not

---

[31] For further discussion of this fragment see D. S. Hutchinson and M. R. Johnson, "4. Iamblichus: Chapter IX, Commentary (25.6.2013)," in *Protrepeticus*.

[32] See R. Bodéüs, *Living Immortals*, p. 82.

matter what the dramatist says about the gods" (*Poetics*, 25. 1460b35–7).[33] The particular religious content of the work "really does not matter," however, not simply because, for Aristotle, "the theology of tragedy is so much a matter of poetic tradition,"[34] but rather because the significance of the work lies, for him, in its effectiveness in reaching the emotional condition he associates with being better able to learn (so that the particular content of the work does not matter as long as it achieves this aim).

Importantly, the significance Aristotle finds in such things as tragedy is *not* in line with the benefits that an ordinary Greek would have attended a religious festival in expectation to achieve. Ordinarily, the participation in such events was considered an essential part of one's religious education and ongoing engagement with worship. In many cases, for example, a representation in a tragedy of a cult associated with a certain deity would have been perceived by the audience, not as a "literary construct," but rather as "an exploratory construct, through which aspects of their cult are articulated, problematized and explored."[35] If so, then audiences valued at least some dramatic performances at least in part on the basis of the religious teachings they conveyed, and the point of Aristotle's remarks must be that audiences are often wrong in their valuation. The popular notion of the value of religious drama as stemming from the truth of its content did not escape philosophers in Aristotle's immediate vicinity. Plato's Athenian in the *Laws* describes how, apart from such things as the myths told to young children, it is also the "spectacles (ὄψεις) which the youth see and hear with the utmost pleasure when presented at sacrifices" that convince those youth of the very existence of gods (X. 887c7-e7). Aristotle's view on these matters, then, does not reflect the consensus. On the contrary, it seems that it would have been quite challenging for Aristotle to establish his thesis that such aspects of Greek culture as religious festivals exhibit contents that are for the most part false, and therefore cannot function as a source of true information about the nature of divinity, and, insofar as they are nevertheless valuable, must have their value elsewhere.

---

[33] R. Parker, "Gods Cruel and Kind: Tragic and Civic Theology" in *Greek Tragedy and the Historian* edited by C. Pelling (Oxford, 1997), pp. 143–60 at p. 148 (reference to source in original footnote).

[34] Ibid.

[35] C. Sourvinou-Inwood, "Tragedy and Religion" in *Greek Tragedy and the Historian* edited by C. Pelling (Oxford, 1997), p. 175. Sourvinou-Inwood discusses here the case of the Tauric cult of Artemis as presented in Euripides' *Iphigenia in Tauris*, which would have represented for an Athenian audience their own local (i.e., Attic) cult of Artemis worshippers. For a competing view see J. D. Mikalson, *Honor Thy Gods: Popular Religion in Greek Tragedy* (Chapel-Hill/London, 1991).

Thus, in the lost works, too, Aristotle seems to have insisted on his rejection of the content of religion, despite the challenges. Nevertheless, he was keen on finding the value in traditional religion, and even locates that value in the ability of traditional religion and its practices to afford a favorable emotional state conducive to learning. This idea comes close to the function we have seen Aristotle should attribute to traditional religion, i.e., initiating philosophical inquiry by engendering in (future) citizens a sense of "wonder" at divinity. The details of the connection must remain a matter of conjecture. Perhaps the emotional condition Aristotle appeals to in his fragments, in which one's emotions are "moderately appeased," is to be understood as either a part or a preliminary stage of the "wondering" at divinity leading potential philosophers to inquire into the gods philosophically. What is worth noting at this point, though, is that in his lost works, too, as far as we can tell, Aristotle was proposing a view of the use of traditional religion for learning that takes it as its basic assumption that the content of that religion is false.

2.5 The Teleological Account of Religion

At this point, one might raise an objection to attributing to Aristotle any natural function for traditional religion, as well as an objection to the particular function I have proposed in what preceded. First, then, one may ask how, given Aristotle's conception and criticism of traditional religion, he could regard its existence in the *polis* as part of a natural social phenomenon (for, surely, there could be no religious institutions without a religion for them to attend to). Aristotle generally attributes the frequent correctness of common beliefs to a natural instinct of human beings for what is true (*Rhet.* 1355a15–17, *EE* 1216b30–1). The content of traditional religion, by contrast, is based, he thinks, on the false anthropomorphic depiction of divinity arising from a cognitive proclivity of "all people" (πάντες/οἱ ἄνθρωποι) (*Pol.* I. 2, 1252b24–7) to envisage gods as humanlike but extraordinarily powerful beings, which in time gives rise to civic religion, in which further false religious myths are added for political purposes. Though this cognitive mechanism is itself naturally present in all humans, then, the false religious content to which it gives rise cannot, in Aristotle's view, be attributed to any human natural instinct for truth. That content would most likely count, in his opinion, as belonging to the conventional opinions of the many, to be contrasted with what "the wise say," which is "in accordance with nature and truth" (*S.E.* 12, 173a29–30). The content of traditional religion, then, turns out to be unnatural in the sense of being merely conventional, a fact that might seem to prevent it from being used naturally by the *polis* (through the relevant natural part of the *polis*, namely the priests) for its purposes. It is perhaps this objection that has led to the attempts, rejected in Section 2.2, at avoiding the need to discover a natural function for traditional religion in Aristotle's view, a function in enabling the *polis* to reach its natural end, even given his evident criticisms of its content.

Second, since it seems safe to assume that the successful use of traditional religion for learning philosophy would not occur regularly, or even frequently in any city, and at any rate not more regularly or more frequently than other uses (since often, and as Aristotle is well aware, the content of traditional religion would simply be taken by the majority of the population at face value), one might ask whether Aristotle could justifiably say that it is the use of religion to stimulate philosophical questioning about what gods are truly like, and so which existing entities properly count as gods, that constitutes the natural function of the phenomenon. After all, Aristotle standardly views natural phenomena as regularities occurring "either always or for the most part" (*Physics* II.8, 199b15–18, 24–6; *PA* III.2, 663b27–9). It seems, *prima facie*, more reasonable to think that traditional religion has a natural function because its content, even if false, would most likely be usually taken to be true.

In fact, however, the function we have been considering can be shown to be perfectly consistent with the principles of Aristotle's political and teleological theories, and both objections can be rejected. It is true that Aristotle does not give an explicit teleological account of how and why religious institutions are needed in any *polis*. So in order to see why the principles of his teleological politics do endorse a natural use in the *polis* of traditional religion for the sake of its role in bringing citizens with the appropriate potentials to a philosophically correct understanding of the nature of (actually existing) god(s), we can compare the "supervision of religious matters" by the priests on behalf of the city to another task that Aristotle claims is necessary for any city to undertake and which he does discuss in detail – the acquisition of wealth. Aristotle's discussion of this task is useful for responding to both of the points mentioned. First, Aristotle views one form of wealth acquisition as natural, and as making natural use of money, which is itself an unnatural convention. And second, that form of wealth acquisition is for Aristotle natural even though it does *not* occur "either always or for the most part."[36]

---

[36] On natural wealth acquisition in Aristotle as an exception to his principle that the natural occurs "either always or for the most part" see J. Annas, "Aristotle's *Politics*: A Symposium: Aristotle on Human Nature and Political Virtue," *Review of Metaphysics* 49.4 (1996), pp. 731–53 at pp. 731–3.

Aristotle discusses the art of "wealth acquisition" (ἡ χρηματιστική) in *Politics* I. 8–10, and in particular its relation to the art of "household management" (ἡ οἰκονομική) and the question regarding its naturalness. First, he makes the point that the art of wealth acquisition is not the same thing as the art of household management: the latter is concerned not with *providing* resources, but rather with *using* them (I. 8, 1256a10–13). However, Aristotle says, whether wealth acquisition is a natural part of household management is a highly contested issue (1256a13–14). Aristotle's own position is that wealth acquisition in fact takes two forms, one natural and one unnatural, and it is only the first, natural form that can be considered a natural part of household management. Wealth acquisition is called natural when it is directed at the procurement of "true wealth" (ἀληθινὸς πλοῦτος), consisting in the external and instrumental goods of the kind (e.g., food) and amount necessary for the self-sufficiency of the *polis* and so the flourishing life of its individual members (1256b30–1; 9, 1257a34–5). It is also *limited* to this kind and amount of goods (8, 1256b35–7). The *polis*, according to Aristotle, ensures the regular supply of necessary goods for its members by (gradually) developing an economic system. First, there arises a barter or exchange (μετάδοσις) of commodity for commodity (C-C)[37] among individual households (I. 9, 1257a15–30). Aristotle says that this practice is natural, and its result does not itself count as wealth acquisition. However, barter, when practiced regularly, gives rise to wealth acquisition over time, since it leads to the need for exchanges that exceed the local context, and so requires the transportation of natural goods, not all of which are "easy to carry" (εὐβάστακτα) over long distances, and this inevitably leads to the invention and use of money (1257a28–41). The exchange of necessary goods through the mediation of money (C-M-C), on Aristotle's theory, is the first form of "wealth acquisition" (ἡ χρηματιστική), and is the only *natural* form of it.

As we would expect, what makes certain kinds of wealth acquisition *unnatural*, for Aristotle, is, most basically, their being directed at the

---

Annas says: "Clearly the uppermost idea in Aristotle's mind here [sc. *Politics* I. 8–10] is that of the natural not as the usual but as the ideal, something not actually found in the world as it is" (ibid., p. 733). As we shall see, though, Aristotle thinks that natural wealth acquisition is feasible, i.e., in the "city of our prayers" he describes in *Pol.* VII–VIII and which he thinks is feasible as well.

[37] The abbreviations used hereafter (C-C, C-M-C, M-C-M, and M-M [where C stands for "commodities" and M for "money"]) are used by S. Meikle ("Aristotle on Money," *Phronesis* 39.1 [1994], pp. 26–44), and date back to Karl Marx's *Das Kapital*. My translation of key technical terms in Aristotle's economic theory is based on C. D. C. Reeve, *Aristotle: Politics*.

acquisition of unnatural wealth. In *Pol.* I. 9, 1257b1 ff., he introduces a new kind of wealth acquisition – commerce (ἡ καπηλική) – which is, broadly speaking, the use of money to buy commodities that are then resold with the aim of obtaining a greater sum of money (M-C-M). Unlike natural wealth acquisition, which is aimed at the acquisition of natural goods in just the quantities needed to maintain a natural life of moderation and justice, commerce is aimed at profit through the accumulation of money, which Aristotle says seems to be wholly conventional and unnatural (φύσει δ' οὐθέν), since it does not directly contribute to the acquisition of necessities, as is exemplified by the myth of king Midas (1257b10–23), who accumulated and hoarded gold. Elsewhere, Aristotle alludes to the etymology of the Greek word for money (νόμισμα) to argue that it is due, not to nature, but to convention or law (νόμος) (*EN* V. 5, 1133a28–31).[38] Money, if it is to count as wealth at all, then, is to be distinguished from natural wealth (*Pol.* I. 9, 1257b19–20), and therefore commerce, whose aim is to obtain and accumulate money, is also unnatural.

It is rather curious, and a source of many interpretative confusions, that Meikle, a leading contemporary interpreter of Aristotle's economic theory, speaks of money on Aristotle's view as having its own (canonical) nature (i.e., nature as spoken of in the *Physics* II sense of an internal principle of change and of being at rest). He says:

> . . . it is . . . typically Aristotelian to find out what something really is by looking for its mature form: "what each thing is when fully developed we call its nature, whether we are speaking of a man, a horse or a family" (*Pol.* I, 1252b32 f). This method would lead to the conclusion that it is in the nature of money to become an end.[39]

Meikle contrasts this "nature as an end" with the usage of money as a means, e.g., for buying necessities through natural wealth acquisition, and his conclusion is inevitably that "Aristotle is in two minds about money," and is thus "inconsistent."[40] Any apparent inconsistency dissipates, however, once we attend to the fact that, for Aristotle, money is in fact entirely due to convention, and does not exist by nature. On his view, natural wealth acquisition employs money as a tool, but nevertheless it remains a natural activity due to the naturalness of its end (obtaining natural wealth, like food, and in general whatever material things are needed for living well a decent daily life). Commerce, by contrast, is unnatural, because it is

[38] See F. D. Miller, *Nature, Justice and Rights in Aristotle's* Politics (Oxford, 1995), p. 78.
[39] Meikle, "Aristotle on Money," *p.* 34.
[40] Ibid., p. 38.

engaged in with a view to obtaining what is unnatural (i.e., money), and in fact an unlimited amount of it (I. 9, 1257b23–30; cf. II. 7, 1267a41-b5), rather than merely using it as a tool for the procurement of what *is* natural and is needed for a flourishing life.

Money, for Aristotle, is only usable as such for exchange. This feature distinguishes money from material goods such as those used for barter prior to the introduction of money, as is shown by the following passage from *Politics* I. 9, 1257a6–13:

> The use of every possession is twofold, both uses being [uses of the possession] *per se* (καθ᾽ αὐτό), but not *per se* in the same way. Rather, one is proper to the thing and one is not, e.g. the wearing, and the exchange, of a shoe. For both are uses of a shoe, for the person who gives a shoe to him who needs it in exchange for money or food [is making use of] the shoe *qua* shoe. But [this is] not the use that is proper to it. For it has not come into being for the sake of barter.

Here, Aristotle claims that there are two different uses of a given commodity *as such*, its proper use and a use that is not proper to it, the proper one being its use to satisfy the need for which it is specifically designed. Selling a shoe to someone who would use it for the specific purpose for which it was made, i.e., wear it, for instance, would be using the shoe *qua* shoe. It would not be a proper use of the shoe, however, since shoes are meant to be worn, not to be used in exchange. Now, the non-proper use of shoes, say in exchange, can be a natural use, as long as it serves a natural purpose. Barter (C-C) is "not contrary to nature" (1257a28–9), though the commodities exchanged have their own uses, separable from their exchange value. It is only the end in view of which the use of such things is made that determines whether or not it is natural, or, for that matter, unnatural. Whether or not a given use of money *qua* money is natural would be determined, much as in the case of shoes, then, by the end pursued. Like shoes, the use of money for exchange is a use of it as such but, in fact, it is the *only* use of it as such, because money just *is* a conventional means for exchange: it is, in other words, only valuable insofar as people agree to exchange it instead of exchanging goods directly. Money may also be used *as such*, that is to say in exchange, both for acquiring natural wealth and for accumulating more money. But whereas the former use of money as such is natural, the latter is not.

Naturally, Aristotle expects to see in his ideal *polis* commerce being forsaken in favor exclusively of natural wealth acquisition (VII. 6, 1327a25–31). He views this option as feasible. Aristotle's "*polis* of our prayers" is importantly only ideal in the sense of being the best *possible* city, and is therefore perfectly capable of realization, in his opinion (VII. 4, 1325b39).[41] Its economy is based on the procurement of necessary goods (τῶν ἀναγκαίων: VII. 6, 1327a27) by its citizens' selling other such goods of which the *polis* happens to possess more than enough. Hence, it is focused on arriving at, and maintaining, self-sufficiency (αὐτάρκεια) for citizens in living a good life, as opposed to surplus of either money or material goods, ones which do not have a use in that sort of life.

Several things may be learned about Aristotle's view of institutionalized religion from comparing it with his account of wealth acquisition.[42] (*a*) Aristotle's analysis of wealth acquisition shows that he can consistently view the religious institutions in the city as natural, as we have supposed he must, even while maintaining that the content of traditional religion is unnatural. Just like money, for him, the content of traditional religion is conventional. But, again just like money, it gives rise to a practice the maintenance of which is the chief responsibility of certain institutions that are in turn *conditionally* necessary for any city, as we have seen. The analogy may be extended further. (*b*) One important implication of the unnaturalness or conventionality of money is that its role in a natural process, such as the activity of natural wealth acquisition, requires that it be used as means for the attainment of a *limited* natural purpose. Once we pursue money with no limit, the process itself becomes altogether unnatural. Similarly, with the content of traditional religion, we may suppose that, for Aristotle, it cannot have its natural social use in itself, or in (engendering) the belief of the members of society in it, but must rather be used for, and limited to, the attainment of a further purpose in the *polis*, and a natural one, in order to count as having a natural role in a teleological process.

---

[41] See R. Kraut, *Aristotle: Political Philosophy*, p. 192.

[42] That we are not misguided in utilizing the analogy between money and the content of traditional religion to understand Aristotle's view of the latter is supported by the fact that Karl Marx, in *Das Kapital* as well as in earlier works, makes constant use of the same analogy. The influence of Aristotle's philosophy on Marx's thought is well known, and is acknowledged by Marx himself, e.g., in the *Capital* (I. Ch. 1. Sec. 3). Marx's own analogy is explicit in his "*On the Jewish Question*," "*Comments on James Mill*," and, most maturely, in the *Capital* I, where he compares the "religious world," which is for him a "reflection of the real world," to the conventional man-made representations concerning the origin and nature of the value of goods (through a process that he calls "commodity fetishism") (Ch. 1. Sec. 4). The conclusions Marx draws from the analogy are, needless to say, quite different from (if not the polar opposite of) Aristotle's. Marx not only thinks of a non-monetary, nonreligious society as possible, but he positively recommends it. In his view, "commodity fetishism and the god of commodities, money, prevail in a social system that is inhuman, unnatural, anti-nature" (A. Nelson, *Marx' Concept of Money* [New York, 1999], p. 179). Aristotle, on the other hand, thinks of (the uses of) both social phenomena as natural necessities. This difference, however, must not deter us from appreciating the significant similarity between their theories, which permit (and make use of) the analogy between the phenomena in question to begin with.

(*c*) Money, unlike such artifacts as shoes, as we have seen, does not have a use value over and above its exchange value. It exists by convention, and is only valuable insofar as it is endowed with value by traders and their clients. By analogy, the content of traditional religion, apart from the value given to it by those who practice the religion, is totally valueless, since, for Aristotle, it is altogether false.

We may use our findings to counter the objections mounted at the beginning of this section. First, the content of traditional religion need not be true (as opposed to conventional, and hence unnatural) in order to be naturally used for the purposes of religious institutions, when those are established under proper state oversight, any more than money needs to be natural (as opposed to unnatural in the sense of being conventional) in order to be used naturally for the purposes of the offices attending to natural wealth acquisition. Second, with the content of traditional religion sharing with money the properties of (*a*) being conventional, and thus unnatural and consequently (*b*) having a natural use that is limited to the achievement of some natural end, and (*c*) being valuable only insofar as it is valued by its users, an option becomes readily available for viewing it as usable in a natural process by the city without even being *accepted* as true. Money, for Aristotle, can, and in the ideal *polis* must, be used naturally by the *polis* for the purpose of natural and limited wealth acquisition, without itself being perceived as unlimitedly valuable. Indeed, as we have seen, Aristotle thinks that once money *is* perceived as worthy of being pursued without limit, the result is the unnatural process of commerce (M-C-M), or, what is even worse, and which has not yet been mentioned, "usury" (ὀβολοστατική), which "makes a profit from money itself, and not from the very thing money naturally procures" (M-M) and is therefore "the most hated sort [of wealth acquisition], and for the best reason" (I. 10, 1258b2–4).

Similarly, the natural use of traditional religion, in Aristotle's theory, would be limited to the natural function that it can achieve, that is, according to my suggestion in Section 2.3, the generation of just enough "wonder" (θαυμασία) at the divine in people with the appropriate potentials to get them to begin their philosophical inquiry. Suppose certain people do "wonder" at the gods as a result of their exposure to the content of traditional religion, but, rather than embarking on a philosophical journey, they decide to dedicate their lives to that content. The "lover of myths" (φιλόμυθος), whom Aristotle contrasts with the philosopher at *Met.* A. 2, 982b18–19, is such a person. Unlike philosophers, then, the *philomuthoi*, or "lovers of myths," pursue the content of traditional religion without limit, and thus fail to use this content naturally (i.e., they fail to see that it is only useful up to the point of motivating them to inquire into the nature of *real* gods, which is required for a fully philosophical and flourishing human life). In this they resemble those traders who pursue an unlimited amount of money, and thus, according to Aristotle, fail to use money naturally (i.e., they fail to see that it is only useful in exchange up to the point of enabling them to acquire natural wealth, which is required for a self-sufficient, and hence for a flourishing, life).

Now, even if religion would not unfailingly (or even usually) lead up to theoretical apprehension and activity, its necessary and natural use for that end would not be called into question. Aristotle sees money in his day as being mostly used in an unnatural way for the purposes of commerce, as opposed to natural wealth acquisition (I. 9, 1257b33–4). Nevertheless, he also thinks that abandoning commerce in favor of natural wealth acquisition is not only to be recommended, but is also actually feasible, in the "*polis* of our prayers" (VII. 6, 1327a25–31), which, in turn, he makes clear, is in itself quite feasible (VII. 4, 1325b39). Similarly, it is possible, or even likely, that a considerable percentage of Aristotle's readers in his day (and afterwards)[43] would have taken the content of traditional religion that he mentions (and that they have been otherwise exposed to) at face value, believing that it reflects the truth about, e.g., the nature of gods or the existence of divine providence. In response to such a scenario, Aristotle would simply say that such people, just like the merchants of his period, are engaging in an unnatural activity. In ideal circumstances, he would add, religion in the *polis* would function differently. In the best achievable *polis*, that is, the task of the priesthood would be the propagation of the contents of traditional religion for the purpose of getting people to engage in good human activities, culminating in philosophical activity for those who are capable of it.

2.6 The Use of Religion for Social Stability and the Enhancement of Moral Virtue

If we accept the foregoing teleological account of traditional religion based on the *Politics*, then the usefulness of this phenomenon would turn out to

---

[43] This is reflected, e.g., in the twelfth-century commentary on the *NE* by Eustratius of Nicaea/Michael of Ephesus. At X. 8, 1179a22–32, the author renders "if there comes to be any care for human affairs by the gods, as is thought. . ." as "if there is divine care for human beings . . . just as it seems to the best philosophers, and it seems to be the truth . . . (ὥσπερ δοκεῖ τοῖς ἀρίστοις κατὰ φιλοσοφίαν, καὶ δοκεῖ ἀληθεύειν . . .) (603. 10–12, Wendland).

rest on (*a*) the falsity of its content, and (*b*) the apprehension, ideally by the entire citizenry (though not necessarily by the entire population, which would include noncitizens as well), of this falsity. The function of traditional religion that we have dealt with, i.e., enabling the learning of first philosophy through the production in citizens of "wonder" (θαυμασία) at the gods, certainly is in line with these two requirements. I wish now to examine two alternative uses that also seem to fit the bill (i.e., meet criteria [*a*] and [*b*]), and show why they are, unlike the function we have discovered, insufficient for explaining why traditional religion is conditionally necessary in the *polis*, in Aristotle's view.

First, then, and as we have already seen, Aristotle himself accepts the use of traditional religion for securing social stability and adherence to law by deceiving certain people (in the ideal city, specifically noncitizens) into believing in the false contents of traditional religion. Legislators, Aristotle thinks, have introduced myths for their political purposes in the past (*Met.* Λ. 8, 1074b5), and may easily continue to do so even in ideal political circumstances (*Pol.* VII. 16, 1335b12–16). This use retains (*a*) the falsity of the content of traditional religion. It also (*b*) would normally entail the existence in the *polis* of those citizens who would reap the benefits of living in a safe society as a consequence of the false beliefs in the traditional gods of other members of their city. In fact, in Aristotle's ideal *polis*, the entire citizenry would enjoy this advantage, since it would invariably consist (at least) of virtuous men of practical wisdom (*phronimoi*), whom Aristotle expects to reject anthropomorphism with regard to divinity, as we shall see shortly. The only people that Aristotle thinks might still be controlled by religion in such political circumstances (which is in line with the example of the pregnant women dealt with before) are women and noncitizens (slaves, *perioikoi*), who in his opinion are, for different reasons, intellectually inferior.[44] Should we assume, with some scholars, then, that this use would be sufficient for

---

[44] For Aristotle, women's capacity for practical deliberation (τὸ βουλευτικόν) is "non-authoritative" (ἄκυρον) (*Pol.* I. 13, 1260a13). Elsewhere, he speaks of them as having a natural impairment (*GA* IV. 6, 775a15 ff.). A natural slave, on his theory, is a man who shares in reason (ὁ κοινωνῶν λόγου), though only to the extent of perceiving (αἰσθάνεσθαι), rather than positively having (ἔχειν), it (*Pol.* I. 5, 1254b22–3). This condition is due to an impairment of one of the two psychological features necessary for rational action, "intelligence" (διάνοια) and "spiritedness" (θυμός). Aristotle thinks of cold temperature as harmful to intelligence, and of heat as harmful to spiritedness, for which reason Greeks, who inhabit a region located between Asians and Europeans, both of whom are for him natural slaves, have a perfectly balanced combination of both features, and are thus alone naturally suited to rule as masters (VII. 7, 1327b23–33).

explaining the conditional necessity of traditional religion in the *polis* in Aristotle's view?[45]

Second, we might introduce a *new* use for traditional religion, based on Aristotle's theory, which would be in line with (*a*) the falsity of its content, (*b*) the realization by the entire citizenry of its falsity. As was just mentioned, Aristotle is commonly agreed to have addressed his *Nicomachean Ethics*, which he explicitly writes "not so that we might know what virtue is, but in order that we may become good" (II. 2, 1103b26–8), to those citizens of respectable upbringing who have come to be acquainted with ethical facts through experience, and are now on their way to learning the explanations of these facts.[46] These ought to include, apart from prospective students of philosophy, future politicians who are not necessarily either interested in, or capable of, philosophizing.[47] Throughout the *NE*, Aristotle makes it clear to this audience that the belief in traditional gods must be rejected. He claims that the gods "appear to be ridiculous when considered by reference to us" (γελοῖοι [. . .] φαίνονται πρὸς ἡμᾶς ἀναφερόμενοι: I. 12, 1101b19–20), and denies true gods any activity attributable to human beings, with the exception of theoretical contemplation (X. 8, 1178b7–23). Aristotle, then, expects even the well-educated (but nonphilosophical) Athenian citizens of his day, including these students of his, not to think anthropomorphically about the gods.

However, still in the same work, Aristotle makes positive references to the very traditional gods whose existence he convinces his audience to renounce. In VII. 1, for instance, he speaks of three "conditions of character" (τὰ περὶ τὰ ἤθη) which should be avoided: vice, lack of self-control, and beastliness, with three opposite conditions of character (to be pursued), respectively: virtue, self-control, and "that virtue which is over and above us, which is something heroic and divine" (1145a15–27). Aristotle describes the third of these positive conditions, the possessors of which either are or become gods, as arising "through an excess of virtue" (δι' ἀρετῆς ὑπερβολήν), by which he clearly means excess of virtue of character (cf. *Pol.* III. 13, 1284a3–17, 1284b25–34). The condition of beasts, then, is

---

[45] R. Mayhew, "Impiety and Political Unity: Aristotle *Politics* 1262a25–32," *Classical Philology* 9.1 (1996), pp. 54–9 at p. 58. See also T. K. Lindsay, "The 'God-Like Man' versus the 'Best Laws': Politics and Religion in Aristotle's *Politics*," *The Review of Politics* 53 (1991), pp. 488–509 especially at pp. 497–500. Broadie, S., "Aristotle," in *The History of Western Philosophy of Religion* v. 1, edited by G. Oppy and N. Trakakis (Durham, 2009), pp. 79–92 at p. 89.

[46] See M. F. Burnyeat, "Aristotle on Learning to Be Good," in *Essays on Aristotle's Ethics* edited by A.O. Rorty (Berkeley, 1980), pp. 69–92, especially at pp. 71 ff.

[47] L. S. Pangle, *Aristotle and the Philosophy of Friendship* (Cambridge, 2003), pp. 8–16. Cf. R. Bodéüs, *The Political Dimensions of Aristotle's Ethics*, J.E. Garrett trans. (Albany, 1993), esp. ch. 1.

here said to be a bad one for humans to be in, not (solely) because beasts lack reason, but because even at their best they lack moral virtue. Gods, on the other hand, are to be imitated, as far as humanly possible, not (merely) because they transcend us intellectually, but because they have an excess of moral virtue, so much, in fact, that their condition can no longer itself be called (mere) virtue.

Surely, this characterization of the gods is incompatible with true gods as Aristotle conceives of them and describes them to the audience of the *NE*, so that the "gods" to whom this condition is ascribed here must be those "gods" whose existence Aristotle's audience has already been told should be denied, i.e., the traditional gods of Greek religion. This is also confirmed by the example Aristotle gives of a possessor of the condition in question, Hector, who, according to Priam, "was nothing like the child of a mortal man, but of a god" (*NE* VII. 1, 1145a21–22; cf. *Iliad* xxiv. 258 ff.), namely one of the Olympians. The members of the audience of Aristotle's *NE*, who are not meant to be deceived into thinking that traditional gods actually exist, are nevertheless encouraged to develop their character with a view to the condition of just these fictional gods. Being exposed to depictions of such gods on a daily basis, beginning in childhood (perhaps when one would still believe in their existence), must be thought by Aristotle as helpful for achieving that end, since Aristotle views imitation as a naturally inherent feature of human beings, at the basis of their cognitive development (*Poetics*, 1448b5–8). The presence of such depictions in the experience of children is due to traditional religion (and its institutions), whose sociopolitical function might therefore be thought to consist in its use for moral education and the development of character virtue.

But there are good reasons to think that Aristotle would not view either of the two uses I have mentioned as necessary in order for the *polis* to exist as such, that is in accordance with human nature, and that therefore we cannot employ these uses to provide a complete and satisfactory explanation for why it is that he thinks of traditional religion as being necessary in this way. First, though Aristotle clearly thinks of the condition of character that he associates with the traditional gods as worthy of being pursued (*NE* VII. 1, 1145a15–27), and though it seems reasonable to assume that the more exposure one has to (morally enticing depictions of) such gods the more likely one is to develop the condition in question, it is unclear whether such an experience is a necessary condition for arriving at that condition. For, (1) it is not entirely clear that Aristotle thinks imitation of appropriate role models is a necessary condition for gaining character virtue, and (2) Aristotle seems to think of the "divine or heroic virtue" as being simply an excessive version of human character virtue, so that, at least in a society that has sufficiently virtuous agents among its members, it should be sufficient to spend time in the vicinity of the most virtuous agents in one's environment in order to get a sense of (and point of reference for) the closest approximation to the "divine or heroic virtue" that one could reasonably be expected to achieve.

Second, as we have seen in Section 2.1, when Aristotle says that religion might be useful for convincing pregnant women to exercise, he says that it would be easy (ῥᾴδιον) for the legislator to use religion in this way. Though this might mean that legislators *should* use religion for such a purpose, it does not follow that they *must* do so, given sufficiently good alternatives (VII. 16, 1335b12–16).[48] Again, in *Metaphysics* α. 3, Aristotle speaks of the "mythical and childish features" (τὰ μυθώδη καὶ παιδαριώδη) in the laws as prevailing over our knowledge of these laws (995a3–6). Even if the features in question require there to be traditional religion, it is still not obvious that these features themselves are necessary for the *polis* in order for it to enact its laws and ensure the adherence to them. Finally, in the passage with which we began, Λ. 8 1074a38-b14, Aristotle certainly associates traditional religion with its use for persuading the masses, and this use might therefore be thought to constitute the whole of the natural function of traditional religion. But, even if the passage is meant to indicate such a function (and not just the way in which religion has been used in the past), there is no reason to assume that it refers exclusively to the use in question. The text says that mythology has been used "with a view to persuading the masses *and* (καί) for its usefulness in supporting the laws and bringing about the general advantage" (1074b4–5). If we do not take the first καί to be epexegetical, then the second part of the sentence would indicate a more general advantage of mythology for the purpose of keeping the laws. It seems plausible that this advantage would include, e.g., the use of traditional religion for developing character virtue in citizens, since in *NE* X. 9 Aristotle presents a detailed account of the two principal ways by which the *polis* might ensure the adherence to its laws, corresponding to the two uses of traditional religion we have been considering in this section. The two ways are through (1) fear, in the case of "the many" (οἱ

---

[48] As we have also seen in Section 2.1 (p. 51), one might think, for instance, that the employment of one further task (ἔργον) that Aristotle says is necessary for any city, namely the use of weapons, would be sufficient for maintaining social stability, since Aristotle, at any rate, does explicitly state that it is necessary for that purpose (ἀναγκαῖον . . . ἔχειν ὅπλα πρός τε τὴν ἀρχήν: 1328b7–10), which is more than he does for religion.

πολλοί) (1179b10–13), and (2) habituation (and later on, reasoned arguments), in the case of citizens (b20–6).

Further, if we do not take the *second* καί, in 1074b5, to be epexegetical either, then we may even take the passage to include a reference to a third use of traditional religion, which would promote the "general advantage" of the *polis*, such as the function of traditional religion of enabling philosophical activity. At most, then, what 1074a38-b14 can conclusively show is that all three uses might *conjointly* constitute the necessary function of traditional religion. Though this is in principle possible, there is, as we have seen, evidence supporting the necessary function we have proposed, and no reason to accept the necessity of the other two uses.

2.7 Conclusion

Aristotle views the content of traditional religion, characteristically involving mythical, anthropomorphic depictions of the gods, as false. Nevertheless, he also thinks of traditional religion, and its institutions, as being necessary for any *polis* to exist as such, i.e., according to its natural purpose. Consequently, the natural role of religion in the *polis* would be based on the realization at least by a select few (and in the ideal *polis* by all mature citizens) of the falsity of its content. Several uses are in line with this requirement, and with Aristotle's theory more generally. First, the *polis* uses religion to deceive certain people (say, noncitizens) for the purpose of controlling their behavior. Second, religion might usefully cultivate the character virtues of (potentially) all citizens of the *polis*, by ensuring their continual encounter with depictions of excessively virtuous agents (the traditional gods), beginning in childhood. Third, religion is useful for the learning process of crucially important subjects, in particular "first philosophy." Since the objects of this science are (actually existing) gods, sparking one's "wonder" (θαυμάζειν) at gods (generally speaking), through an exposure to traditional (and fictional) gods, would be the first step toward engaging in this science (since the inquiry into any subject X requires an initial "wonder" at X).

It is the third use that is the most suitable candidate for providing traditional religion with a natural function that would explain its conditionally necessary role in the *polis* according to Aristotle's view. Among other reasons, it is only this use that makes explicit reference to the subject matter of religion (i.e., the gods). Unlike other uses of religion, like maintaining social stability and developing moral character, in other words, it seems that sparking one's interest in the gods must be carried out by means of those institutions whose prerogative is to attend to matters relating to the gods. Moreover, based on Aristotle's theory and principles, traditional religion in fact turns out to be necessary in order to ensure the occurrence of "wonder" at gods in future philosophers and consequently their arrival at knowledge of "first philosophy." Interestingly, prominent medieval followers of Aristotle have included similar uses to the three we have dealt with in their accounts of the function of (specifically) the anthropomorphic aspect of (their) religion, granting a special status to the third. A case in point, to which we shall return in Chapter 5, is the view of Moses Maimonides, a self-proclaimed Aristotelian, whose furious rebuttal of anthropomorphism in relation to divinity (in the form of a negative theology) has been, as Hilary Putnam puts it, much more radical than that of "both Islamic and Christian theologians."[49] When Maimonides acknowledges the presence of anthropomorphic depictions of God in the *Torah* (as opposed to explaining them away), he assigns to them several different uses, assuming all the while, as Aristotle does, that they are themselves false. At times, then, he speaks of certain beliefs, such as the belief in an angry and revengeful God, as being, though unqualifiedly false, also useful for "the removal of exploitation and the instillment of virtue" (*Moreh Nevukhim* [*Guide of the Perplexed*], III. 28). These two uses correspond exactly to the first two uses of traditional religion that we have found in Aristotle.

At other times, Maimonides speaks of a different use of simplistic, false descriptions of God:

> When a person begins with metaphysics (lit. "divine wisdom" [אלעלם אלאלאהי]), there shall occur not only confusion with regard to belief but a complete annihilation thereof. Such a person would resemble an infant who is being fed wheaten bread, meat and wine. This would surely kill that infant, not because these are unnatural foods for human beings, but because of the weakness of the child, precluding it from digesting and making use of them. This is why these true opinions [sc. the truths of metaphysics] are concealed, are only hinted at, and are deliberately taught by the wise in the most mysterious ways, not because they contain some evil content or are destructive of the principles of faith (as those fools believe, who only think themselves to be philosophers) but rather they are hidden because of the incapability of the human mind to receive them at the beginning [of the educational process]. (Ibid. I. 33; trans. following Friedländer)

Here Maimonides comes remarkably close to the natural function we have assigned to traditional religion in Aristotle's theory. Metaphysical truth, he

[49] H. Putnam, "On Negative Theology," *Faith and Philosophy* 14 (1997), pp. 407–22 at p. 407.

says, is to be attained gradually, after those who are fit for receiving it have been exposed only to some premeditatedly obscure version of it for the appropriate amount of time. The metaphysical truths that Maimonides has in mind here are themselves closely related (at times, identical) to those in Aristotle's theory. He describes God, e.g., much like Aristotle's prime mover, as "the intellect, and the intellecting, and the intelligible" (אלעקל ואלעאקל ואלמעקול) (I. 68, 112:14). Leaving aside the highly controversial question of whether or not Maimonides could have done so in consistency with his negative theology (or whether such descriptions are themselves for him further means of hiding the "ultimate" truth revealed only via negative theology),[50] it is clear that at least more obviously anthropomorphic depictions of god are to be counted, for him just as for Aristotle, as serving the purpose of leading one toward a philosophical investigation that culminates in the apprehension of the true nature of God.

At this point we should mention one further feature shared by Aristotle and Maimonides. For both, the most desirable goal for human beings to try and achieve is an approximation to the condition of the Aristotelian god, i.e., the exercise of one's intellect in theoretical contemplation (Aristotle: *NE* X. 8, 1178b18–23; 1179a22–32; *Met.* Λ. 7, 1072b14–18; Maimonides: *Guide* I. 1, I. 18, I. 34, I. 54, III. 8, III. 27, III. 51 [the celebrated palace allegory], III. 54).[51] On this view, then, it is a certain commonality between human beings and god(s) that accounts for (the possibility of) human flourishing or perfection, which is in turn itself understood as a form of *imitatio dei*. If we focus on Aristotle in this regard, we see that he insists that what makes human beings human is in fact the presence in them of something divine, namely the intellect (νοῦς: *NE* X. 7, 1177b34–1178a7). As it turns out, then, the anthropomorphic, mythical depiction of divinity provided by traditional religion might play an importantly broader role with a view to the attainment of philosophical knowledge than simply to motivate an inquiry into "the gods." It may further, that is, motivate an inquiry into gods *as they are related* to human beings, i.e., *qua* intellectual beings the sharing in the activity of which constitutes the most preferable way of life for us.

The use of traditional religion for the purpose of attaining philosophical knowledge, then, might explain Aristotle's initially puzzling reference to the "supervision of religious matters" as being of primary importance

---

[50] For a very reasonable solution see E. Z. Benor, "Meaning of Reference in Maimonides' Negative Theology," *The Harvard Theological Review* 88 (1995), pp. 339–60.

[51] For a discussion of these and other relevant texts see, e.g., H. Kreisel, "*Imitatio Dei* in Maimonides' *Guide of the Perplexed*," *AJS Review* 19.2 (1994), 169–211 at 179–81.

among the different tasks (ἔργα) to be fulfilled in the *polis* (πέμπτον δὲ καὶ πρῶτον τὴν περὶ τὸ θεῖον ἐπιμέλειαν: *Pol.* VII. 8, 1328b11–12). For, in accepting such a use, we are accepting this task as enabling an activity that Aristotle views as the pinnacle of human endeavor. Moreover, even if religion would not unfailingly, or even usually, lead up to theoretical apprehension, its necessary and natural use for this purpose would not be called into question, just as money, whose natural use is rarely if ever achieved, in Aristotle's view, nevertheless has this natural use, which is in principle perfectly capable of being exercised, under the right set of political circumstances. Under such proper political circumstances, the offices concerned with overseeing religious affairs would propagate the contents of traditional religion for the purpose of getting people (with the right potentials) to philosophize. Whenever the latter is accomplished, religion would make its most relevant contribution to the natural functioning of the *polis*, which, as Aristotle says, comes to be merely for the sake of living, but exists for the sake of living well (τοῦ εὖ ζῆν: I. 2, 1252b29–30).

CHAPTER 3

Humans, 'Eternal Humans' and Gods: The Usefulness of Traditional Gods for the Imitation of the Divine

3.0 Introduction

In the first two chapters I presented Aristotle's criticisms of the content of traditional religion as they emerge both from the extant corpus and from the lost dialogues, which reject anthropomorphism with respect to the gods in general, and in particular the attribution to them of beneficence and providence. The discussion in those chapters also supported the conclusion that Aristotle's criticisms are not meant to deny traditional religion a legitimate role in individual as well as civic life. In Chapter 2, I showed that, in the *Politics*, Aristotle in fact views religious institutions, and the class of citizens maintaining them, as necessary for any correctly organized *polis* to exist as such, since they perform a crucial sociopolitical function. In particular, I have argued, Aristotle thinks that religion is required for arriving at the knowledge of first philosophy, which he views as the highest intellectual achievement and the highest human good, and thus its achievement is among the most important purposes for which a *polis* existing according to human nature itself exists. Aristotle does think that religion is also useful in other ways, e.g., insofar as it encourages the masses to accept and support legitimate social and political authority. But it is its role in enabling individual human beings to come to know and understand the ultimate truths of first philosophy, and thus engage in the highest human good, that he thinks makes religion and its institutions indispensable to any well-ordered *polis*. Religion excites one's "wondering" (θαυμάζειν) at the gods by presenting traditional depictions of them. This sense of wonder leads one to inquire into the nature of gods. Eventually, assuming one possesses the appropriate potential and is proceeding in the right way, this inquiry leads to an apprehension of the true nature of divinity and the ability and will to engage actively in the contemplative knowledge of god, thus sharing in the very knowledge that is god's own essence.

The gods of traditional religion are anthropomorphic. It is this feature that Aristotle thinks attracts potential philosophers to such gods, since human beings are naturally pleased by things that are akin to themselves. Once enthusiastic about (alleged) gods that in many ways resemble them, the prospective philosophers begin their research into the nature of true gods, with whom they would turn out to share much less in common. Nevertheless, in Aristotle's theory, there remains an important feature that humans do, or can, share in common with those beings that he thinks exist and should be regarded as true gods, namely rational activity, in particular theoretical contemplation (*NE* X. 8, 1178b18–23). By engaging successfully in that activity, human beings are in fact capable of enjoying the way of life of the true gods, if only intermittently and for brief periods of time (*Met.* Λ. 7, 1072b14–18). And so, when religion acquaints us with human-like alleged gods, or, alternatively, with "eternal humans," as Aristotle calls them (B. 2, 997b8–12), it is not merely an effective tool for generating interest in a philosophical topic. It also raises the question concerning the relation between human beings and gods, the answer to which is the key to the best condition of life humanly achievable.

We can see that this is so in the final lines of *NE* X. 8. In giving his final argument in favor of taking contemplative activity based on knowledge and understanding to be complete or endlike *eudaimonia*, Aristotle encourages his audience to value most highly the exercise of their intellect by referring to the divine providence that would have been conferred upon the persons capable of engaging in such contemplation, had there been providential gods. This has come to be known as the "*theophilestatos* argument":

> Furthermore, the person who actively exercises the intellect and is its servant (τοῦτον θεραπεύων) would seem to be the person in the best condition and the most god-loved (θεοφιλέστατος). For if there comes to be any care for human affairs by the gods, as people think, it would in fact be reasonable for them to be pleased by what is best and most akin to them (εἰ γάρ τις ἐπιμέλεια τῶν ἀνθρωπίνων ὑπὸ θεῶν γίνεται, ὥσπερ δοκεῖ, καὶ εἴη ἂν εὔλογον χαίρειν τε αὐτοὺς τῷ ἀρίστῳ καὶ συγγενεστάτῳ) (and this would be the intellect) and to do favors in return (ἀντευποιεῖν) to those who love and honor this most of all (on the grounds that by doing so they are taking care of their friends) and who act correctly and beautifully.[1] And

---

[1] Taking ἐπιμελομένους to agree with αὐτούς, i.e., the gods who are pleased by and return a favor to human beings engaging in theoretical contemplation. Translators standardly take ἐπιμελομένους to refer to the human beings pleasing the gods by exercising their intellect (see ad loc., e.g., Irwin *Aristotle*: Nicomachean Ethics; Crisp, *Aristotle*: Nicomachean Ethics). Though this option is certainly

it is clear that all of these things belong most of all to the wise person. This person, then, is the most god-loved. And it is plausible that this person is also the most *eudaimōn*, so that, by this argument too, the wise would be *eudaimōn* in the highest degree. (1179a22–32)

It is important in interpreting this argument to pay proper attention to the phrase in Greek that I translate as "as people think," namely ὥσπερ δοκεῖ.[2] This is often misconstrued, as, for example, in T. Irwin's translation: "as they seem to," which indicates that Aristotle himself thinks the gods probably do take an interest in human affairs.[3] But Aristotle clearly does not think that there are any providential gods who are capable of being pleased by, loving, or "returning a favor to" any particular kind of person more than another (see Chapter 1 and Section 3.2). He also clearly expects his reader to be aware of this, since he speaks earlier in the same chapter of benevolent actions as "unworthy of the gods," to whom we may only attribute theoretical contemplation (1178b7–23).

Thus in the passage just quoted Aristotle motivates his readers (or listeners) to "be servants of their intellect" by appealing to the accepted idea in Greek traditional religion that the gods reward those who serve them through sacrifices or through honoring what they hold in high regard, as Zeus does with justice among humans or Hera, with the sanctity of marriage vows. These are gods that both he and they realize are fictional. But, as he and they realize, the true gods are intellects themselves, pure ones whose whole being consists in active contemplative knowing and understanding.[4] So, if like the traditional gods the true gods rewarded any human beings for anything they did, it would be for devoting themselves to their intellects by acquiring knowledge and understanding and actively engaging in contemplative theoretical activities. Hypothetically retaining from traditional religion the idea that the gods do reward their servants, Aristotle seeks in this argument to motivate his audience to acquire the needed knowledge and understanding and to devote themselves to its

---

possible, it misses the parallel between ἐπιμελομένους and ἐπιμέλεια in line 1179a24, and resorts to a clumsy understanding of τῶν φιλῶν at 1179a28 (e.g., as "things that are dear to them", as in the translation by W. D. Ross).

[2] Cf. J. Burnet (ed. and comm.), *The Ethics of Aristotle* (London, 1900), p. 467.

[3] T. Irwin (trans. and comm.), *Aristotle:* Nicomachean Ethics, p. 167.

[4] At least, this is unqualified true of such gods as the first unmoved mover. One possible exception is the celestial bodies. These count for Aristotle as gods, although they have material natures, and may even share in sense perception. But in their case, too, the intellect may be considered "pure," since it most probably operates completely independently of their perceptual capacity (if indeed they have one). See Section 3.1.

active exercise in as much sustained contemplation as possible throughout their remaining lifetime.

That traditional false ideas about the gods (e.g., that they give rewards) are still expected to appeal to Aristotle's audience at this stage in their intellectual development is revealing. Traditional religion would presumably be even more useful for prompting one toward an initial inquiry about the gods while one may still not even have questioned the content of that religion. The *theophilestatos* argument also shows that the inquiry in question, which is initiated by traditional religion, is in fact twofold. It implies that one must not simply inquire into the nature of divinity, but also into the relation between humans and gods. Specifically, one must ask how he or she might approximate the condition of (true) gods, since such an approximation, according to the *theophilestatos* argument, must be feasible. The answer, ultimately, and again in keeping with that argument, is that one might do this by exercising one's intellect in a contemplative activity of knowing and understanding ultimate truths, in particular truths about the true gods of Aristotle's metaphysics.

Presumably, one realizes, either from the very start or at some time along the inquiry, that it is not the condition of *traditional* gods, but rather that of the actually existing ones, that one should aspire to attain. However, it *is* the traditional gods, or the conception of these, that motivate one toward the inquiry outlined. (In fact, it seems from the *theophilestatos* argument that there is merit in using traditional ideas about the gods even for convincing those who are aware of the identity of the true gods, and who may even be themselves already in a position to engage in the activity of such gods, to do so.) The active exercise by human beings of first philosophy, whose objects are the true gods, is the highest human good, according to Aristotle's theory. And thus, bringing about this highest human good in a *polis*, as the product of the common effort of all the citizens, constitutes the ultimate sociopolitical role for the practice of traditional religion.

In this chapter I aim, first, to explain in detail why, in Aristotle's theory, the gods of traditional religion are the proper tools for motivating people with the appropriate potential toward an inquiry into the issues just mentioned, namely (*a*) the nature of true gods and (*b*) the way in which humans may approximate these entities; and second, to give an account of the purpose of the inquiry into (*a*) and (*b*), so as to show just what it is that Aristotle thinks we might gain by practicing traditional religion in the right way. In Section 2.1, I deal with issue (*a*). I distinguish between, and compare, the main classes of things that Aristotle uses the word "god(s)" to designate, namely the divine *nous* and unmoved mover(s) of the heavens in *Metaphysics* Λ, the celestial bodies, and the gods of traditional Greek religion. It is not a coincidence that Aristotle calls all such things "god(s)," since he is in fact committed to a definition of "god" that all the things in question meet. Traditional gods, then, are the appropriate class of things to lead one toward an inquiry concerning true gods, because they both are convenient items for human beings to identify with, and are in fact appropriately called gods.

In Section 3.2, I turn to issue (*b*). The gods of traditional religion share, not only in the definition of "god," but also in that of "man." Though powerful and everlasting, these gods also lead political and social lives, engage in practical deliberation, have various (human) needs, and are therefore not strictly speaking self-sufficient, as true gods according to the proper definition of gods must be. These features make traditional gods effective in raising the question of how and to what extent, being human, one might imitate the activity characteristic of gods, that is to say rational or intellectual activity. In the case of those beings that Aristotle takes to be true gods, the activity in question is, more specifically, self-contemplation with knowledge and understanding of this self. In his *Ethics*, moreover, Aristotle in fact encourages his readers to imitate *that specific* kind of activity, as far as possible.

In Section 3.3, then, finally, I go on to consider Aristotle's idea of the human imitation of divine self-contemplation. At first glance, it may seem puzzling that Aristotle recommends self-knowledge for beings (i.e., humans) who can, through first philosophy, apprehend intelligible objects much nobler than themselves (e.g., gods). However, I will argue, Aristotle thinks that it is only through self-cognition that human beings can reach self-sufficiency and attain the best condition available to them, where self-cognition includes both the knowledge and perception of one's own character and particular qualities and, ultimately, an understanding of one's own essence as intellect. The latter culminates in the knowing or understanding of one's intellect "at its peak," and this, Aristotle says, is identical to the activity in which god in fact consists, although we may engage in it only after having gone through the learning process we have described, and even then only in an imperfect, divided, and non-eternal way. Approximating the condition of the gods successfully, for us, involves knowing our limitations by comparison to them. By the time we find ourselves in that condition, then, we have resolved both of the main issues prompted by our exposure to traditional religion and its gods, dealt with in the first two sections of this chapter. First, we possess an understanding of the nature of true gods. Second, we engage in a human version of the activity of these very gods, knowing that such an imitation is as close as we can get to the divine and makes us as well off as we may hope to be.

3.1 "Eternal Humans" – Gods: The Nature of the Divine

Aristotle's working definition of god in *Metaphysics* Λ, which seems to have been a relatively standard one, is "the best [and] eternal living thing" (ζῷον ἀίδιον ἄριστον: 7, 1072b28–9).[5] J. DeFilippo importantly notes that, contrary to conventional assumptions, here in Λ. 7 Aristotle ascribes the various features of this definition (DeFilippo focuses on the predicates "eternal" and "living thing") to his prime mover *prior to* claiming that it is god, and that therefore Aristotle infers that this prime mover is god *from* the fact that it is alive and eternal, rather than the other way around.[6] The fact that the prime mover is god, in other words, is established by the conformity of this entity, as its existence and nature are established by philosophical analysis, to an already formed conception of what being a god is. Similarly, and more formally, the *Topics*, in the context of explaining the mistake of giving the differentia as a genus in a definition, gives the example of mistaking immortal to be the genus of god, with the implication that the *correct* definition of god would be "immortal living thing" (ἀθάνατον ζῷον), with "living thing" functioning as genus and "immortal" as differentia (IV. 2, 122b12–17). The absence of the superlative adjective "best" (ἄριστον) in this definition, and its presence in that of the *Metaph.* Λ. 7, need not call the intended identity of the two into question, if we take "best eternal/ immortal living thing" to indicate a relation, not to other immortal living things, but to (all) *mortal* animals.[7] In *Topics* III. 1 Aristotle says that the *proprium* (ἴδιον) of what is better (τοῦ βελτίονος) is better (βέλτιον) than the *proprium* of the worse, and then explains:

---

[5] For a discussion of this definition and its similarity to the one found in the pseudo-Platonic *Definitions* (i.e., "immortal living thing self-sufficient with regard to happiness"), see S. Menn, "Aristotle's Theology," in C. Shields (ed.), *The Oxford Handbook of Aristotle* (Oxford, 2012), pp. 422–64 at p. 423 and p. 452 n. 4.

[6] J. DeFilippo, "Aristotle's Identification of the Prime Mover as God," *The Classical Quarterly* 44.2 (1994), pp. 393–409 at p. 404.

[7] Nor should the substitution of "eternal" (in the *Metaphysics*) for "immortal" (in the *Topics* and the pseudo-Platonic *Definitions*) be a cause for concern. Aristotle elsewhere "slips" from speaking of the "immortality" of his true god to speaking of his "eternal life" (*De caelo*, 286a9; cf. *Topics* IV. 5, 126b36–127a2). In *Met.* Λ. 7, he may deviate from the precise terminology of the general definition of god that he is employing, foreknowing that the subject matter of the specific discussion to follow is his true god (or a plurality of true gods), which is (or are) of course both immortal and eternal.

e.g. [the *proprium*] of "god" [is better] than that of "human being." For whereas they do not differ at all from each other with regard to what is common between them, with regard to their *propria* (τοῖς δ' ἰδίοις) the first surpasses the second. (116b13–17)

As Alexander of Aphrodisias notes in his commentary on the text, the thing with regard to which "human being" and "god" are identical, for Aristotle, is their genus, i.e., "living thing," which as he notes they both also share with "horse" (235. 18–21, Wallies).

As for the relevant notion of *proprium*, god's *proprium* being better than human being's and both better than horse's, there are two options. Aristotle uses the term to designate a property counter-predicating with the subject it is a property of, which either (*a*) does not indicate the essence (τὸ τί ἦν εἶναι) of the subject in question or (*b*) does signify the essence of the subject, in which case it is identical with the definition of that subject (*Topics* I. 4, 101b17–25; 5, 102a18-ff.). More precisely, he tends to use a "broad sense" of *proprium*, encompassing *propria* of both types, and a "narrow sense," referring exclusively to *propria* of type (*a*).[8] Whatever is true of type (*a*) *propria*, type (*b*) *propria* must be at least included in those *propria* that Aristotle considers better or worse relative to the things of which they are *propria* being better or worse than one another, so that the relevant sense of *proprium* here should be the "broad" sense. For, type (*b*) *propria*, being definitions, signify what their subjects *are*, and so, the relation of being better or worse than one another applies to them as much as it does to the subjects themselves.[9] Aristotle explicitly mentions the (type (*b*)) *proprium*

---

[8] For a helpful discussion of this distinction see S. Slomkowski, *Aristotle's* Topics (Leiden, 1997), pp. 76–7. Slomkowski mentions various occurrences, especially in book V of the *Topics*, where the broad sense of *proprium* is actually used (cf. V. 4, 132b8–18; 132b19–34; 5, 134a18–25; 7, 137a21-b2). We shall discuss one further example, from V. 1, 128b19–20, shortly. J. Barnes counts twenty-seven out of the thirty-six *topoi* in book V in which the meaning of *proprium* is indeterminate between type (*a*) and (*b*) ("Property in Aristotle's *Topics*," *Archiv für Geschichte der Philosophie* 52 [2009], pp. 136–55 at p. 141).

[9] Alexander speaks of the *propria* of "god," "human being," and "horse" as being, in this context, "immortality" (ἀθανασία), "being receptive of knowledge" (τὸ ἐπιστήμης δεκτικόν), and "being able to neigh" (τὸ χρεμετιστικόν), respectively (ibid., ll. 21–5). In doing so, he seems to miss the mark, in that "immortality," for instance, is neither a type (*a*) *proprium* of god, since it (i.e., the quality of being immortal) is part of its definition (it is the differentia), nor the type (*b*) *proprium* of god, since it is not a full definition (furthermore, "immortality" need not, on its own, counter-predicate with "god," since it is said to belong to things that do not qualify as living things, and are therefore not gods, such as the heaven as a whole [ὁ πᾶς οὐρανός: *De caelo* II. 1, 283b26–284a1] and the perpetual motion [κίνησις] in it [*Physics* VIII. 6, 259b25–26]). Perhaps by ἀθανασία Alexander means to refer to the property of being an immortal *living thing*, in which case it would perhaps function as a type (*b*) *proprium*. In any event, my interpretation of *Topics* III. 1, 116b13–17 as pertaining (also) to type (*b*) *propria* still stands, seeing that we have Aristotle's "broad sense" of *proprium* at our disposal.

of god when he says that "[a *proprium* that holds] always is like [the *proprium*] of god, of being an immortal living thing" (V. 1, 128b19–20).[10] In saying that *this proprium* is better than the equivalent one in the case of "human being," "horse," and presumably all other animal species, Aristotle effectively says that the definition of god as an immortal animal already includes the predicate "best" (ἄριστον), the explicit presence of which in the *Metaphysics* Λ. 7 version of this definition may therefore be (justifiably) deemed redundant.

Viewing Aristotle's definition of god as unified, and as one to which he commits himself, e.g., by using it in his appraisal of his prime mover as god, one would expect him to accept any object that meets this definition, that is to say, any immortal living thing, as a god. The heavenly bodies are a case in point. Aristotle thinks of both "the courses of the planets" (αἱ φοραὶ τῶν πλανήτων) and "the nature of stars" (ἡ τῶν ἄστρων φύσις) as eternal (*Metaph.* Λ. 8, 1073a30–5). He also thinks of such objects as living things, as he makes clear by saying in *De caelo* that we must not think of them as inanimate (ἄψυχα) bodies, but rather "take them [sc. the ἄστρα of 292a11] to be partaking of life and action" (*De caelo*, II. 12, 292a18–21). This is supported by further passages in *DC* in which Aristotle says that the heaven is "animate" (ἔμψυχος) and has a "principle of change" (ἔχει κινήσεως ἀρχήν: II. 2, 285a29–30), and that its action (πρᾶξις) is of the same kind as that of animals and plants (12, 292b1–2).[11]

---

[10] R. Bodéüs seems to confuse the type (*b*) *proprium* of god here (namely *Topics* V. 1, 128b19–20) with the differentia of god at IV. 2, 122b12–17 (*Aristotle and the Theology of the Living Immortals*, trans. J. E. Garrett [Albany, 2000], p. 115).

[11] Two further passages in *De caelo* II, on the other hand, suggest that the movement of the heavenly bodies is not due to a soul. In II. 1, 284a27–8, Aristotle says it is not reasonable to assume that the universe persists eternally "by a soul constraining [it]" (ὑπὸ ψυχῆς . . . ἀναγκαζούσης), and in II. 9, 291a23, he says that the motion of the heavenly bodies can be "neither animate nor forced" (οὔτ' ἂν ἔμψυχον οὔτε βίαιον). The apparent contrast between these two groups of texts prompted a controversy dating back at least to the Byzantines (H. A. Wolfson, "The Problem of the Souls of the Spheres from the Byzantine Commentaries on Aristotle", *Dumbarton Oaks Papers* 16 [1962], pp. 65–93, at pp. 68–ff.). According to Simplicius (*in De caelo*, 388. 16–19, Heiberg), some philosophers (whom he opposes) went as far as denying (at least distinct motive and rational) souls to the heavenly bodies on Aristotle's behalf. Most recently, D. Blyth argues that in 284a27–8 and 291a23 Aristotle denies only the existence of a heavenly self-motive soul that acts on a celestial body "in a way contrary to that body's own nature" ("Heavenly Soul in Aristotle," *Apeiron* 48.4 (2015), pp. 427–65 at p. 441 and nn. 22–3; cf. J. Moreau, *L' âme du monde*, p. 115). Thus, on Blyth's view, 285a29–30 can still be taken to establish that the heavenly bodies are ensouled (contra R. Bodéüs, *Living Immortals*, p. 45, p. 120), but not that they possess either "intelligence or self-movement" (Blyth, "Heavenly Soul," p. 446). However, Aristotle cannot possibly attribute nonrational souls to the heavenly bodies consistently, since he thinks both that (*a*) nonrational soul capacities are inferior to the intellect (*NE* X. 7, 1177a20–21), and that (*b*) human beings, though they are rational animals, are inferior to the heavenly bodies, which are "more divine" (VI. 7, 1141a33-b2). It seems reasonable

Stars, for Aristotle, as it turns out, are immortal living things. According to the definition presented in this section, then, they must qualify as gods, for him. And, indeed, they do. Apart from referring to them in the context of the aforementioned discussion as "divine bodies" (τῶν σωμάτων τῶν θείων: 292b32), and as "more divine" (θειότερα) than human beings (*NE* VI. 7, 1141a33-b2), Cicero reports Aristotle to have said that the "stars must be counted among the gods" (*in deorum numero astra esse ducenda*: *N.D.* II. 15. 42=*De phil.* Fr. 21a, Ross). This is in line with the use of the definition of god in Aristotle as we have construed it, since the reason Aristotle gives for this last statement, according to Cicero, is that the stars, occupying the ethereal region which "always moves and is lively" (*semper agitatur et viget*), are endowed with perception and intelligence (*sensum . . . et intellegentiam*) (ibid.). If we may add to the fact that stars are living things the further fact that they are immortal, as we have seen Aristotle state elsewhere and as he seems to suggest here,[12] we may conclude that, for him, stars are to be counted as gods *because* they meet his definition of god as we have unpacked it in this section.

The fact that the stars count as gods for Aristotle shows that we were correct in taking the predicate "best" (ἄριστον) in the version of the definition of god in *Metaph.* Λ. 7 (as the "best and eternal living thing") to indicate a relation between the class of things that qualify as gods and that of all other (namely mortal) living things. For Aristotle regards both his prime mover and the unmoved movers of the heavenly bodies, as well as the heavenly bodies themselves (including, as we have just seen, individual stars), as gods, whereas he certainly is committed to there being a hierarchy

---

to conclude, then, that Aristotle does think of the heavenly bodies as having rational souls (which is also in line with Cicero's report, as we shall presently see).

[12] It is true that Cicero speaks in this passage of stars as "coming into being in aether" (*gigni in aethere*), which would, if taken at face value, deny them eternity (though it would not necessarily deny them immortality). However, this is clearly meant to contrast with the sublunar animals having their origin (*ortus*) in "earth, water and air," and whose generation out of such inferior elements makes it "absurd" for there not to be animals made of the celestial element (aether), which is superior and consequently most conducive to life (*ad gignenda animantia aptissima*). The statement thus seems to me to take the form of a rhetorical paromologia, in which a loose and non-literal concession is made of a characteristic feature of animals (i.e., birth) to the case of stars, in order to connect the latter with living things, and establish their status as living things in their own right. The eternity of stars is retained throughout, by their placement in a region of perpetual and eternal movement and eternal liveliness, as the upper, ethereal region is described in the passage. In any event, taking the statement literally would clash, not only with the extant Aristotelian corpus, but also with testimonies ascribed to the lost works (ὡς ἀναλλοιώτοις: Olymp. *in Phd.* 26. 22–27. 4 [Norvin]=*De phil.* Fr. 24, Ross), and, more importantly, with Cicero's own report, in which he attributes to Aristotle, for instance, the view that the courses of the stars are "in all eternity settled and immutable" (*in omni aeternitate ratos immutabilesque*: *N.D.* II. 37. 95–96=*De phil.* Fr. 13a, Ross).

between those kinds of being, where the movers of the celestial bodies are superior in goodness to the celestial bodies,[13] and both are presumably inferior in some way to the prime mover.[14] This hierarchy may even turn out to imply that higher-rank divine entities (e.g., the prime mover) are "more divine" (θειότερα) than lower-rank gods (e.g., stars) for Aristotle, in which case the predicate "best," when attributed to the former, would indicate a relation to the latter (and not only to non-gods).[15] Nevertheless, inasmuch as all immortal living things are collectively best (ἄριστα), in the sense we have outlined, the term "god" applies to all of them. Now, since the hierarchical structure of gods should include all immortal living things, there is no reason for it to exclude, in principle, anthropomorphic gods, such as those of traditional Greek religion. Aristotle of course denies the existence of such beings. But this does not mean that he also denies their being the kind of thing that he has in mind in using the term god *if* they existed.

This last statement requires clarification. When Aristotle, in *Metaphysics* B. 2, 997b8–12, criticizes those who say that "there are gods, but in human shape" for "positing nothing but eternal human beings," he means to criticize the mode of reasoning (in this case, the projection of ordinary human experience onto superhuman affairs) by which people come to believe, erroneously, in the existence of such beings (see Chapter 1). Indeed, since that belief attributes eternality to a type of being (i.e., a human) a part of whose form (namely, the nutritive soul) normally dictates a movement of "growth and decay" (*De anima* III. 9, 432b8–14), its content almost amounts to a *contradictio in adjecto*, on Aristotelian grounds.[16] Nevertheless, Aristotle certainly acknowledges the ability of people to imagine such "eternal

---

[13] Generally, in Aristotle's paradigm of action, the agent affecting change in a patient without itself being changed thereby is of a higher kind than the latter. Cf. *GC* I. 7, 324a24-b6, and the discussion thereof in S. Menn, "On Dennis De Chene's *Physiologia*," *Perspectives on Science* 8.2 (2000), pp. 119–43 at p. 136.

[14] Cf. R. W. Sharples, "Aristotelian Theology after Aristotle", in D. Frede and A. Laks (eds.), *Traditions of Theology: Studies in Hellenistic Theology, Its Background and Its Aftermath* (Leiden, 2002), pp. 1–40 at p. 8.

[15] This seems to be suggested by *De caelo* I. 9, 279a12-b3, where Aristotle outlines a notion of the "divine, primary and highest" as that which is unchangeable because there is nothing more divine than it which would be required in order to change it.

[16] It is for this reason, it seems, that Aristotle does not attribute a nutritive soul to the heavenly bodies, focusing rather on their intelligence, and possibly on their perception. Presumably, for him, the necessity of having at least such a soul in order to count as a living thing only applies to the sublunar realm (at any rate, it surely does not apply to the prime mover) (cf. *DA* II. 2, 413a20–32). This interpretation is supported by Alexander's denial (on behalf of Aristotle) of a nutritive faculty to the heavenly bodies (Simplicius in *DC* I. 8, 263. 18–21, Heiberg). Though be it noted that Alexander thinks they should not have sense perception either (ibid., II. 8, 463. 3–6). See H. A. Wolfson, "Problem of the Souls," pp. 76–8.

humans," and indeed the high place of such imaginary gods in the collective consciousness of his day. As absurd as it is to think of the gods as digesting nectar and ambrosia, and as useless as it may be to consider the truth of such ideas seriously (οὐκ ἄξιον μετὰ σπουδῆς σκοπεῖν), Aristotle knows full well that such ideas are not only thinkable, but are ordinarily thought, backed up by the authority of such figures as Hesiod (*Met.* B. 4, 1000a9–19). Now, had "eternal humans" miraculously existed, they would be immortal living things, and hence, by Aristotle's definition, gods. It is in this sense that I say that the traditional gods of Greek religion, albeit fictional for Aristotle, do not deviate from Aristotle's understanding of the term, and that they must therefore be included as referents in any general statement that he might make about gods as such.

Furthermore, the "eternal humans" functioning as gods in traditional religion share quite a significant common denominator with those gods whose existence we know Aristotle to affirm, against, say, "eternal brutes" or "eternal plants," insofar as "eternal humans," like all of Aristotle's gods, are *rational* immortal living things. As we have seen, the essence of god, captured in its full definition, includes by implication its being better than those living things that do not meet its definition. Since "eternal brutes," supposing they could exist, would lack intellect (unless they be zoomorphic gods of the kind commonly found in ancient religions, and which standardly share in deeds presupposing reasoning power), there is a real sense in which they would be *worse* than other, mortal, living things that *do* possess it (i.e., humans); for Aristotle thinks of the nutritive and perceptual capacities as inferior to the intellect (*NE* X. 7, 1177a20–21). It is no coincidence, therefore, that he regards the intellect as godlike (θεῖος), and attributes it to every entity that meets his definition of god. This attribution, it appears, follows from that very definition.[17]

In fact, on the picture that emerges from our discussion so far, the hierarchy that Aristotle sees between the different kinds of god, culminating

---

[17] Blyth (2016) has recently argued that it is only in *Met.* Λ. 9, and not yet in Λ. 7, that Aristotle identifies his Prime Mover, or God, as intellect, and that he does so by first presenting and then defending the common belief (found in Plato, Euripides, Anaxagoras, Xenophanes, and Diogenes) that the intellect is divine. But, as we have seen, the definition of god accepted and employed in Λ. 7 (1072b28–9) already directly implies that god must possess intellect. Even if one interprets Λ. 9, 1074b16, with Blyth, as indicating a common belief in the divinity of the intellect, one need not "dispense with the idea that at the start of ch.9 Aristotle is referring to a previously established identification of the Prime Mover as an intellect" (ibid., pp. 80–1). For, we have seen that the definition of God in Λ. 7 is *both* (*a*) based on a common (philosophical) belief (traced by Menn back to the pseudo-Platonic *Definitions*) *and* (*b*) (following DeFilippo) also accepted by Aristotle and applied by him to his prime mover in that chapter; see p. 91 and p. 91, nn. 5-6.

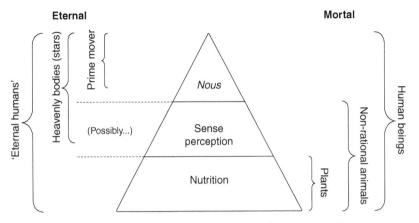

Figure 3.1 The relation between the hierarchy of eternal living things
and that of mortal living things.

in the prime mover, is in perfect correlation with the degree to which the beings in question are *purely* intellectual. This hierarchy is thus the inverse of that of the sublunary living things, among which one ensouled thing is ranked higher than another the more soul capacities it shares in, although both hierarchies, of course, have the intellect for their highest point. We may represent the relation between the two using Figure 3.1.

The intellect (i.e., prime mover), Aristotle says, has itself as an object of thought because it must think the "most godlike" of things (θειότατον: *Met.* Λ. 9, 1074b15–35),[18] and he suggests that, specifically in the case of humans, their intellect is either objectively godlike or the "most godlike" (θειότατον) thing in them (*NE* X. 7, 1177a15–16). This "most godlike" thing, as we can infer from the preceding discussion and diagram, and as we would expect given the literal meaning of the adjective, qualifies as such because it is the thing the having of which, or in the case of the prime mover *being* which, is the most in accord with the essence and definition of god (which, as we have seen, includes its being better than all mortals). "Eternal humans," though qualifying as gods, are at the bottom of the divine pyramid, so to say, since they possess both a perceptual and a nutritive soul in addition to intellect.

---

[18] It is interesting to note, in this respect, that Aristotle is said to have called the Delphic inscription "know thyself" the "most godlike" (θειότατον) (Plu. *Mor.* [*Adv. Colot.*] 118c=*De phil.* Fr. 1 Ross).

The heavenly bodies assume an intermediate position, since they are eternal, intellectual beings lacking a nutritive soul, though they are also movable material substances. They might possess sense perception, though there is a long history of debate on this issue.[19] Plutarch of Chaeronea, Galen, Plutarch of Athens and Simplicius, for example, ascribe sense perception to the heavenly bodies on Aristotle's behalf.[20] We have already mentioned Cicero's testimony to the same effect.[21] It is yet a further question whether the sense perception Aristotle would have attributed to these beings is at all comparable to that of sublunar living things, and, if so, which senses it ought to include. What seems to be generally accepted, though, is that sense perception, if they have it, must benefit them not by maintaining their (already invulnerable) existence, but by enhancing their lives in some other way. Thus, Olympiodorus the younger, in his commentary on Plato's *Phaedo*, says that, for Aristotle, the heavenly bodies (τὰ οὐράνια) possess "only sight and hearing" (ὄψιν μόνην καὶ ἀκοὴν), as opposed to the entire range of animal senses, the ones that on Aristotelian theory require the sense of touch, since one should attribute to them only those senses that contribute to well-being (πρὸς τὸ εὖ) (4. 9. 1–4 [Westerink]=*De phil.* Fr. 24, Ross), and not the mere continued existence to which the senses of touch, taste, and smell contribute for those animals that possess them.[22]

However, it is more likely that, if Aristotle indeed thinks the heavenly bodies share in perception, he nevertheless denies them the perception of any external perceptible objects, be they visible, audible, or otherwise. Aristotle claims that if the intellectual activity in which the divine intellect consists would have as its object something composite (σύνθετον), then that intellect "would change" (μεταβάλλοι γὰρ ἂν) in going through parts of the whole, which leads him to think that the divine intellect in

---

[19] In *De anima* III. 12, for example, Aristotle says that "It is impossible for a body to have a soul and a discerning intellect, but not to have sense perception, being non-stationary, but generated – but nor [is it possible for it to lack sense perception if it is] ungenerated" (434b3–5). Here, too, Aristotle seems to commit himself to attributing sense perception to the heavenly bodies (but see the controversy surrounding the interpretation of this passage, e.g., in Polansky, *Aristotle's* De anima, ad. loc.) For a survey of the controversy see H. A. Wolfson, "Problem of the Souls," pp. 77–ff. The controversy revolves around the interpretation of *De anima* III. 12 and several other key texts.

[20] See H. A. Wolfson, "Problem of the Souls," pp. 77–81. Cf. Plutarch of Chaeronea – *De musica*, 25; Plutarch of Athens – Philoponus *in De anima* III. 12, 599.35 Hayduck; Simplicius, *in De anima* 320.29 Hayduck; Simplicius – *in De anima* 106. 25–9 Hayduck and *in De caelo* 463. 6–12 Heiberg.

[21] See p. 94.

[22] Olympiodorus seems to be drawing (rather loosely) on Aristotle's view that touch (perhaps in conjunction with its derivative, taste) is essential for any animal, with all the other senses being (at least in the case of rational living things) for the sake of well-being (τοῦ εὖ ἕνεκα: *DA* III. 12, 434b22–4; cf. *De Sensu* I, 436b14–437a5).

fact simply thinks itself (*Met.* Λ. 9, 1075a5–10).[23] Similarly, for Aristotle, a heavenly body is necessarily unchanging (ἀναλλοίωτον) and unaffected (ἀπαθές) (*DC* I. 3, 270b1–4). Specifically, it is "insofar as they move, in this respect and no other, that they can become otherwise, according to place, if not according to substance" (*Met.* Λ. 7, 1072b5–7).[24] If so then, similarly to the restriction on the object of theoretical contemplation by divine intellects, the heavenly bodies, if they are percipient, could only perceive a non-composite object. And so, again following the case of divine contemplation, divine perception should amount to self-cognition. This option is available to Aristotle. In *Met.* Λ. 9, he speaks of the self-cognition necessarily occurring alongside the cognition of any objects. He gives as examples of such self-cognition both self-knowledge, later associated with the identification of intellection with the intelligible object (ἡ νόησις τῷ νοουμένῳ μία) in the theoretical sciences (i.e., in the case of the activity in which the divine intellect consists), and self-perception (1074b35–1075a5).[25]

On the other hand, such figures as Alexander, Philoponus, and Themistius deny sense perception to the heavenly bodies, often claiming that these entities, which are eternal and impassible (i.e., cannot undergo change), are in no need of sense perception either for their being or for their well-being, in Aristotle's view.[26] Now, we may grant that the heavenly bodies are in no need of sense perception for the performance of their proper, eternal, intellectual activity. This activity, being eternal and unchanging, must be entirely separable from the material constitution of those bodies. So, unlike sublunar rational animals (humans), and like the prime mover, the heavenly bodies engage in an intellectual activity that does not depend upon sense perception (through the mediation of *phantasia*). That is not to say, however, that they necessarily lack sense perception. It might be that in their case, perhaps uniquely, a perceptual soul and a noetic one coexist independently, without cooperation or interrelation of

---

[23] For an analysis of this discussion see K. Oehler, "Aristotle on Self-Knowledge," *Proceedings of the American Philosophical Society* 188 (1974), pp. 500–1.

[24] I read "ταύτῃ γε" in 1072b6 with Jaeger in the 1957 OCT (which I translate as "in this respect and no other"). Note, however, that Bonitz (1848) reads "ταύτῃ [δέ]," and also mentions the possibilities of omitting δέ (citing Alexander) or replacing it with δή (citing Cod. A^b; see *Observationes Criticae in Aristotelis Libros Metaphysicos* [Berlin, 1842], p. 150).

[25] See Oehler, "Aristotle on Self-Knowledge" (1974), p. 497: "The experience of the reflexivity inherent in all perception goes beyond the concrete content of any particular perception; it is an experience of a property common to all perceptions."

[26] See Wolfson, "Problem of the Souls," pp. 77–81. Cf. Alexander – Simplicius, *in De anima* 319–21 Hayduck, Philoponus, *in De anima* III. 12, 395–6 Hayduck; Philoponus – in *De anima* III. 12, 595.39 and 596.12 Hayduck; Themistius – *in De anima* 123. 29–31 Heinze.

any kind. Whether this was in fact Aristotle's view might be impossible to determine based on the extant texts. For present purposes it suffices to say that the heavenly bodies, for him, are eternal living things, and are therefore gods, ranking higher than traditional gods, because they do not possess a nutritive soul, but lower than other gods (e.g., the prime mover), since they are not purely intellectual beings, either because they share in perception (i.e., self-perception) or merely because they have bodies and are moved.

Importantly, the inferiority of certain types of god as gods gives them a certain usefulness over their superiors, so far as human beings are concerned. For it is precisely what makes some gods inferior to others, namely the "impurity" of their intellect, which is accompanied in their case by other soul capacities, that (naturally) brings them closer to the kind of being a human being is. As a result, the lower some gods are in rank, the easier it would be for us to identify with them, and thereby gain access to gods in general and knowledge of divinity, including and culminating in the prime mover. Such an identification is paramount in Aristotle's overall project. As we have seen in Chapter 2, Aristotle thinks that it is a sense of "wonder" at the gods that initiates the process of learning about their true nature, and, as a matter of psychological fact, he thinks, such a sense of wonder is most likely to be engendered in one by something that is akin to oneself.[27] This fact is echoed by Aristotle's own philosophical method. Even those scholars who see an abysmal disparity between the intellect of human beings and that of god in Aristotle's ultimate view agree that (at least) in *Met.* Λ. 7 he draws on a presumed similarity between the two in order to establish our ability to understand god's (particularly the prime mover's) occupation.[28] He speaks there of the prime mover as having an "occupation" (διαγωγή) identical to the best one achievable by us, only extended to eternity (1072b14–18).

The similarity between (the proper activities of) human beings and the prime mover establishes the status of the latter as a living thing (since "the activity of intellect is life, and [the prime mover] is such an activity," 1072b26–7), and this fact, combined with the eternity of the prime mover already established, enables the identification of it as (a) god, using, as we

---

[27] See p. 64. Cf. *Rhet.* 1371a30–2, 1371b12–15.
[28] J. Beere, "Thinking Thinking Thinking: On God's Self-Thinking in Aristotle's *Metaphysics* Λ. 9" (2010), esp. at. p. 5 and p. 27.

have seen, the readymade definition: "immortal/eternal living thing." It is perhaps the reliance on the comparison with human beings for the application of the genus of god to the prime mover that explains why the predicate "best" (ἄριστον) is stated explicitly in the Λ. 7 version of the definition of god, although it is also included, as discussed earlier, by implication in the *Topics* IV. 2, 122b12–17 version (namely "immortal living thing"). For it is by being of the same genus as the best mortal living things, i.e., humans, that the prime mover is here shown to belong to the class of the (absolutely) best living things, i.e., immortal living things (that is to say, gods), since it also happens to be eternal. Now, since it becomes gradually less clear in what way the activity of the prime mover really resembles human thought as *Metaphysics* Λ progresses,[29] an understanding of what it means for us to share in something as godlike as *nous* may only be plausibly attained by considering our relation to gods who resemble us in other respects as well.

It is understandable that it would seem, and often does seem, impossible for us to overcome the gap between human thinking and the activity of the prime mover, and thus to feel kinship with the prime mover, by anything like a direct comparison. A similar result holds, in fact, for a subclass of gods that are less purely intellectual and hence have more in common with us than does the prime mover, namely the heavenly bodies. Although these resemble us, not only in being rational, but also in having bodies, motion, and possibly even sense perception, as we have seen, Aristotle implies that it is nevertheless quite difficult for human beings to feel any kinship with them, as he says that people tend to think of them, wrongly, as mere bodies and as "completely inanimate" (ἀψύχων δὲ πάμπαν: *De caelo* II. 12, 292a18–20). But it is clear that Aristotle does not think of the anthropomorphic gods of traditional religion as difficult objects for humans to identify with, since he himself compares them to "eternal humans" (and, as a matter of fact, such gods were of course standardly worshipped in his immediate environment). Indeed, it is clear that it is precisely on account of the similarities between human beings and such fictional gods that Aristotle criticizes the belief in the existence of the latter. Let us investigate the basis for human beings' identification with these gods further.

---

[29] Beere, ibid., p. 3: "In fact, the resulting theory of god's thought is so strange that one might start to wonder why god's activity counts as thought at all."

3.2 Humans – "Eternal Humans": The Divine in Human Beings

Arguably the most elementary difference between the natures of human beings and the true gods that emerges from Aristotle's discussions in the ethical and political works, and one which is at the center of the difficulty in understanding the basis for the analogy Aristotle occasionally makes between the proper activities of both, is the level of self-sufficiency (αὐτάρκεια) of humans in comparison to gods. This difference is apparent in the following famous remarks Aristotle makes in *Politics* I. 2:

> He who is incapable of partaking in a community (κοινωνεῖν), or is in no need of a community due to (his) self-sufficiency, is no part of a *polis*, so that he is either a beast or a god (ἢ θηρίον ἢ θεός).[30] The impulse toward this kind of community, then, is found in everyone by nature. And he who first established [such a community] was responsible for the greatest goods. For, just as a human being is the best of the animals when perfected, thus also, when he is separated from law and justice, he is the worst of them all. (1253a27–33)

It is *because* of his self-sufficiency (δι' αὐτάρκειαν), according to what Aristotle says here, that god (or a god) has no need for social interaction or a community (κοινωνία) of whatever kind. On the other hand, the first construction of a *polis* is responsible for the greatest goods for *humans*, since (Aristotle implies) it is conducive to their being perfected (τελειοῦσθαι). Whatever it is that god's self-sufficiency consists in, then, it may not reasonably be adopted by a human being as an ideal to be attained directly. If god's condition is to be taken as an ideal to be imitated, such an imitation must not be taken to involve the renunciation of life under political organization, since that would result in the deterioration of a human being to the point of being "the worst of all [animals]," and not in the best human life, as would have been intended. The unique nature of humans forces them to arrive at the best state achievable by them in a unique way, namely via a political life, which would be appropriate neither for beast nor for god. Nevertheless, the traditional gods, Aristotle's eternal humans, *are* commonly thought to partake in politics, and even to be ruled by a king, a thought that results, as Aristotle recognizes, from a tendency to think anthropomorphically (I. 2, 1252b24–7; cf. Sections 1.1 and 2.5).

---

[30] One is reminded here, once again, of the definition of god in the pseudo-Platonic *Definitions*. Cf. p. 91, n. 5.

Moreover, the self-sufficiency of the true gods denies them any moral behavior or consideration. In the *Nicomachean Ethics* I. 9, immediately after mentioning the ways in which *eudaimonia* might be thought to be acquired,[31] Aristotle says:

> If anything (else) is (also) a gift of the gods to humans, it is reasonable that *eudaimonia* should be god-given (εἰ μὲν οὖν καὶ ἄλλο τί ἐστι θεῶν δώρημα ἀνθρώποις, εὔλογον καὶ τὴν εὐδαιμονίαν θεόσδοτον εἶναι), and particularly inasmuch as it is the best among human things. But this question would perhaps be more appropriate for another inquiry. But even if it is not god-sent, and comes to be through virtue and some sort of learning or training, it is apparently among the most divine things (τῶν θειοτάτων). For that which is the prize and end of virtue is apparently the best thing, and something both godlike and blessed (θεῖόν τι καὶ μακάριον). (1099b11–18)

The conditional in this passage does not reflect merely "some uncertainty in [Aristotle's] words" or an intuitive feeling that "the common belief in divine providence" was "incompatible with his own idea of god in its strictest form" as W. J. Verdenius claims.[32] Both its protasis and its apodosis are clearly taken by Aristotle to be false, both here and elsewhere. Apart from his explicit attribution of the acquisition of the two kinds of virtue (i.e., virtues of thought and virtues of character) to the two methods given in this passage as alternatives to divine beneficence (i.e., to learning [μάθησις] and habituation [ἄσκησις], respectively), later on, in *NE* II. 1–2 (pointing against the apodosis, that *eudaimonia* is god-given), and from his general dismissal of anthropomorphism already discussed in Chapter 1 (pointing against the protasis, that gods give gifts to human beings at all, as well as the apodosis), the description of gods in X. 8 directly excludes the possibility of their bestowing any gifts upon anybody (again, contra the original conditional as a whole). There, Aristotle says that it is unworthy of the gods to attribute to them bountiful deeds: "To whom will they give?" (since they live totally separately from human beings, and are of course in no need of financial or material aid themselves) (1178b7–18). Indeed, Aristotle there denies any action to the gods, save theoretical contemplation on the basis of metaphysical knowledge and understanding, with the conclusion that it is the latter that is most of the nature of *eudaimonia* (1178b18–23).

---

[31] Aristotle is drawing here, as on an established question with an established range of possible answers, on the opening lines of Plato's *Meno*.

[32] W. J. Verdenius, "Aristotle's Religion," pp. 60–1.

It is interesting that, in the discussion following this conclusion, arriving at which confirms the status of the conditional from I. 9 as a counterfactual, Aristotle introduces a similar conditional, i.e., in the "*theophilestatos* argument"quoted in Section 3.0: "If there comes to be any care for human affairs by the gods, as people think, it would in fact be reasonable for them to be pleased by what is best and most akin to them (and this would be the intellect) and to do favors in return (ἀντευποιεῖν) to those who love and honor this most of all" (X. 8, 1179a24–9). The protasis here ("if there comes to be any care for human affairs by the gods"), like that of the original conditional of I. 9 ("if anything is a gift of the gods to humans"), hypothesizes a possibility of divine providence. Again, far from "the truth of the antecedent [being] assumed," as S. Broadie says,[33] Aristotle must expect his reader to assume that it is false, and similarly for the apodosis. Again, the characterization of the gods appearing previously in the same chapter (cf. 1178b7–23) suffices to show that they are not the kind of beings to be capable of "caring for," let alone of loving, "being pleased by" (χαίρειν), or "returning favors to" (ἀντευποιεῖν) anyone. These are obvious and deliberate anthropomorphisms, which are designed to contrast with Aristotle's own rigorous analysis of the divine and its properties. In Chapter 1, we saw that Aristotle not only generally rejects the idea of divine intention and providence, but also views our *philia* toward the gods as unreciprocated (cf. e.g., *MM* II. 11, 1208b26–31) specifically because god, being completely self-sufficient, is in no need of friends, and will therefore have none (*EE* VII. 12, 1244b7–10). It is for the same reason, we now see, that Aristotle's true gods need not and cannot function in any moral or political context. As Aristotle puts it in *Pol.* VII. 1, 1323b21–6, god's happiness depends on no external goods (and hence, we can add, on no interaction with anybody else), but rather only on himself and the quality of his nature.

According to Aristotle, then, real gods do not act morally either toward one another or toward anyone else. Their self-sufficiency forbids it. Even justice (or just actions) are inapplicable to them, since they cannot "have an excess of" things that are "good without qualification" (*NE* V. 9, 1137a26–30). Again, Aristotle is quite aware of ordinary opinion, which

---

[33] S. Broadie, "Aristotelian Piety," *Phronesis* 48.1 (2003), pp. 54–70 at p. 61, n. 22. See also R. Bodéüs, *Aristotle and the Theology of the Living Immortals*, trans. J. E. Garrett (Albany, 2000), p. 10: "This passage [i.e. 1179a24–30] manifests a view that . . . has every intention of conforming to ordinary beliefs concerning divine benevolence." Bodéüs (ibid. p. 153) attempts to link this passage to Aristotle's remark about "the opinions of the wise" at 1179a17 in the same chapter, but these discussions are clearly separate, as is shown by the beginning of a fresh discussion between them, at 1179a20 (σκοπεῖν . . . χρή).

does attribute moral characters to the gods. Clearly, when he speaks in the *theophilestatos* argument of *NE* X. 8 of the idea that there is some "care (ἐπιμέλεια) for human affairs by the gods, as people think (ὥσπερ δοκεῖ)," he refers to the gods of traditional Greek religion, which are commonly believed to pay heed to, and take active part in, human life. These gods are neither apolitical nor amoral, and Greek culture is of course rife with examples of stories about them engaging in moral considerations and behaving accordingly, both toward one another and toward human beings. Naturally, Aristotle recognizes the existence of such a behavior among those gods (whose existence he of course rejects). Thus he says, for instance, that we attribute to the gods indignation, a feeling associated with good character (*Rhetoric* II. 9, 1386b14–15), which is the "mean between envy and spite" (*NE* II. 7, 1108a35-b1; cf. *MM* I. 27, 1192b18–19; *EE* II. 3, 1221a3). In fact, he adds, indignation is itself made into a god(dess) – *Nemesis* (III. 7, 1233b26).[34] The (fictitious) class of traditional gods, then, is distinct from self-sufficient gods like the prime mover, to whom neither morality nor politics is relevant. This does not go against their meeting Aristotle's definition of god. That definition, as we have seen, merely requires of a god to be an immortal living thing, as well as to be rational, so as not to be inferior to any mortal species, like human beings, in any respect. Traditional gods, it is true, are not *superior* to humans in every respect, as (say) the first unmoved mover might be, but this only means that, had they ever existed, they would be lower-rank gods, rather than not gods at all.

Being equal to humans in (having a) moral character, and superior to them in being gods, the "eternal humans" deified by popular religion form a class of (nonexistent) beings whose features constitute a subset of the union of the features of human beings and the first unmoved mover. The intersection between all three classes, i.e., the intellect, which, apart from being in existence, is the only feature known to be common both to humans and to the prime mover, is thus accompanied by a much wider range of properties from both beings in the class of anthropomorphic (or traditional) gods.

Conceiving of, and relating in some way to, such gods (say, by wondering at them), then, might open up new possibilities of exploring the way in which human beings share in something divine, i.e., the intellect, as part of their nature, and the extent to which their nature might allow them to enhance their share in it. One might begin this investigation by considering

---

[34] Cf. Hesiod, *Works* 200; *Theog.* 223.

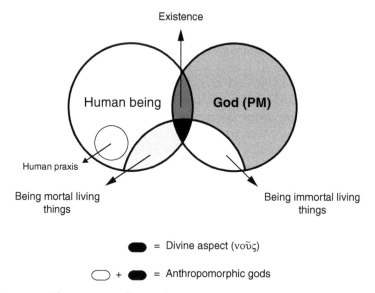

Figure 3.2 The properties of human beings, traditional gods, and the prime mover.

the case of morality just mentioned. Moral (or morally relevant) action, understood as the product of practical deliberation, is common to us and to the traditional gods. Such deliberation counts for Aristotle as an exercise of one's intellect (namely the practical intellect [νοῦς πρακτικός], which Aristotle says differs from the speculative [θεωρητικός] intellect only in the end pursued [τῷ τέλει: *De an.* III. 10, 433a14–15]). And so, traditional gods, or "eternal humans," share in the practical intellect both *qua* humans and *qua* eternal living things, that is to say, both insofar as they are "political animals" whose natures are such as to necessitate social interactions in order to flourish, as well as insofar as they are gods, whose full definition includes by implication noetic activity, which sets them apart from (and above) nonrational animals.

In her discussion of the human approximation of the divine life according to Aristotle, G. R. Lear makes an important distinction between two possible reasons why Aristotle denies that actually existing gods have moral properties. This distinction helps us see just what I mean by the usefulness of the traditional gods for stimulating human investigation into, and coming to understand, our relation to the divine via a consideration of the practical intellect:

> Now Aristotle thinks it is absurd to imagine the gods as possessing moral virtue ([*NE* X. 8,] 1178b10–21), but not because there is anything per se

undignified about exercising practical reason when in political circumstances. What is unworthy of the gods is the thought of their being tied to (much less finding their leisure in) political circumstances in the first place.[35]

The gods referred to here are of course those eternal living beings that Aristotle takes to be actually in existence, such as the first unmoved mover. That these gods do not engage in practical deliberation, Lear says, is no indication of the status of such an activity, e.g., as unworthy of them, but only of the particular circumstances surrounding the nature of such beings, including, as we have seen, their self-sufficiency, which translates into (*inter alia*) complete political and moral independence, and due to which there is no reason for them (and, consequently, no possibility for them) to deliberate.

Now, we need not accept Lear's own controversial argument for the godlikeness of political life, which relies on a very specific reading of *NE* X. 8,[36] in order to appreciate her general point. It is indisputably true that Aristotle views practical deliberation as an exercise of intellect, and the intellect as godlike, so that he is committed to viewing practical deliberation as an application of something godlike, one mode of whose exercise enables human beings to share in god's proper contemplative activity with metaphysical knowledge and understanding.[37] Human beings are confronted with situations, and are endowed with properties, totally inapplicable to (say) the prime mover, that predispose them to engage in intellectual activity for practical purposes. The activity in question remains, of course, of the intellect, and it is thus comparable to the activity of Aristotle's true gods. If those gods were "thrown into" political circumstances, their intellectual nature would manifest itself in engagement in practical deliberation and

---

[35] G. R. Lear, *Happy Lives*, p. 195.

[36] According to Lear, Aristotle commits himself in *NE* X. 8 to thinking of moral action, based on practical deliberation, as godlike, since he says there that (*a*) nonrational animals cannot be happy because they do not participate in contemplation in any way (cf. 1178b22–28), and therefore (*b*) any human life that is happy would be so (for him) due to its proximity to divine contemplation, and (*c*) "a fortiori, the happy *political* life must be happy in virtue of its godlikeness." Lear, *Happy Lives*, p. 195 (emphasis mine). However, it seems reasonable to suppose that, whichever view of political life and its relation to human flourishing he holds, in the discussion in question Aristotle deals exclusively with the philosophical life and the flourishing afforded by *it*. Otherwise, we are forced (with Lear) to attribute to Aristotle, *inter alia*, the view that practical reasoning is a "contemplation . . . of a sort" (Lear, ibid.; cf. θεωρία τις: *NE* 1178b32).

[37] V. Caston, "Aristotle's Two Intellects: A Modest Proposal," *Phronesis* 44.3 (1999), pp. 199–227 at p. 203: "when Aristotle speaks of the practical intellect (ὁ πρακτικὸς νοῦς) and the theoretical intellect (ὁ θεωρητικὸς νοῦς), we are inclined to take this only as a statement about two different capacities ([*De anima*] 3. 10, 433a14–17). No one supposes for a moment that Aristotle is referring to two distinct *intellects*."

in the rational behavior based thereon. It is of course completely impossible for such a scenario to occur, for instance in the case of the prime mover, since that would absurdly reduce this being to insufficiency, which is incompatible with its being the particular thing that it is.

Lear says: "if the gods," again referring to the gods that Aristotle takes to exist, "were political, that would imply that they were dependent (and perhaps even mortal) creatures."[38] The anthropomorphic gods of traditional religion, or "eternal humans," to return to Aristotle's own terminology, enable the elimination of the parenthetical remark in Lear's statement, by straddling immortality and human nature. These gods, although fictional, can function as thought experiments through which we may envisage the hypothetical scenario discussed (and perhaps even accept it, of course solely on the basis of imagination), in which (real) gods are "thrown into" the human condition or, more precisely, into a political context. By concluding, on the basis of this thought experiment, that the godlike modes of life in such a context would involve virtuous behavior and therefore a (correct) use of one's practical intellect, one can appreciate one's own share in the divine as tenable by such a behavior, and appreciate it on *purely Aristotelian grounds*. The upshot is both theoretical and practical. Imagining the gods as political and moral beings helps us appreciate Aristotle's view of human beings, not just as having, but indeed as essentially *consisting* in, something divine (i.e., in νοῦς: *NE* X. 7, 1177b34–1178a7),[39] and, through this appreciation, one may acquire in addition a criterion for determining which type of behavior would *most fully realize* one's own share in the divine (and consequently lead to one's [complete] flourishing or happiness).

Of course, practical deliberation is not our only, indeed not even our primary, mode of exercising our rational capacity. Higher (κρείττων) than it, says Aristotle, is the contemplative activity of the intellect (ἡ . . . τοῦ νοῦ ἐνέρεγεια . . . θεωρητικὴ οὖσα: *NE* X. 7, 1177b19–20). A human life is more godlike, and hence happier, the more it is dominated by this latter kind of activity (1177b26–1178a8). Although more godlike than any other activity achievable by us, and in fact in a sense constituting the real nexus between us and the real gods (X. 8, 1178b21–22), the human version of that activity differs from its divine expression. In particular, just as practical wisdom (φρόνησις) and the life corresponding to it are "closely entangled with our passions" (συνηρτημέναι . . . τοῖς πάθεσι) and "belong to

---

[38] G. R. Lear, *Happy Lives*, p. 195.
[39] For further discussion of this passage see G. R. Lear, *Happy Lives*, pp. 190–1.

ourcompositenature," andareconsequentlyentirely "human" (ἀνθρωπικαί),
the (theoretical) activity of the intellect, though it is carried out in separa-
tion (κεχωρισμένη) from all connection to our passions and indeed our
bodies, is also, in the case of humans, in need of "external supplies" (τῆς
ἐκτὸς χορηγίας), though to a lesser degree than its practical counterpart
(1178a19–25). This account hearkens back to Aristotle's discussions of cognition in *De anima*, in which it is established that the (human) soul never
thinks (νοεῖ) without a *phantasma* (III. 7, 431a16–17). Since *phantasia* presupposes the possession of sense perception (III. 3, 428b11–15), this feature
of human thinking distinguishes it from the thinking of, at the very least,
all immaterial gods.[40]

   The relevance of the conception of "eternal humans" to the exploration
of the relation between the intellectual activity of humans and that of the
real (and immaterial) gods may therefore be extended to include the case
of theoretical contemplation. Practical reasoning, unlike contemplation, is
entirely foreign to the true gods, but so is the use of *phantasmata* in theoretical reasoning. Since this use is, again, necessarily foreign to incorporeal
gods, we may invoke "eternal humans" once more to aid us in learning the
sense in which human thinking (νοεῖν) is godlike. This invocation becomes
all the more useful when one comes to consider the differences (already
alluded to) between the human activity of theoretical contemplation on
the basis of metaphysical knowledge and understanding and the proper
activity of the prime mover.

3.3 Humans – ("Eternal Humans") – Gods: The Human Imitation of the Divine

So far, we have seen why traditional, anthropomorphic depictions of gods
are the proper tools for motivating people to learn of (*a*) the existence
and nature of what Aristotle takes to be actually existing gods, as well

---

[40] It would also seem to distinguish it from the thinking of certain material gods, e.g., the heavenly
bodies. It is true that these beings may have sense perception, as well as voluntary movement, which
Aristotle says is only possible given desire (τὸ ὀρεκτικόν), which in turn necessitates *phantasia* (*De
an*. III. 10, 433b28–9). But one may do well to handle the material from *De anima* carefully when
applying it to anything other than sublunary living things (just as one must take Aristotle's statement that contemplation [θεωρεῖν] necessarily occurs in conjunction with some *phantasma* [III. 8,
432a8–9] as admitting of exceptions, at the very least in the case of the prime mover). As J. Owens
notes, "there is very little [in Aristotle] about the soul of the heavens," so that their cognitive apparatus remains vague (Owens, "Relation of God," p. 220). Even if the heavenly bodies turn out to
possess *phantasia*, though, this need not necessitate that *phantasia* be involved in their intellectual
activity (see also p. 160).

as (*b*) the common denominator between human beings and those true gods – namely the intellect. That arriving at knowledge concerning these matters, for the sake of which traditional religion operates in a *polis* established according to nature, is of immense significance in Aristotle's view, is already clear. The science dealing with the nature of true gods is the "most divine and most honorable" (θειοτάτη καὶ τιμιωτάτη), being both about, and worthy of being practiced by, true gods (*Met.* A. 2, 983a5–7). And thus humans, since they are in principle capable of practicing this science too, are capable of achieving, if only temporarily, the best possible life activity, precisely by understanding and pondering the truths of this science (Λ. 7, 1072b14–18). It is less clear, however, what Aristotle thinks this approximation of the condition of the divine by human beings amounts to in detail, and exactly how he recommends to bring it about.

Particularly confusing, at first glance, is his recommendation in more than one place to imitate god's activity not, or not only (or directly), by engaging in the activity of knowing and understanding the nature of divine objects, but by engaging in self-reflective thought (*MM* II. 15, 1213a14–15; *EE* VII. 12, 1244b26–7, discussed presently). What could be gained by concentrating one's intellectual attention on such lowly objects (relative to divine beings) as oneself (a human being)? The answer to this question turns out, somewhat paradoxically, to be, as I will argue, that human beings benefit from self-knowledge because, for Aristotle, we are *both* "lowly" *and* divine. Our lack of self-sufficiency, manifesting itself in our political nature *inter alia*, forces us to form friendships in order to (gradually) learn about ourselves. As the culmination of the process, however, we gain an understanding of our true nature, which *is* divine (namely we gain knowledge of ourselves *qua* intellects). Fully knowing ourselves as we truly are includes, and culminates in, knowing the best application of our nature and engaging in it, which is identical with the contemplative activity that constitutes the nature of Aristotle's true gods. Finally, since the traditional conception of divinity, as has been shown by the discussion in Section 3.2, is useful for the realization both of our human limitations, in particular the lack of self-sufficiency in human beings relative to the true gods, and of the fact that we nevertheless share in the divine as (the most essential) part of our nature, traditional religion turns out, here too, to be beneficial for getting human beings to actually engage in the human/divine activity in which we approximate god itself.

In order to understand the relationship, just sketched, between human rational activity and divine contemplation in Aristotle's theory, we need to focus on three corresponding texts, from *MM* II. 15, *EE* VII. 12, and

NE IX. 9, whose explicit topic is the relationship between human self-sufficiency and friendship. In the *Magna Moralia* II. 15, Aristotle (or the Aristotelian for whose authorship we owe this work)[41] raises the question whether the person who possesses all good things already and so is self-sufficient will have any need for a friend. Will that person be self-sufficient in this as in other matters? Aristotle proposes, and immediately rejects, the analogy between the self-sufficient person and god for the purpose of answering this question (1212b33–1213a10):

> The comparison customarily derived from god [ἐκ τοῦ θεοῦ] in discussions [ἐν τοῖς λόγοις] is incorrect there, nor would it be useful here. For if god is self-sufficient and does not need anyone, it does not follow that we will need no one. For this is the kind of thing that is said in discussions about god. For since, as they say, god has all the goods and is self-sufficient, what will he do? For he will not sleep. He will contemplate [θεάσεται] something, then, they say. For this is the finest and most appropriate thing to do. What, then, will he contemplate? For if he is going to contemplate something other [than himself], he will contemplate something better than himself. But this is absurd, that there should be something better than god. Therefore, he will contemplate himself. But this is absurd. For we evaluate the human being who examines [κατασκοπῆται] himself as ignorant. It will be absurd therefore, they say, that god will be contemplating himself. What, then, will god contemplate? Never mind that: we are inquiring about human self-sufficiency, not that of god – whether the self-sufficient man will need friendship or not.

That god does not need friends is not only "said" (λεγόμενος), but is rather a well-established and "evident" (φανερόν) fact, for Aristotle (*EE* VII. 12, 1244b7–10).[42] This fact is based on the self-sufficiency (αὐτάρκεια) in god's nature, which, as we have seen,[43] allows him to live independently, not only of friends, but indeed of any social or political interaction, by contrast to humans, who have an innate impulse for political organization in which alone, in fact, they may flourish.

It is this difference in nature between human beings and god that Aristotle must rely on when he says, in the passage just quoted, that the analogy between them is inappropriate either here (ἐνταῦθα, i.e., in the case of self-sufficiency and friendship) or there (ἐκεῖ, i.e., in the discussions about the object of god's contemplation). Although, in the discussion Aristotle

---

[41] See J. M. Cooper, "The *Magna Moralia* and Aristotle's Moral Philosophy," in *Reason and Emotion* (Princeton, 1998), pp. 195–211.

[42] See Section 1.2.

[43] See Section 3.2. Cf. *Pol.* I. 2, 1253a27–33.

refers to, it is said that it would be absurd for god to be contemplating himself (ἄτοπος . . . ὁ θεὸς ἔσται αὐτὸς ἑαυτὸν θεώμενος), this alleged absurdity is inferred on the ground that we tend to evaluate a *human being* behaving in this way as ignorant or imperceptive (ὡς ἀναισθήτῳ ἐπιτιμῶμεν). However, since god's self-sufficiency rests on his unique nature, it is irrelevant to our consideration of what human self-sufficiency involves. And, by the same token, god's own self-sufficient nature is not to be determined by reference to human self-sufficiency, so that Aristotle can endorse the condemnation of the "self-examining" human being (as he seems to, by using the first person plural "ἐπιτιμῶμεν"), while maintaining that self-contemplation *just is* the proper activity of god, that is to say of the divine *nous* whom he designates as god in *Metaphysics* Λ. 7. Aristotle positively argues, in what scholars have noticed are two parallel discussions in *EE* VII. 12, 1245b14–19 and *Met.* Λ. 9, 1074b33–5, that since (1) god, or the divine *nous*, knows or understands (νοεῖ) that which is best, and (2) god itself is that which is best or most excellent (τὸ κράτιστον), therefore (3) god or the divine *nous* "always νοεῖ the same simple thing, namely itself."[44] God's knowing or understanding, as Aristotle puts it in Λ. 9, must be knowing or understanding *of* knowing or understanding (1074b34–5: ἡ νόησις νοήσεως νόησις).

Of course, there is a sense in which Aristotle *does* recommend god's proper activity to human beings, and recommends it to them, furthermore, *qua being* the proper activity of god. In *Nicomachean Ethics* X. 8, Aristotle tells us that god's activity, which "is distinguished in blessedness," is contemplative, and that therefore the human activity most akin (συγγενεστάτη) to this must be the most constitutive of *eudaimonia* (εὐδαιμονικωτάτη) (1178b21–3). Here, Aristotle seems to *endorse* the comparison (concerning human beings) that is "customarily derived from god in discussions" (*MM* II. 15, 1212b33–4), using it to determine the activity most appropriate for humans. Furthermore, in the *MM* passage, immediately after comparing human beings with god and mocking the "self-examining" human being, Aristotle mentions the opinion of certain wise people that self-knowledge is "a most pleasant" thing (ἥδιστον: 1213a14–15). On the ground that "knowing oneself" (τὸ αὑτὸν γνῶναι/εἰδέναι/

---

[44] S. Menn, *The Aim and the Argument of Aristotle's* Metaphysics (a work in progress: <www .philosophie.hu-berlin.de/institut/lehrbereiche/antike/mitarbeiter/menn/contents/>), chapter III γ2, pp. 19–20 and n. 31; Cf. J. Brunschwig, "*Metaphysics* Λ. 9: A Short Lived Thought-Experiment?" in M. Frede and D. Charles (eds.), *Aristotle's* Metaphysics Lambda (Oxford, 1997), pp. 275–306 at pp. 304–5.

γνωρίζειν: 1213a14–15, 26) for humans is impossible to accomplish directly (or, introspectively), Aristotle offers his own method, involving a "second self" (ἕτερος ἐγώ), that is to say a friend, by observing whom alone one would gain self-knowledge just as one sees one's own face only by looking into a mirror (1213a7-b2). Although human "self-examination" is mocked, and the comparison between humans and god is declared irrelevant to understanding human self-sufficiency, then, clearly there is more to be said on both points. It is not the goal of knowing oneself that Aristotle objects to, but only one method of achieving that goal, i.e., solitary introspection. Similarly, he rejects the analogy with god, not absolutely, but only insofar as it might be taken to imply that direct self-knowing is available to humans as it is to god. To be retained from the analogy is the need of self-knowledge for self-sufficiency, whether or not this also requires having friends (which in the human case it does).

Discussing exactly the same topic (i.e., the relationship between self-sufficiency and friendship) in the *Eudemian Ethics* VII. 12, Aristotle begins again from an analogy between the self-sufficient person and god:

> If he who lives virtuously is happy, why would he need a friend? For the self-sufficient man is in need neither of useful people, nor of comforters, nor of society. He himself living with himself suffices [for him]. And this is most clear in the case of a god. (1244b5–8)

And again, just as in *MM* II. 15, the analogy is immediately rejected. Aristotle suggests we may have missed the mark "owing to the juxtaposition" (sc. of man with god) (διὰ τὴν παραβολήν: 1244b21-3). In what follows (1244b24 ff.), he goes on to explain why it is that the analogy in question *is* misguided, that is to say, why in order to approximate divine self-sufficiency as far as they can humans, unlike gods, need friendship. Now, Aristotle says at the end of *EE*, in VIII. 3, 1249b16 ff., that the best choice or acquisition of naturally good things, for example friends, is that which promotes the contemplation of god, and that the worst choice is that which hinders one from contemplating god. With the standard (ὅρος) for determining the goodness of acquiring this or that naturally good thing being the contemplation of god, then, the self-sufficiency with which *EE* VII. 12 is concerned, and for which friendship would turn out to be needed in the human case, seems to essentially involve the knowing of god, which is also the sole activity of god himself, by virtue of which *he* is self-sufficient.

To return to 1244b24–ff., where Aristotle sets out to explain why friendship is needed for human self-sufficiency, we find as a starting point an explication of (human) life in terms of perceiving and knowing (αἰσθάνεσθαι καὶ γνωρίζειν) (familiar from *De anima*), and the implication that living-together, as friends do, just is perceiving-together and knowing-together. With the implicit question of why it is that such things as perceiving and knowing *along with one's friends* would be useful for attaining self-sufficiency, Aristotle seems to go on to say that what is most choice-worthy (αἱρετώτατον) for each person is *self*-perception and *self*-knowledge (ἔστι δὲ τὸ αὑτοῦ αἰσθάνεσθαι καὶ τὸ αὑτὸν γνωρίζειν αἱρετώτατον ἑκάστῳ: *EE* VII. 12, 1244b26–7).[45] The text allows for various readings of the kind of activity that Aristotle is concerned with here.[46] We may read the pronouns, for instance, not only as reflexive ("knowing *oneself* as object [τὸ αὑτὸν γνωρίζειν]),[47] but also as subjective ("*oneself* knowing" [τὸ αὑτὸν γνωρίζειν]).[48] The reflexive reading is undoubtedly the one most in accord with the discussion in *MM* II. 15, 1213a13–26, and this fact gains added importance when we consider the similarity between the *EE* and the *MM* on the issue of the friend as "another Heracles" or "a second self" (cf. *EE* 1245a30).[49] Its occasional rejection by scholars,[50] then, implies a doctrinal discontinuity between the two works. I believe we can and should avoid this result.

In order to see why Aristotle should argue in *EE* VII. 12, 1244b26–7 that self-cognition is the "most choice-worthy" thing "for each person," we must first ask just what it is that Aristotle means by "self-cognition" in this context. Since self-knowing and self-perceiving are also discussed later on in *EE* VII. 12 (1244b29–ff.), we may begin by clarifying the notion of

---

[45] Reading "τὸ αὑτοῦ αἰσθάνεσθαι καὶ τὸ αὑτὸν γνωρίζειν" with Bonitz instead of Sylburg's "τὸ αὐτὸ αἰσθάνεσθαι καὶ τὸ αὐτὸ γνωρίζειν." Walzer-Mingay, in the OCT, follow Bonitz, whose reading seems to be well supported upon examination of the manuscripts. Bonitz rightly directs the reader in this regard to a comparison with 1244b33, 1245a4, 36 and b1. See H. Bonitz, *Observationes Criticae in Aristotelis quae feruntur Magna Moralia et Ethica Eudemia* (Berlin, 1844), p. 76.

[46] J. Whiting, "The Pleasure of Thinking Together: Prolegomenon to a Complete Reading of *EE* VII. 12," in F. Leigh (ed.), "*The* Eudemian Ethics *on the Voluntary, Friendship and Luck*" (Leiden, 2012), pp. 77–154 at pp. 91–2 and pp. 103–ff.

[47] This reading is supported, for instance, in R. Sorabji, *Self* (Chicago, 2006), p. 235.

[48] A. Kosman, "Aristotle on the Desirability of Friends," *Ancient Philosophy* 24 (2004), pp. 135–54 at p. 138.

[49] Ibid. p. 136. Kosman, who seems to call into question the authenticity of the *Magna Moralia*, has no qualms about interpreting the two discussions we are dealing with from *MM* and the *EE* as incongruent. For him, the explanation of the desirability of friends in *MM* II. 15 "[is not the explanation] that is at work in the *Eudemian Ethics*. There a different argument is offered . . ." (ibid.). See also J. Whiting, "Thinking Together," p. 123.

[50] A. Kosman, "Desirability of Friends," p. 138; J. Whiting, "Thinking Together," pp. 105–6; C. Osborne, "Selves and Other Selves in Aristotle's *Eudemian Ethics* vii 12," *Ancient Philosophy* 23 (2009), pp. 349–71, at pp. 349–52.

self-cognition there. There are two (closely related) candidate notions readily available in Aristotle's theory, and both seem to make an appearance in the text we are considering. Cognition, be it perceptual or intellectual, according to him, involves, apart from the actual cognition of the object, (1) becoming in the act of cognition somehow identical with the object cognized (and thus cognizing oneself by cognizing the object to which one is in a sense identical) (*De anima* II. 5, 418a3–6; III. 4, 430a3–4) and (2) cognizing that one is cognizing (III. 2, 425b12–25; *Met.* Λ. 9, 1074b34–ff.). [51] In our text, Aristotle first says that our desire to know is not simply a desire for knowing to occur (e.g., to some other person), but rather a desire for knowing to occur in oneself, a desire for oneself to be actively engaged in knowing (1244b29–34). This seems to be a demand for the cognition of one's cognizing, or cognition's cognition of itself ἐν παρέργῳ, as it is called in *Met.* Λ. 9, 1074b36.

In the discussion that follows, the *former* kind of self-cognition, namely the cognizing of oneself by cognizing the object to which one has become in some way identical in the act of cognition, is introduced. Aristotle seems to argue as follows (1244b34–1245a10). Life and the good are desirable (their opposites being undesirable), and therefore it is also (naturally) desirable for us to be alive and to be good. Also desirable are what is perceived and what is known (their opposites being, again, undesirable). To be perceived and to be known, therefore, is also itself desirable. Since by perceiving and knowing we become (at least in some sense) identical with the objects perceived and known, and since being known and perceived is desirable, as has just been said, it follows that it is desirable to perceive and to know. Here, the relevant notion of self-cognition is that of cognizing an object to which one has thereby become (in a way) identical. It may seem, then, that one or both of the notions we have mentioned, i.e., becoming like the object cognized and cognizing that one is cognizing, are exclusively what Aristotle has in mind in speaking of self-cognition in this chapter as "most choice-worthy." But, if that were the case, it would be unclear why Aristotle construes 1244b24–ff. as a discussion of the necessary role *friendship* plays in the attainment of human self-sufficiency, since both of the kinds of self-cognition in question are provided by cognizing any object whatsoever and do not require having friends.[52]

---

[51] On the importance of distinguishing between these two admittedly connected self-referential aspects of cognition in Aristotle see K. Oehler, "Aristotle on Self-Knowledge," pp. 493–506 at p. 498.

[52] Cf. p. 113. A. Kosman, for example, who does recognize the connections we have noted between *EE* VII. 12, *De anima* and *Metaphysics* Λ. 9 ("Desirability of Friends," pp. 141–3), seems to think that

Remarkably, Aristotle's next comment in the chapter is that "indeed, choosing to live with others may seem foolish, from a certain vantage point" (1245a11–12). By saying this, Aristotle recognizes that, if all we mean by self-knowledge or self-perception is the cognition of objects that we have become similar (or somehow identical) to in virtue of that cognition, or our cognition of ourselves as engaging in such a process, then we may just as well carry on cognizing on our own. In order to settle the question of the relevance of our friends, however, "the truth must be examined based on the following point," namely that, as is familiar from *MM* II. 15, a friend is a "second self" (a29–ff.). It is more promising, then, to follow *MM* II. 15, which is clearly related to the text we are dealing with, and to suppose that in discussing self-knowing in *EE* VII. 12 (as well as self-*perceiving*, though *MM* II. 15 focuses on self-knowledge) Aristotle has in mind also the more specific kind of cognition whose object just is oneself (or a substitute for oneself, a mirror-image, so to speak, such as one's friend is supposed to function). It is *this* type of self-cognition, it seems, that he mentions in 1244b26–7 as the "most choice-worthy" thing for every individual.

In the language of *Met.* Λ. 9, the self-knowing (or perceiving) aimed at must extend beyond the knowing (or perceiving) ἐν παρέργῳ of one's knowing (or perceiving) to oneself as the direct object of one's cognition. That this aim is modeled on the activity of the divine *nous*, as Aristotle describes it, is clear. What is not clear, yet, is why Aristotle thinks this aim is "the most choice-worthy" one for human beings. He certainly thinks there are more godlike (θειότερα) things by nature than human beings, e.g., the heavenly bodies (*NE* VI. 7, 1141a33-b2), and these (not to mention the prime mover) must count as more worthy objects of knowledge. Indeed, as we have seen, *EE* VIII. 3 tells us that a thing counts as choice-worthy precisely by virtue of exhibiting a contribution to the contemplation of god, which therefore seems to be itself the *most* choice-worthy thing of all. As J. Whiting legitimately asks: "[W]hy should it not in fact be *more haireton* for a subject to know someone or something superior

the two kinds of self-cognition we have mentioned so far in connection with these further texts, namely cognition of one's cognition and cognizing one as one becomes identical to a further object of cognition, exhaust all the references in *EE* VII. 12 to self-cognition. He concludes, partly on that basis, that Aristotle proposes in the *EE* "shared consciousness, rather than self-consciousness, as the fruit of friendship" (ibid. p. 152). J. Whiting similarly recognizes the connections between the texts in question (e.g., "Thinking Together," p. 120), which she also utilizes to reject the reading of *EE* VII. 12 as "arguing that the self-sufficient agent *needs* a friend in order to achieve *self*-knowledge" (ibid. p. 123).

to himself – for example God or the starry skies above – than to know himself."[53]

The answer to Whiting's question is that self-cognition, of the last kind we have been considering, namely one's cognition of oneself directly as such, both leads to the contemplation of god and is in a sense ultimately identical to it. The process may be described using the following discussion from *EE* VII. 12. First, one engages in "vulgar" pleasures (τὰ φορτικά) with one's friend, and thereby perceives oneself, which gives one an initial grasp of one's own character, appearance, qualities, etc. To these one then adds "the more divine pleasures" (τὰς θειοτέρας ἡδονάς) (1245a37–9), whereby one obtains a deeper apprehension of one's own nature, which, as Aristotle says both in this treatise and elsewhere, contains (primarily) the "divine element" within one, namely *nous* (*EE* VIII. 2, 1248a26–7; *NE* X. 7, 1177b28). Full knowledge of one's true nature as *nous* would naturally include, indeed culminate in, the realization of the best possible application of such a nature. This further knowledge is tantamount to the knowledge of god, who just is the best, eternally activated life of which we as human beings are capable of partaking, if only for brief periods of time (*Met.* Λ. 7, 1072b14–18).[54]

---

[53] J. Whiting, "Thinking Together," pp. 105–6. cf. p. 124. The purpose of this statement in Whiting's paper is to support the "subjective" reading of *EE* VII. 12, 1244b26–7 against the "reflexive" reading, which I support.

[54] We are now in a position to reply to one of the main arguments mounted in the secondary literature against reading *EE* VII. 12, 1244b26–7 as suggesting that it is self-cognition that is the most choice-worthy thing for every individual (ἔστι δὲ τὸ αὑτοῦ αἰσθάνεσθαι καὶ τὸ αὑτὸν γνωρίζειν αἱρετώτατον ἑκάστῳ). A. Kosman is concerned about harmonizing this reflexive reading with what follows the sentence in question. Aristotle goes on to say that, if one were to "cut off" and posit knowledge "itself by itself" and its opposite, there would be no difference between such knowledge and someone else knowing instead of oneself (1244b29–32). Since this last point has to do with subjects of knowledge, Kosman argues, so must the preceding line, for "why should the lack of reflective perception generate any such difficulty?" ("Desirability of Friends," pp. 137–8). As we have seen, Aristotle's "objective" point in 1244b26–7, namely that self-cognition is the most choice-worthy thing for every individual, marks the beginning of an elaborate account in that chapter of what self-cognition is, the reason for its choice-worthiness, as well as why, in the human case, it requires friendship. The "subjective" point of lines 1244b29–34, namely that one desires cognition more when it is accompanied by one's cognition of one's own cognition, alludes to one kind of self-cognition, and one that any normal instance of cognition, of whatever objects, would include. Since Aristotle thinks this kind of self-cognition occurs whenever one cognizes, there is every reason for him to worry that a "lack of reflective [cognition]," understood thus, would result in a subjectless cognition, contra Kosman (ibid.). But this is not the only kind of self-cognition that Aristotle discusses in this text. Second comes self-cognition in the sense of oneself becoming in a sense identical to one's object of cognition and the consequent cognizing of oneself by and while cognizing that object of cognition due to the (quasi-)identity relation in question. And, finally, there is the cognition of oneself as such, for which alone friendship is necessary, and which is the notion most relevant to Aristotle's discussion of self-sufficiency in this chapter. It is *this last* type that Aristotle has

Aristotle is therefore consistent in claiming both that (*a*) self-cognition is the most choice-worthy thing for every individual (*EE* VII. 12, 1244b26–7), and that (*b*) the contemplation of god is the standard for all good choices (*EE* VIII. 3), because, according to his theory, a human being *is* in fact among the most choice-worthy objects of knowledge. We have already seen that Aristotle thinks of each person (ἕκαστος) not only as having intellect for his or her highest element, but also as being essentially constituted by intellect (*NE* X. 7, 1178a2–3).[55] Aristotle is justified in speaking of human self-knowledge both as "most pleasant" (*MM* II. 15 1213a14–15) and as "most choice-worthy" (*EE* VII. 12, 1244b26–7), then, since this knowledge ultimately amounts to knowledge of intellect. We know from the *Metaphysics* that the self-knowing activity of the intellect (in this case, god) is pleasure (1072b16), and that it is "most honorable" and "best" (A. 2, 983a5) and hence most choice-worthy for whomever is capable of it (including god). Insofar as humans have (or are) intellect, which is divine (*NE* X. 7, 1177b28), then, their self-knowing would amount to such an honorable and pleasurable activity.

Granted, the self-knowledge that is prescribed in *EE* and *MM* is not confined to the contemplation of intellect. The *EE* makes this crystal clear by coupling self-knowing (αὐτὸν γνωρίζειν) with self-perceiving (αὑτοῦ αἰσθάνεσθαι) (1244b26–7), though in both cases it is evident from the context that the relevant notion of self-knowledge includes knowledge of the sum of one's individual characteristics, not all (indeed plausibly not even most) of which could be subsumed under the activity of a self-knowing intellect. This knowledge therefore merits the use of verbs such as γνῶναι, γνωρίζειν, and εἰδέναι, as opposed to θεάσεσθαι (consistently used in *MM* II. 15, 1212b33–1213a10 for the self-reflective activity of god) or νοεῖν (attributed to god in *EE* VII. 12, 1245b16–18). Moreover, it may be argued that even that part of human self-knowledge that does focus on one's consisting essentially in intellect would not compare with the knowledge of first philosophy or of god, since the latter involves knowing intellect, not generally speaking, but specifically "*qua*" god, that is to say *qua* the activity of knowing or understanding that is the cause or first principle of the ordered universe (cf. *Met.* A. 2, 983a8–9).

Nevertheless, if, as we have assumed, Aristotle thinks of the cognition of one's own physical appearance, character, etc., as a starting point for

---

primarily in mind in calling self-cognition "most choice-worthy" in 1244b26–7, though the other two forms of self-cognition are of course necessary in order to attain it.
[55] See Section 3.2.

coming to know one's own true nature, then he may legitimately also think that self-knowledge *in toto*, namely as encompassing both of the kinds of reflexive cognition just mentioned, is the most choice-worthy thing for every individual human being. For, the endpoint of the process, that is to say one's knowing or understanding of one's own true nature, in its best form, Aristotle thinks, *just is* a version of god's absolutely self-sufficient condition, albeit an imperfect, non-eternal, and temporally divided version (Λ. 9, 1075a7–9).[56] Knowing the intellect *qua* god, then, is equivalent to knowing oneself as one would be in the best condition one may ever attain (except that it might also include the proviso just mentioned, namely that this would be only a temporary instantiation of god's condition, which is eternal). There is a real sense, then, in which self-cognition, when fully achieved, includes, as its topmost part, the knowledge of god, namely the activity of metaphysical knowing and understanding that god simply *is*.[57] Furthermore this, it seems to me, would be the case whichever content we end up attributing to the knowing or understanding of Aristotle's god, a debated issue we cannot hope to resolve here and do not need to.[58] Thus,

---

[56] K. Oehler goes further, and argues that the aspiration for self-reflective cognition, in Aristotle's view, is inherent to all living things, and is in all such cases comparable to divine self-knowing, which is "only the purest form of the same self-reference, which [Aristotle] met with in other forms of life of all kinds"; he quotes *EE* VII. 12 1244b24–1245a10 in support of his view, "Aristotle on Self-Knowledge," pp. 505–6. There is something to be said for this suggestion. Aristotle says, at 1245a9–10, that one wishes to live *always* (ἀεί), because one wants to know always, which is in turn because one wants to be oneself the object known (τὸ γνωστόν). At least if we read "ζῆν ἀεὶ βούλεται" as (or *also* as) "wants to live always" as opposed to "always wants to live" [M. M. McCabe brings up the possibility of reading ἀεί here as "janus-faced": "Self-Perception in *Eudemian Ethics* VII. 12," in F. Leigh (ed.), "*The* Eudemian Ethics *on the Voluntary, Friendship and Luck*" (Leiden, 2012), pp. 43–76 at p. 58 n. 63.], and similarly for "βούλεται ἀεὶ γνωρίζειν," this statement immediately reminds us of *De anima* II. 4, in which Aristotle says that the nutritive or reproductive faculty is that by which all (sublunar) living things act "so as to share in eternity and the godlike as far as is possible for them" (ἵνα τοῦ ἀεὶ καὶ τοῦ θείου μετέχωσιν ᾗ δύνανται: 415a23–b1). Percipient and/or rational animals, Aristotle seems to be adding here (in the *EE*), aspire to and may share in "eternity and the godlike," not only by propagating their species, but also by engaging in self-cognition, the highest form of which is the activity characteristic of god.

[57] An interesting analog is to be found in the (pseudo?) Platonic *Alcibiades* A, in which Socrates says that "this [sc. knowing and thinking] seems to resemble god, and anyone looking at it and knowing all that is divine, god and thought (φρόνησις), would as a result know himself too most of all" (133c4–6). R. Sorabji notes the influence this text must have had on Aristotle in forming his thoughts about self-knowledge, but goes on to say, contrary to my view, that Aristotle (in *MM* II. 15 and *EE* VII. 12) differs from Plato in being interested, not in one's knowledge of human nature, but rather specifically in one's knowledge of "particular actions seen as his or her own and as good or enjoyable," *Self*, pp. 233–4.

[58] The main controversy surrounds the question of whether or not the self-knowing of the divine *nous* would include (also) the knowing of multiple (perhaps all) intelligible objects. K. Oehler, "Aristotle on Self-Knowledge," p. 493, traces the modern exclusivist line, which he adopts, to E. Zeller's *Die Philosophie der Griechen in ihrer geschichtlichen Entwicklung* (Leipzig, 1921), p. 382, followed by

it is reasonable for Aristotle to think, based on his conception of human beings and god(s), that the former can, and ought to, imitate the self-reflective activity of the latter, with the appropriate modifications, in order to become self-sufficient and live happily in the highest degree.

The modifications in question point to the *dis*-analogy between human beings and god, which amounts in the *EE*, as it did in the *Magna Moralia*, to a difference in the particular way in which self-knowing is to be had by either. Aristotle suggests that it is only insofar as the original anal-ogy between the two suggests that humans can be self-sufficient without friendship that it is useless, the reason being that "for us well-being (τὸ εὖ) is with regard to another, but as for him [sc. for god] – he is himself his own well-being" (1245b18–19).[59] What began as an outright rejection of the analogy between god and human beings with regard to the issue of friendship both in the *MM* and in *EE*, then, turns out to be a fundamental reliance on it with regard to their proper activities. Not only is it possible for god to set an example for human behavior, according to Aristotle, but the *excellent* activity of humans, that is to say their *eudaimonia*, is in fact modeled on that of god. The problematic application of the analogy in the case of friendship presents a mere difference in practical detail between the attainment and nature of the proper activities of god and humans, but cannot call into question the essential commonality between them, i.e., that they are both contemplative activities aimed, either exclusively or as a crucial step, at the contemplator him- or herself as an object.

It is interesting, however, and at first glance curious, that in *Nicomachean Ethics* IX. 9, the third text dealing explicitly with the topic of the relation

---

W. D. Ross, B. Russell, F. M. Cornford, and W. K. C. Guthrie. As prominent defenders of the inclusivist interpretation, Oehler mentions H. J. Kraemer in "Grundfrgagen der Aristotelischen Theologie," *Theologie und Philosophie* 44 (1969), pp. 363–82 and pp. 481–505, and L. Elders, *Aristotle's Theology* (Assen, 1972), p. 257 ff. For a more recent discussion, favoring the exclusivist reading, see J. Brunschwig, "*Metaphysics* Λ. 9," esp. p. 288 and S. Menn, chapter IIIγ2, esp. n. 31.

[59] C. A. Gartner, in her doctoral dissertation, offers an alternative interpretation of this line, according to which the comparison between god and human beings does not allude merely to a difference in *means* toward attaining self-sufficiency, but rather to a difference between two relevant *kinds* of self-sufficiency. In particular, human self-sufficiency (or *eudaimonia*), in her view, consists not only in individual, but also in mutual, well-being. Our need for friends, then, would be for the latter type of well-being, not for something like individual self-knowledge of which god would be the paradigm (*Aristotle's Eudemian Account of Friendship* [PhD Dissertation, Princeton University, 2011], p. 130). This interpretation has two consequences that my interpretation so far has attempted to avoid. First, as Gartner recognizes, it makes, much like the views of Kosman and Whiting, for a discontinuity between the *MM* and the *EE* (ibid., pp. 127–8). Second, it also seems to be at odds with the fact, which is at the heart of my interpretation, that Aristotle thinks the best state achievable by human beings *just is* (a non-eternal instance of) the very activity that god *is* (*Met.* Λ. 7, 1072b14–18; 9, 1075a7–9).

between friendship and self-sufficiency, god is left unmentioned.[60] This is not the place to discuss this chapter in detail.[61] It suffices for our purposes to point out that it is not only god that is missing from the arguments in this chapter for the necessity of friendship for human self-sufficiency: self-knowledge is also not spoken of. Instead of the various references in *MM* II. 15 and *EE* VII. 12 to self-knowledge (αὑτὸν γνῶναι/εἰδέναι/γνωρίζειν), IX. 9 talks only of self-*awareness* (αἴσθησις). These two omissions cannot be coincidental. As we have seen, both *MM* II. 15 and *EE* VII. 12 conclude that friendship is necessary for human self-sufficiency by establishing friendship as a precondition for self-knowledge. But the fact that gaining self-knowledge is in the first place relevant for self-sufficiency, in both arguments, is grounded in an analogy between human beings and god. It is the reflexive intellectual activity of god that provides the paradigm for human self-sufficiency, in both the *MM* and *EE* texts in question, where the aim is one of explaining human beings' need for friendship in order to imitate the divine successfully.[62]

The arguments of *NE* IX. 9 seem to take a different strategy in arguing for the role of friendship in human self-sufficiency, and the fact that they mention neither god nor self-knowledge supports our interpretation of the essential connection between these two features in the arguments of *MM* and *EE*. Since it is only in these two texts that Aristotle argues for his view that friendship is necessary for self-sufficiency by alluding to the self-knowledge that it facilitates, his overall view of this issue turns out to be unified and consistent.[63] However, Aristotle does compare human beings

---

[60] See S. Stern-Gillet, *Aristotle's Philosophy of Friendship* (Albany, 1995), p. 132.

[61] For such a discussion see J. M. Cooper, "Friendship and the Good in Aristotle," in *Reason and Emotion* (Princeton, 1998), pp. 336–56 at p. 338.

[62] Of course, the human self-knowledge leading to such an imitation would include knowledge of things completely inapplicable to god, such as the "knowledge of one's character and qualities, motives and abilities" (J. M. Cooper, ibid., p. 341; cf. τί ἐστι καὶ ὁποῖός τις ὁ φίλος: *MM* II. 15, 1213a10–11). And so, even if, as R. Norman suggests, the self-thinking of the prime mover is "the same activity that human minds perform when they engage in abstract thought," and therefore "God's happiness is not generically different from man's" ("Aristotle's Philosopher-God," *Phronesis* 14 (1969), pp. 63–74 at pp. 67–72), such an activity would, in the human case, still be *preconditioned* on something quite distinct from divine contemplation (although, as we have noted, it might also ultimately get remarkably close to such a contemplation, given the intellectual nature of human beings).

[63] S. Stern-Gillet (*Aristotle's Philosophy of Friendship*, p. 134) argues that ". . . all three *Ethics* contain statements to the effect that, for whatever reason, self-knowledge cannot be direct and immediate," with the result that friendship is required. However, she limits self-knowledge in this context to knowledge of one's moral virtue (ibid., pp. 54–6). A. O. Rorty ("The Place of Contemplation in Aristotle's *Nicomachean Ethics*," *Mind* 87 (1978), pp. 343–58 at p. 355) seems more accurate, as does Z. Hitz ("Aristotle on Self-Knowledge and Friendship," *Philosopher's Imprint* 11 [2011], pp. 1–28 at

to god elsewhere in the *NE*. As we have seen,[64] he establishes, both in I. 9 and in X. 8, the status of the activity that he considers best for human beings *on the basis of* an analogy with the proper activity of god, which is contemplative (X. 8, 1178b21–2), and indeed self-reflective, since contemplation is most pleasant and perfect when it is performed by a "subject in good condition and in relation to its most excellent (σπουδαιότατον) object" (X. 4, 1174b21–3), and god is of course such a subject as well as such an object.

Aristotle brings up the analogy with god in the parts of the *NE* where he does so by introducing the traditional conception of gods as anthropomorphic, benevolent, and providential agents. Such gods would grant humans happiness as a gift (I. 9, 1099b11–18), and would "be pleased by" wise human beings and "return them the favor" (X. 8, 1179a22–32). As we have seen in Chapter 2, Aristotle thinks that the role of traditional religion in the *polis* is to motivate citizens to inquire philosophically into the nature of divinity by introducing them to anthropomorphic gods. If this inquiry is successful, the citizens would be in a position to practice first philosophy, which is the top human good and therefore the natural end of any correctly organized *polis*. In the present chapter, we have seen that it is not merely the nature of the true gods, but also the relation between divine and human nature, that one must understand in order to reach this desired goal. We have seen, further, that the gods of traditional religion can be used as a mitigating factor for the relevant comparison between human beings and Aristotle's real gods, particularly the prime mover.

---

p. 25) who says that, for Aristotle: "Contemplative friendship, to the extent that it includes appreciative knowledge of one's nature, resembles God yet more than moral friendship, where one only appreciates the goodness or beauty of one's actions." But both Rorty and Hitz base their conclusions on *NE* IX. 9, rather than *EE* VII. 12 or *MM* II. 15. Similarly, C. H. Kahn reads *NE* IX. 9 as arguing that (perfect) friendship involves the recognition of the friend's true self – which both friends share in common *qua* human beings – namely *nous* (which is the same, at least in kind, as the god of *Metaphysics* Λ) ("Aristotle and Altruism," *Mind* 90 [1981], pp. 20–40 at pp. 34–40). But since Kahn also focuses on IX. 9, which mentions neither god nor self-knowledge, he has to resort to linking this chapter to the (controversial) discussion of the active *nous* in *DA* III. 5. Lastly, M. D. Walker argues that, on Aristotle's view, friendship initiates a process of coming to know oneself, whose endpoint is the contemplation of god, whereby one comes to fully grasp one's own nature as *nous* ("Contemplation and Self-Awareness in the *Nicomachean Ethics*," *Rhizai* VII [2010], pp. 221–38). But, once again, Walker focuses on *NE* IX. 9 and not *EE* VII. 12 or *MM* II. 15. Walker is content to speak of the "self-awareness" mentioned in IX. 9 as encompassing the self-knowledge spoken of in the *EE* and *MM* chapters (ibid., p. 222, n. 3), and even as being ultimately equivalent to self-*contemplation* (p. 230, and n. 17). But this is clearly reading too much into the self-*awareness/perception* (αἴσθησις) exclusively spoken of in *NE* IX. 9. Further attention to the *EE* and *MM* would also relieve Walker of the need to rely on Plato's *Alcibiades* A in order to corroborate his interpretation of Aristotle (ibid. pp. 226–9; cf. p. 119, n. 57).

[64] See pp. 87 ff.; pp. 103 ff.

Such a comparison suggests that human rational activity, consisting in both practical deliberation and theoretical reasoning, and culminating in the contemplation of god, is the closest approximation of god's self-sufficient state that humans can reasonably expect to achieve. The role of anthropomorphic gods here is to show that this is the case by illustrating the fact that it is the ability to perform precisely this kind of activity that *real* gods would have performed had they been subject to human limitations (or, alternatively, by illustrating the fact that it is this kind of activity that real gods would have conferred upon human beings had divine providence been possible, since it is most godlike, or that it is just the kind of activity that real gods would have identified with and repaid with gratitude and favor).

It is by means of this comparison, which yields both an analogy and a dis-analogy between human beings and god, that one comes to learn of the best possible state one could aspire to as the closest approximation to that of god (i.e., the actually existing gods, such as the prime mover). As we learn from the *MM* and *EE*, one also comes to learn through this comparison about one's reliance on others, in particular on one's friends, on the way toward reaching that state. Here the traditional conception of gods again becomes relevant. Anthropomorphic gods exhibit a mode of behavior that deviates significantly from anything applicable to an actual god. But that mode of behavior is nevertheless a crucial step toward approximating the condition of god. Thus, acting morally and civilly, sharing one's life with one's friends, none of which is even remotely attributable to such beings as the prime mover, are preconditions for knowing and perceiving oneself, e.g., knowing one's moral properties and character traits. But, such self-knowledge and self-perception, according to Aristotle, are in turn a prerequisite for knowing or understanding one's own true nature. Since this nature is essentially intellectual, fully knowing it involves understanding what its best activity consists in. To understand this, finally, just is to understand god, because god essentially consists precisely in that best activity.

Traditional religion, according to Aristotle, is necessary in order for any *polis* to exist and thrive, because its anthropomorphic conception of gods leads citizens to inquire into the true nature of divinity. This inquiry, in turn, necessarily involves learning of the relation between human beings and the divine, for which the gods of traditional religion are also useful. Having undertaken these inquiries, some citizens would prove capable of engaging in excellent contemplative activity, which is modeled on, and may even stand a chance of periodically becoming identical to, the proper activity of god. These citizens would owe a long-standing debt to the traditional religion with which they were raised for its role in enabling them to lead flourishing lives, and would, as Aristotle might hope, recognize the importance of maintaining the institutions of that religion for future generations to benefit similarly.

CHAPTER 4

Aristotle on the Possible Uses of the Myths of "The Ancients"

4.0 Introduction

Aristotle's various references to the myths of traditional Greek religion, especially as related in Homer and Hesiod, permeate his *corpus*. He references those myths in his discussions of topics as diverse as metaphysics, ethics, politics, and music. Aristotle is as likely to use such myths as evidence for or illustrations of his own theories as he is to rebut them or dismiss them out of hand. The question naturally arises as to whether or not Aristotle uses any discoverable criterion in deciding to "approve of one of these ancient accounts and reject the other."[1] It is tempting to answer the question in the negative. As John Palmer succinctly puts it, "it appears to be simply that underlying one account [Aristotle] detects a view in agreement with his own, while underlying the other he discerns a view that he wants to reject."[2]

However, once we attend to the uses that Aristotle himself ascribes to myths in general, we would be in a position to assess at least some of his reasons for rejecting or criticizing the content of certain myths. It is true that Aristotle deems some myths useless beyond redemption, due to their unintelligibility. However, he also thinks that all myths are necessary for philosophical instruction, and that at least some of them are useful for social stability and moral habituation as well. In addition, he thinks that some myths can usefully reflect the norms and standards of the period in which they were composed. In what follows I shall show that when Aristotle is willing to consider the content of myths he generally has these uses in mind (specifically, he has in mind the non-necessary uses of myths just described). Thus, whenever the content of a myth is intelligible but turns out not to be based on or indicative of any truth whatsoever, Aristotle can

---

[1] J. Palmer, "Ancient Theologians," pp. 181–205 at p. 201.
[2] Ibid.

still explain the usefulness of the myth using one of the other normal uses of religious mythology.

4.1 Underlying Truths

The most explicit statement of Aristotle's view concerning the truth underlying certain myths concerning the gods is in a passage we have already dealt with *in extenso* in the previous chapters – *Metaphysics* Λ. 8, 1074a38-b14. It is worth quoting the passage in full once more for our present purposes:

> It has been transmitted to us through the ancients and very-old ones, and has been passed on to future generations, in the form of a myth, that these [sc. the highest substances, acting as primary movers of the heavenly bodies] are gods, and that the divine encloses the whole of nature. The rest has been added, mythically, with a view to persuading the masses and for its usefulness in supporting the laws and bringing about the general advantage. For they say that they [sc. the gods] are man-shaped or resemble certain other animals, and [they add] other things, which are consequent on or similar to those already said. If one were to take the first point by itself, separately from those [additions], namely that they think the first substances are gods, they would be thought to have spoken excellently (lit. divinely), and though every art/science and philosophy have probably been discovered as far as possible and destroyed again and again, these opinions of theirs have been preserved like remains up until now. The ancestral opinion, that we have obtained through the first ones, is clear to us only to this extent.

According to what Aristotle says here, at least in the case of some myths one may discover, beneath the layers of fictitious anthropomorphic representations of the gods and other falsehoods, indications of such truths as the existence of the unmoved movers of the heavenly bodies and spheres and their causal relation to the natural world. However ancient the "ancients and very old ones" possessing the requisite philosophical knowledge are in Aristotle's view, he quite clearly thinks that truth-bearing myths of the kind he mentions include some of the myths familiar to him from his immediate cultural environment ("these opinions of theirs have been preserved like remains up until now").[3]

---

[3] I here leave open the question of whether or not the inclusion of truths in myths is at least sometimes intentional. As we shall see, R. Bodéüs suggests that for Aristotle authors revealing truth in their myths generally do so unintentionally (see p. 134, n. 17; cf. R. Bodéüs, *Aristotle and the Theology of the Living Immortals*, pp. 82–3). But I see no evidence for this view. If anything, since Aristotle regards the use of traditional religion for philosophical instruction as its necessary function (as we have seen in Chapter 2), he might expect at least certain myths (e.g., ones introduced by philosophers who are

It is therefore not surprising to find a reference to a Homeric example of such a truth-bearing myth in Aristotle. In *MA* IV, discussing the necessary existence of an unmoved entity that is external to the universe and causes motion within it, Aristotle says:

> And for that reason Homer would appear to those who believe thus to have spoken well: "You will not drag Zeus, the highest of all, from the heavens down to earth, not even if you wear yourselves out: hang on [to your chains], all you gods and all you goddesses." For that which is wholly immovable is incapable of being moved by anything. (699b35–700a3; cf. *Il.* VIII.20–22)

As Palmer rightly notes, the truth which Aristotle detects in Homer's words here is "on a par with the view that the divine encompasses the whole of nature, which he attributes to the ancients in *Metaphysics* Λ. 8."[4] These words also correspond, indeed more immediately, to the first truth ascribed to the ancients in Λ. 8, concerning the unmoved movers as being gods.

Aristotle does not restrict the truths to be discovered as underlying certain myths to these two metaphysical facts, however. When he says, after describing these facts, that "the rest has been added mythically" (1074b3–4), he has in mind the mythological additions to the particular facts in question, not mythology in general. Again, when he says that "the ancestral opinion . . . is clear to us only to this extent" (1074b13–14), i.e., to the extent that we can manage to separate it from what has been "added mythically" to it, he does not mean to say that it is only to the extent that we are able to detect these two particular metaphysical truths within a myth that we may clearly apprehend any underlying and true ancient opinion whatsoever. Rather, he means to say that the opinion regarding the two particular metaphysical facts under discussion is only clear to us as the audience of a myth concealing those truths to the extent that we may isolate those truths, while leaving open the question regarding the possibility of extending that occurrence to further cases (i.e., further myths concealing further truths).

Indeed, Aristotle does seem to think of certain myths as containing grains of truth regarding other, and in fact non-metaphysical, facts. In

---

fully aware of the function of religion) to intentionally allude to philosophical facts (though this, be it noted, is not at all required in order for traditional religion to perform its natural necessary function, according to our analysis above). We shall return to this point in the conclusion to this chapter (Section 4.6).

4 Palmer, "Ancient Theologians," p. 200.

Pol. II. 9, he mentions two factors causing the perilous revering of wealth in a city as being (a) a lawgiver who, legislating only with a view to a half of the population in a *polis*, i.e., males, "is utterly careless with regard to women" (1269b21–2), and (b) the men of the city being "controlled by women" (γυναικοκρατούμενοι) (1269b24–5). Sparta is given as an example of a *polis* that has suffered from both symptoms (1269b19: ἐκεῖ [sc. in Sparta]; 1269b31–2). Aristotle links at least the second problematic features of Sparta to the nature of warlike people in general, who are especially prone to an excessive preoccupation with either heterosexual relations (as in the case of the Spartans) or homosexual relations (as in the case of the Celtics) (1269b24–7). He then goes on to say the following:

> For it seems it was not irrational of the first [poet] composing the myth to couple Ares with Aphrodite. For all such [sc. warlike] people seem to be inclined toward a communion with either men or women (1269b27–31).

Here Aristotle refers to a standard myth, appearing for instance in the *Odyssey* (VIII.266–366). He means to say that this myth, much like the one described in *Met.* Λ. 8, is an addition of fictitious content (here, the communion of Ares and Aphrodite) to an underlying basic truth.[5] The basic truth in question, though, is here not a metaphysical, but a sociopsychological one: it is the truth concerning the fact that people of a warlike nation develop a tendency toward excessive sexual desire.

4.2 Social Stability

Occasionally, Aristotle mentions myths in order to reject the views or theories on which they seem to be based. A case in point is his recurring discussions of the myth of Atlas. In *DC* II. 1, he commends "the ancients" (οἱ μὲν ἀρχαῖοι) for having assigned the heavens or upper regions to the gods, thereby establishing the status of the latter as alone being "immortal" (ἀθάνατον: 284a11–13). He takes this true opinion to be compatible with (and presumably indicative of) his own preceding arguments for the perfection of the heavens, which includes their being incorruptible, ungenerated, incapable of being affected by any "mortal annoyance" (θνητῆς δυσχερείας), and effortless (284a13–18).

Aristotle's immediately following remark is that:

> For this reason, one must not suppose the case to be in accordance with the myth of the ancients (τῶν παλαιῶν), who say that [the world] is in need of

---

[5] As C. D. C. Reeve points out in his translation of the *Politics* ad loc. (n. 99).

some Atlas for its preservation. For those who contrived this story (λόγον) seem (ἐοίκασι) to have the same supposition as those who came later. For they [sc. the mythologists]⁶ laid down for it [sc. for the heavens], mythically (μυθικῶς), animate constraint, as if⁷ [their myth were] about (the) upper bodies having weight and being earthy (284a18–23).

Whether or not the ancients (οἱ ἀρχαῖοι) who hold the correct opinion regarding the immortality of the heavens are the same as the ancients (οἱ παλαιοί) responsible for the misleading portrayal of Atlas, Aristotle clearly means to contrast the truth of that opinion with the falsity of that myth, in a way resembling the contrast between the true opinion of the "ancient and very old ones" and what has been later on added to it "mythically" (μυθικῶς) according to the passage from *Met.* Λ. 8.

Indeed, as was the case with the *MA* IV passage discussed in the previous section, and as Palmer again notes, the correct opinion of the ancients spoken of in *DC* II. 1 regarding the immortality of the heavens as the dwelling place of the gods clearly has an affinity to the correct opinion of the "ancient and very old ones" spoken of in *Met.* Λ. 8 regarding the divine as encompassing the whole of nature, and even more so (though Palmer, again, does not note this feature) to their correct opinion that the unmoved movers of the heavens are gods.⁸ This similarity emphasizes the truth Aristotle finds in the first ancient opinion that he mentions in *DC* II. 1. By contrast, the second ancient opinion mentioned in that chapter is taken by Aristotle to be entirely false. Consequently, Palmer raises the question of whether there is any criterion by reference to which Aristotle might be said to "approve of one of these ancient accounts and reject the other," and ultimately concludes that the only criterion emerging from Aristotle's treatment of myth is conformity to his own philosophical principles and taste.⁹ A more careful comparison between *DC* II. 1 and *Met.* Λ. 8, however, provides us with a better criterion, as I shall presently argue.

---

⁶ The subject of ὑπέστησαν in 284a23 can be either the mythologists (οἱ συστήσαντες τὸν λόγον) or the philosophers who came later (οἱ ὕστερον). This is reflected by W. K. C. Guthrie's two different translations of 284a20–3: "[T]hose who made up that story seem to have had the same notion as later thinkers, that is, they thought that in speaking of the upper bodies they were treating of bodies which were earthlike and had weight, when they posited for the heaven the constraint of a living being," *Aristotle* On The Heavens (*Loeb Classical Library*) (Cambridge, 1939); "It looks as if those who made up that story had the same notion as later thinkers, who spoke of the higher bodies as if they were earthy and had weight, and for that reason assumed for it just like the mythologists a constraint dependent on soul" ("Development of Aristotle's Theology," pp. 162–71 at p. 169).
⁷ Manuscripts *F* (Laurentianus 87. 7), *H* (Vaticanus 1027), and *M* (Urbinas 37) read ὥσπερ instead of ὡς.
⁸ Palmer, "Ancient Theologians," p. 201.
⁹ Ibid.

The first thing to notice is that Aristotle does not in fact attribute the erroneous "opinion" or "account" regarding the weight and earthiness of the bodies of the upper region directly to the ancient authors of the myth of Atlas. The opinion or account in question is merely said to be "in accordance" with that myth (κατὰ τὸν . . . μῦθον: 284a18–19), and of the ancient composers of the myth it is merely said that they "*seem* to" (ἐοίκασι) share that supposition (284a20–2). It is then said that the mythologists, in composing the story of Atlas, spoke of the heavens *as if* representing the erroneous philosophical theory in question mythically (it is also possible that in this sentence, i.e., 284a22–3, it is not the mythologists who are spoken of at all; see p. 129 n. 6). For all we know, then, Aristotle may be thinking of the erroneous account of the heavens by later philosophers as simply resembling the myth of Atlas, so that using it as a source of truth would amount to an erroneous interpretation possibly deviating completely from the intention of its original authors.

Aristotle's discussion of the same myth in *MA* III seems to support this possibility. There, Aristotle says that

> Those composing mythically (μυθικῶς) [the story of] Atlas having his feet on the earth seem to have uttered the myth because of thought (ἀπὸ διανοίας), as this [character] is just like a diameter turning the heavens around the poles. And this would happen to be in accordance with reason, due to the fact that the earth remains still. However, it is necessary for those who say those things to say that the earth is not a part of the universe, and, besides (. . .) the force of the earth at rest must be as great as that which the whole heavens and that which moves it have. But if this is impossible, it is also impossible for the heavens to be moved by something of this kind from within. (699a27–b11)

Again, a myth concerning Atlas, here specifically the depiction of him as standing on the stationary earth while moving the heavens about, is associated with a philosophical theory. And, again, it is only said of the authors of the myth in question that they "seem to" have had some such theory in mind. This is so, even though Aristotle thinks the theory in question is partially correct. The theory resembling the myth of Atlas as presented in this chapter holds that the earth is stationary, which for Aristotle is true, but it errs in proposing that the heavens are moved by something internal ("either Atlas or whatever else moves the [heavens] internally"), which leads to an impossibility, as Aristotle goes on to argue (in the part of the passage omitted from the preceding quotation). The ancient mythologists speaking of Atlas in this seemingly crypto-philosophical way, though, deserve neither the praise for what the myth apparently gets right nor the blame for what it seems to get wrong. For, in composing the myth, Aristotle means to say, they had no such theory in mind.[10]

Since Aristotle thinks the motivation behind the composition of such stories as the myth of Atlas was not the propagation of a philosophical theory, he may think that stories of this kind have been composed, similarly to the mythical additions to the wisdom of the "ancient and very old ones" discussed in *Met.* Λ. 8, "with a view to persuading the masses and for [their] usefulness in supporting the laws and bringing about the general advantage" (1074b3–5). In other words, just as the true and ancient opinion concerning the unmoved movers of the heavens as being gods and of the divine as encompassing the whole of nature has been supplemented by fictitious myths for the securing of social stability or for moral habituation, the true and ancient opinion regarding the heavens as divine and eternal has been supplemented by a fictitious myth about Atlas moving the heavens with a view to a similar political end.

Hesiod's *Theogony* describes Atlas as one of the four sons of Iapetus and Clymene (507–511). Zeus is said to have determined Atlas' fate (μοῖρα) as having to carry the "broad heavens by mighty constraint on the limits of the earth, before the clear-voiced Hesperides, standing with head and hands unresting" (517–520; cf. *Od.*I. 52–4). Though Zeus is not explicitly said to have determined Atlas' fate as a punishment,[11] listing his fate alongside the obvious punishments endured by his three brothers (Menoetius is struck by Zeus' thunderbolt and is sent to Erebus for his presumptuousness and excessive manhood, Epimetheus accepts the "gift" of Pandora, and cruelly bounded Prometheus has his liver perpetually eaten by an eagle) certainly suggests viewing Atlas as being punished as well.[12] It is fitting, then, that in later sources "Atlas is described as the leader of the Titans in their contest with Zeus, and, being conquered, he was condemned to the labor of bearing heaven on his head and hands."[13]

Now, if Atlas' predicament has indeed been inflicted on him for some such transgression against the gods, according to the mythologists, it is easy to see how Aristotle could have regarded the myth of Atlas as being

---

[10] Finally, in *Metaphysics* Δ. 23, 1023a17–21, the myth of Atlas is briefly mentioned, and is used as an example of the special usage of the verb "to have" (ἔχειν) to signify the impeding by something of another thing's being moved or acting, "as the poets say Atlas 'has' the heavens."

[11] See R. Hard, *The Routledge Handbook of Greek Mythology* (London, 2004), p. 49: "there is no reason to assume that it was regarded as a punishment for some specific offence in the early tradition."

[12] W. Hansen, *Handbook of Classical Mythology* (Santa Barbara, 2004), p. 126.

[13] W. Smith, *A Dictionary of Greek and Roman Biography and Mythology* (London, 1880), p. 406. Cf. *Hyg. Fab.* 150. Smith also seems to assume that Atlas' fate as described in Hesiod is a punishment.

devised for a political purpose, such as the maintenance of social stability. Propagating stories relating the immense suffering undergone by even a mighty Titan for disrespecting the gods would naturally be thought to be conducive to godliness and to have a deterring effect, especially, Aristotle would say, on the masses, who are likely to be persuaded by such stories (*Met.* Λ. 8, 1074b4).[14]

4.3 Moral/Political Instruction

Apart from the use of fictitious myths for persuading and deterring the masses, Aristotle adds, more generally, that such stories are useful "in supporting the laws and bringing about the general advantage" (*Met.* Λ. 8, 1074b5). This leaves room for viewing certain myths as being intended to be used for moral habituation or political instruction, for instance by introducing anthropomorphic gods or heroes who, though entirely fictitious, function as role models for moral and political excellence (see Section 2.6).

In *Pol.* VIII. 5, Aristotle considers the possible beneficial uses of music. As one of these possible uses, he assesses the contribution of music to the development of (character) virtue, for the presumed reason that "just as gymnastics renders the body to be of a certain kind, so also music makes character be of a certain kind, in habituating [one] into being able to rejoice correctly" (1339a22–5). The problem with defending musical education on these grounds, according to Aristotle, is that there does not seem to be any need for people to learn how to *play* music (which is otherwise potentially harmful, as it is inherently vulgar) in order to learn how to *enjoy* it. He thinks that this point is illustrated by the example of Zeus, who "does not himself sing or play the cithara, [as he is portrayed] by the poets" (1339b7–8). Aristotle relaxes his statement in the following chapter (VIII. 6). Learning how to play a musical instrument could improve one's ability to appreciate and enjoy music after all, though this practice must be restricted to a young age and to specific kinds of instrument, *excluding* professional instruments such as the cithara (which has been denied to Zeus) or the flute. Again, Aristotle exemplifies using a myth:

---

[14] Insofar as Aristotle thinks the myth of Atlas resembles some philosophical theories, which he then goes on to refute, as we have seen, one might think that he could also ascribe a use for myths of this kind in philosophical instruction, specifically the use for a dialectical discussion of opposing views for the purpose of clarifying and avoiding errors (*Topica*, 101a34–7). However, though he might think that the myth of Atlas could be put to such a use subsequent to its composition, he seems to think, as we have seen, that its original authors had neither a correct nor an incorrect philosophical theory in mind in composing it.

And the mythical tale (τὸ . . . μεμυθολογήμενον) told by the ancients (τῶν ἀρχαίων) about flutes is also reasonable (εὐλόγως . . . ἔχει). For they say that Athena, having invented flutes, rejected them. It is not base to say that the goddess did so being discontented because of the disfigurement of the face, though it is more plausible that education in flute playing is of no value with a view to intelligence (πρὸς τὴν διάνοιαν), whereas we confer upon Athena both knowledge (ἐπιστήμη) and expertise (τέχνη). (1341b2–8)

Both the portrayal of Zeus as avoiding the cithara and of Athena as avoiding the flute are presented by Aristotle in order to illustrate the problematic aspects of picking up such instruments.[15]

Though Aristotle neither affirms nor denies an original purpose for this portrayal of Zeus, he does say of the myth of Athena that it, in its original form as composed by the ancients, is reasonable for the reasons he goes on to list. Especially when contrasted with the myth of Atlas which, as we have seen in Section 4.2, Aristotle only says seems to be associated with a certain theory, this direct affirmation of the reasonableness of the myth of Athena for its representation of a correct mode of behavior indicates that Aristotle accepts the promotion of such a behavior as the original purpose of the myth. This is also corroborated by the very fact that Aristotle is clearly engaged in an interpretation of the myth, first proposing one acceptable interpretation and then supplementing it with a better one.

4.4 Reflections of the Period

Some myths (or aspects of myths) that Aristotle discusses seem to be useful in a way deviating from the paradigm introduced in *Met.* Λ. 8 and followed so far in our analysis: they can usefully teach us something about the period in which they were originally composed and the norms and practices dominant then. Thus, as we have seen, in *Pol.* I. 2 Aristotle says that

All people say that the gods are ruled by a king for this reason, namely that some of them to this day are, and others in the distant past were, themselves ruled by a king. Just as human beings make the shapes [of the gods] similar

---

[15] For texts such as *Pol.* VIII. 5 as presenting "portrayals of Zeus as models to be imitated," see R. Bodéüs, *Aristotle and the Theology of the Living Immortals.*, p. 267, n. 113 (174). Note that Bodéüs also thinks that myths of the kind presented in this section reflect certain opinions held by their authors or people in their day, albeit unintentionally (see p. 134, n. 17; cf. R. Bodéüs, ibid., pp. 82; 89). In general, it is to be expected that myths intended to encourage a certain kind of behavior would do so based on certain presumptions or beliefs concerning the goodness of that type of behavior. By distinguishing myths of this kind from myths indicating truths, then, I do not mean to deny that the former could *also* be indicative of truth.

to their own, thus [they] also [do this in the case of] the gods' ways of life. (1252b24–7)

By attending to the fact that the traditional depiction of Zeus as king of the gods (prevalent throughout Greek epic poetry, except Homer)[16] in fact derives from the prevalence of kingships at the period during which such traditions have emerged, we may learn two things. First, the depictions in question are fictitious and man-made. Second, the practices and actions depicted in myth in general may be used as sources for learning true facts, not about the gods, but rather about one's predecessors and their (e.g.) social and political circumstances.[17]

However, even though the myths in question or their relevant parts contain a discoverable "grain of truth," insofar as they tell us about the life and times of ancient people, there seems to be a basic difference between such myths and the myths added on to philosophical truths such as the one described in *Met.* Λ. 8. For, whereas Aristotle tells us that the latter myths were intended to achieve a certain purpose, e.g., social stability, the myths (or parts of myths) revealing historical details concerning the period in which they were composed would seem to do so merely coincidentally, as a result of their authors working at a particular time and place. In fact, it is quite plausible to assume that the original authors of these myths would at least in some cases wish for such details not to be exposed, since such

---

[16] See p. 16–ff. Cf. Hesiod: *Theog.* 71, 923; *Works* 668. *Cycle*: *Thebaid*, fr. 3 [Kinkel]; *Cypria*, fr. 6 [Kinkel]. *Hymn to Demeter*, 335. On Homer cf. G. M. Calhoun "Zeus the Father," pp. 1–17. For Homer on Zeus as the *father* of the gods, which is again associated with kingship, see *NE* VIII. 10, 1160b24–7.

[17] See also R. Bodéüs, *Aristotle and the Theology of the Living Immortals*, 89. Bodéüs in fact sees all myths indicative of any truth as reflecting the knowledge or opinions of their authors and their times. Thus, the myth of Ares and Aphrodite only "seems to testify for the thesis that warlike souls are inclined toward eroticism" (cf. *Pol.* II. 9, 1269b27–31), and the myth of Athena as playing the flute merely "seems to indicate that flute-playing is inappropriate for a liberal education aimed at developing the mind" (cf. *Pol.* VIII. 6, 1341b2–8) (ibid., p. 82). In fact, Bodéüs says, such myths as (e.g.) the one about Zeus as avoiding playing the lyre merely reflect the "tradition's feeling that such servile functions are hardly appropriate to a free man's dignity" and, in general, Aristotle appeals to traditional myths in support of philosophical positions concerning (e.g.) humans or society because he thinks that "the anthropomorphism of the mythical imagination occasionally tells us something about humans, or rather about ideas that the authors of myth possessed about humans" (ibid., p. 83). In Aristotle's view, Bodéüs maintains, a myth is "not meant . . . to teach anything about the gods of whom it speaks . . . it aims to create fear or to provoke some other feelings" (ibid.). On this view, Aristotle does not interpret myths allegorically, strictly speaking, because he assumes that any truth they might reveal is only revealed unintentionally. Bodéüs' insistence on this point is related to his overall view of Aristotle as believing in the traditional gods. For if when Aristotle brings up such examples as Homer's portrayal of Zeus as stationary (cf. *MA* 4) he does not mean to interpret the myth allegorically as being concerned with the existence of an unmoved mover, then there is room for thinking, as Bodéüs does, that Aristotle in fact upholds the existence of (e.g.) the traditional Zeus himself (ibid., p. 2).

details are indicative of the fictitious nature of the myths in which they are embedded, as we have seen, and thus render them less believable by the masses who are (at least in some cases) supposed to be persuaded by them.

4.5 Unintelligible and Coincidental Myths

The preceding survey of the various uses of myths should not be taken to imply that Aristotle thinks of all myths as being useful for the purposes we have listed. To be sure, Aristotle thinks some myths, including canonical and influential ones, cannot be used for such purposes, for at least two reasons. First, he thinks some myths are too unclear to be taken seriously.[18] Second, he thinks some myths, which in themselves neither indicate any fact or theory nor contribute to any political purpose, simply follow as consequences from other myths.

The clearest example of Aristotle's charge of certain myths as being too unclear to be considered useful (or to be considered at all) is his discussion of "those around Hesiod" in *Met.* B. 4. After introducing the questions of whether mortal and immortal things share the same kind of principles and, if so, by what do mortal and immortal things differ from one another, Aristotle says (1000a9–19):

> Those around Hesiod, then, and all of the *theologoi*, cared only about the thing convincing themselves, and took no heed of us. For, representing the principles as gods and as coming from gods, they say that those things which do not taste nectar and ambrosia become mortal, clearly speaking as if these words are known to them. And yet, they have spoken "beyond us" about the same application of these causes. For if they [sc. the gods] touch [nectar and ambrosia] for the sake of their own pleasure, then nectar and ambrosia are not causes of being, but if [for the sake] of being, then how, needing nourishment, would they be eternal? – But it is not worth it to look seriously into these subtleties [said] mythically.

The Hesiodic myths about nectar and ambrosia presented in this passage seem to take a stand on the issue with which Aristotle is concerned in this part of his *Metaphysics*. They seem to side with the view that mortal and immortal things share the same divine principles, and differ from each other based on a process they either do or do not undergo (either taking in nectar and ambrosia or failing to do so). However, the significance of the specific terms used in these stories (nectar, ambrosia) is known only to

---

[18] See Palmer, "Ancient Theologians," pp. 182–91.

their authors, not to their audience, and it is also "beyond us" how these stories could avoid an obviously absurd result (i.e., that either nectar and ambrosia are not causes of being or else the gods rely on them for nutrition and are hence themselves mortal). As these myths stand, then, we cannot even assess their meaning, let alone their truth value, as far as Aristotle is concerned.

Naturally, if we cannot understand even the basic terms and meaning of these myths, we cannot judge whether they have been originally introduced for any political purpose such as maintaining social stability or promoting moral virtue. In fact, Aristotle seems to take the overwhelming obscurity of such myths as an indication that they have not been introduced for any such function. For, if in composing such myths the *theologoi* cared only about what convinced them, not paying the slightest attention to their audience (1000a10–11), then we could hardly expect them to have anticipated such myths to provide moral instruction or to persuade the masses toward good and lawful behavior.

Other myths (or parts of myths) are also useless for the purposes we have enumerated so far. Those include myths (or parts of myths) consequent on myths (or parts of myths) having a use for some such purpose. Consider the following example. In *Met.* N. 4, Aristotle raises the question of whether "the good and the best" are among the elements and first principles, or whether they are "later in origin" (ὑστερογενῆ) (1091a29–33). He says that what the *theologoi* say *seems* (ἔοικεν) to agree with those who say that the good and best are indeed later in origin (1091a33–6), since they make Zeus the ruler even though he is preceded temporally by Nyx, Ouranos, Chaos, and Okeanos (1091b4–6). But, whereas the philosophers who side with this opinion have a theoretical reason for doing so (they wish to avoid a *reductio ad absurdum* argument directed at the supposition that the good itself is a principle and an element [1091a36-b3]), the "ancient poets" (οἱ δὲ ποιηταὶ οἱ ἀρχαῖοι) speak similarly (ὁμοίως) for quite a different reason. They "happen to say such things for no other reason than the changing of the rulers of things" (1091b6–8).

Many myths used for the purposes already mentioned presuppose the change of rulership among the gods. To mention one example already given, Atlas' punishment may have been used for deterrence and against impiety in Aristotle's opinion. But, had Zeus always been the undisputed king of the gods (and of all other things), he presumably never would have needed to engage in war with the Titans and hence would not have punished Atlas for siding with the Titans against him. Some features of Greek mythology are themselves useless aside from their ancillary role in supporting the system as a whole, along with those myths within it that are designed for a purpose. Aristotle's point is that we should be careful to recognize these features as such, so that (e.g.) we should not be misled into thinking that they signify a certain philosophical view they only seem to resemble.

The case of the myths that seem to signify the view that the good is not an original principle or element is especially instructive, since Aristotle tells us we in fact have evidence that it is the very opposite view that the ancient poets and theologians actually held. For those *of them* (αὐτῶν) who "mix" mythical expression with non-mythical argumentation, like Pherecydes and others, suppose that the first originator is best (1091b8–10). What Aristotle means to say is that Pherecydes, and others like him, make it clear that the "official" view of the ancient theologians is that the good and best are among the first principles and elements, and that they do so by stating this view using non-mythical modes of presentation. Those myths or mythical features that give us the opposite impression, then, are not in fact meant to illustrate the philosophical point they seem to convey. And, since they do not seem to be designed for any other specific purpose either, but do seem to follow logically from myths that are useful for some such purpose, the conclusion to draw is that they are simply coincidental results and ought to be understood as such.

4.6 Conclusion

In surveying the myths of his day, Aristotle occasionally finds in them traces of philosophical truths. Naturally, these presumed truths correspond to the various conclusions of Aristotle's own views (e.g., his metaphysics and his political theory), for otherwise Aristotle would hardly regard them as truths. However, when Aristotle rejects other myths for being completely false, he does not and need not do so simply by contrasting them with his own theory. Rather, in those cases, Aristotle has the theoretical resources to explain why the myths in question are completely false. In some cases, though the myths in question may seem to present a specific false philosophical view, they are in fact meant to be used for quite a different purpose, such as securing political stability or enhancing moral habituation. Other myths apparently supporting false views are not used for any purpose, but are either merely too unintelligible to be seriously taken to support any view or the coincidental results of other myths. These distinctions help to explain how Aristotle can determine the truth or falsity at the basis of myths based on their intentional use or lack of it.

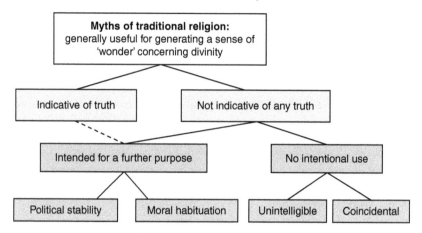

Figure 4.1 The possible uses of myths in Aristotle's theory.

It is Aristotle's view, be it noted, that myths of all the types just described are useful most basically for motivating people to engage in philosophical inquiry into divinity, which he thinks is the necessary political function of traditional religion (as we have seen in Chapter 2). This is why in our survey in the present chapter there has been no appeal to the usefulness of traditional religion and its myths for initiating philosophical inquiry. Precisely because this use constitutes the necessary function of traditional religion, it applies to *all* religious stories. Aristotle would count any mythical story generating a sense of "wonder" at the gods, regardless of the specific details of its content, and regardless of any additional use it might have, as contributing to the necessary function of traditional religion (see Figure 4.1).

However, it is hardly surprising, given his overall view of the function of traditional religion, that Aristotle also finds it reasonable to expect that in some cases certain myths, including those we have reviewed in Section 4.1, would in fact reveal certain philosophical truths when interpreted allegorically. It is true that even if no myth ever contained a grain of truth, traditional religion would still be perfectly capable of fulfilling its necessary natural function in Aristotle's opinion. But the people composing the myths of traditional religion would presumably at least occasionally include those who are cognizant of the function of that religion. And those people (possibly including the "ancient and very old" philosophers Aristotle discusses in *Met.* Λ. 8), Aristotle might think, are likely to include in the content of their myths representations of or hints at philosophical truths of which they are knowledgeable.

Now, the people in question might allude to truths in their myths unintentionally, just as certain people inadvertently include in their myths elements and beliefs belonging to and reflecting their own tradition and culture (as we have seen in Section 4.4). However, Aristotle could also think that they would do so consciously and intentionally, at least on occasion.[19] Philosophers composing myths may well choose philosophical topics as the basis of their myths before and over others, simply because of the association of such topics with the function for the sake of which they compose the myth to begin with, i.e., generating a sense of wonder at divinity with a view to initiating philosophical inquiry into divinity. Indeed, such a choice might hold additional benefits. For instance, myths closely related to phenomena explained by theoretical science – say astronomical phenomena, which merit wonder in their own right (cf. *Met.* A. 2, 982b12–17) – might generate more wonder than others. Again, propagating myths directly related to philosophical topics to a general audience might be useful in distinguishing, at an early stage, between those who are naturally fascinated by philosophical questions, and hence could potentially become philosophers themselves, and those who are not.[20] Finally, myths indicating truths could raise the status of traditional religion in the eyes of those who have access to some such truths, but nevertheless neither comprehend the natural function of traditional religion themselves nor wish to simply accept the position of philosophers on the matter. One or more of these reasons could explain why it is that Aristotle anticipates some truths to underlie the myths of traditional religion, even though he thinks it is unnecessary for any myth to contain or conceal philosophical truth in order for traditional religion to function properly and naturally.

---

[19] Contra R. Bodéüs, *Aristotle and the Theology of the Living Immortals*, pp. 82–3. See p. 134, n. 17.

[20] Granted, both of the reasons just listed may work even if the myths in question are based on *falsehoods* concerning philosophical topics. However, it is reasonable to assume that competent philosophers engaging in myth composition for these additional purposes would choose truths over falsehoods as the basis of their myths, all things being equal.

CHAPTER 5

The Influence of Aristotle's View of Religion on Medieval Jewish and Christian Thought

5.0 Introduction

Aristotle's influence on subsequent theology and philosophy of religion is deep, wide-ranging, and unquestionable. This chapter focuses on two key figures in the development of Jewish and Christian thought in the Middle Ages – Moses Maimonides and Albertus Magnus – and argues that Aristotle's view of the usefulness of traditional religion, as we have interpreted it, is visibly present in the systems of both. Apart from their prominent place and role in their traditions, these two thinkers were chosen for two additional reasons. First, their views are historically related. Albertus' writings are filled with references to Maimonides' work, and he is clearly indebted to Maimonides in his interpretation of Aristotle as well. Second, Maimonides' and Albertus' views complement each other in the ways by which they exhibit Aristotelian influence. Maimonides, on the one hand, is faithfully Aristotelian in his view of the usefulness of the traditional aspects and practices of religion, but his interpretation of Aristotle is not presented as such, but rather is mostly embedded in his own philosophical project in the *Guide of the Perplexed*. Albertus, on the other hand, follows Aristotle (and Maimonides) only up to a point. As we shall see, he thinks for instance that religious poetry, at least as it is used in Christian theology, should not be viewed as means toward philosophical inquiry, but rather transcends philosophical methods and devices by providing a direct and special way of apprehending, appreciating, and enjoying certain truths. Nevertheless, Albertus does present his interpretation of Aristotle as such, in commentaries on Aristotelian treatises (most importantly for our purposes, on the *Metaphysics*).

5.1 Moses Maimonides

In *Guide* III. 26, Maimonides introduces a disagreement among "those believers in the Torah who are people of reason." Whereas some such people attribute a cause (עלה, סבה) and a purpose (גאיה, תכלית) to the Laws, others believe they are willed by God for no particular reason (368:19–24).[1] He then goes on to support the attribution of a cause and a purpose to all Laws (or at least to the "general rule" of every commandment, e.g., the slaughtering of animals, as opposed to its "parts," such as the particular details of Kosher slaughtering), even when their utility is unclear, based on Scriptural evidence, and to interpret apparently conflicting texts in Rabbinic literature as in fact being in agreement with his own opinion.[2] Based on this opinion, Maimonides sets out to classify the 613 commandments of Jewish Law based on the purpose they are supposed to serve. Before doing so, however, he feels the need for a preliminary and general discussion of the purpose of commandments.

According to the general account in III. 27 (371:17), then, the Law is directed toward two goals: the improvement of the body (צלאח אלבדן, תקון הגוף) and the improvement of the soul (צלאח אלנפס, תקון הנפש). These correspond to two types of human perfection. The perfection of the body (i.e., health) is secured by appropriately procuring such things as nutrition, shelter, and baths. These in turn require interpersonal relationships, since, as Maimonides says, obviously echoing Aristotle, humans are naturally political (372:6).[3] The second human perfection, corresponding to the improvement of the soul, consists of becoming rational/intellectual "in actuality" (נאטקא באלפעל, משכיל בפעל), so as to know all there is to know concerning those things that fall within the scope of human

---

[1] Pagination is based on the edition of the Arabic text by I. Joel, דלאלה אלחאירין (Jerusalem, 1930/1). Quoted terms and phrases from the original Judeo-Arabic are accompanied by their Hebrew rendering in Ibbn-Tibbon's translation.

[2] In this context, Maimonides says that the text he is interpreting from *B. T.*, Sanhedrin, 21b would seem to go against the "view agreed upon" (369:26–7 השרש המוסכם עליו, אלאצל אלמגמע עליה), namely the opinion that the Law is purposeful. S. Pines renders the phrase as "universally agreed upon principle," which is far too strong and ignores Maimonides' direct reference to the controversy surrounding this issue at the beginning of III. 26. Elsewhere, I argue that Maimonides does not rely anywhere in the *Guide* on the truth of universal opinions *ipso facto*.

[3] Pines notes that "[t]here is no reason to doubt that Maimonides was acquainted with all the writing of Aristotle known in Moslem Spain, i.e., practically the whole *Corpus Aristotelicum* as we know it. Only one major work was lacking, Aristotle's *Politics*" (S. Pines (trans. and comm.), *Moses Maimonides The Guide of the Perplexed* (Chicago, 1963), p. lxi). As A. Melamed notes, the idea that humans are political animals could have influenced Maimonides through its equivalent formulation in *NE* I. 7 (1097b11); "Aristotle's *Politics* in Medieval and Renaissance Jewish Philosophy (Hebrew)," *Pe'amim* 51 (1991), pp. 27–69 at pp. 30–1. But, as Melamed also goes on to note, based on suggestions by Pines and Berman, Maimonides may well have been influenced by Aristotle's *Politics* indirectly, through his acquaintance with Al-Farabi's *Perfect State* which contains ideas from Aristotle's *Politics* and may be based on an Arabic epitome of it (ibid., pp. 31–32; cf. L. V. Berman, "Maimonides, the Disciple of Alfarabi," *I.Q.S.* 4 (1974), pp. 154–78; S. Pines, "Aristotle's *Politics* in Arabic Philosophy," *Israel Oriental Studies* 5 (1975), pp. 150–60 at pp. 156–7.

knowledge (372:7–9). Here, again, Aristotle (or a particular version of Aristotle) is certainly in the background as the basis for the claim that it is by virtue of an intellect "in actuality" existing within us, due to an overflowing of the so-called "active intellect," that we have access to truth and thereby to intellectual perfection as far as it is humanly achievable (cf. II. 4, 179:17–18).

That Aristotle is so dominantly present in Maimonides' discussion of the two human perfections corresponding to the two main uses of the Law is no coincidence. For these uses themselves correspond to the uses Aristotle ascribes to the content of the traditional Greek religion of his day. First, Maimonides sees the improvement of the body as most basically consisting of attaining bodily health, but he also thinks that, since the means of achieving health require successful social interactions, the commandments designed to achieve health do so by getting people to better interact with one another. This in turn is accomplished by either (a) eliminating mutual wrongdoing by coercing individuals into correct behavior or (b) instilling virtue in them (371:22–5). Maimonides explicitly links these uses of the Law to the proper governing of the state (תדביר אלמדינה, הנהגת המדינה, 8–27). These two uses correspond to two uses Aristotle ascribes to traditional religion. As we have seen in Chapter 2, Aristotle thinks that the content of traditional religion is introduced "with a view to persuading the masses and for its usefulness in supporting the laws" (cf. *Met.* Λ. 8, 1074b4–5). We have also seen that there are reasons for thinking that this use encompasses the coercion of populations into correct behavior (e.g., in legislating a mandatory daily walk for pregnant women to the temple of Artemis) and the moral habituation of future citizens (e.g., by confronting them with depictions of gods or heroes with "superhuman" character virtue, like Hector). And just as Aristotle thinks of the anthropomorphic depiction of Artemis, though useful for persuading people to behave in certain ways, as fictitious, Maimonides thinks of the opinion that God is angry with whomever disobeys Him, an opinion in which belief is "necessary" (III. 28, 373:12 צרורי, הכרחית) if political stability is to be maintained, as false. For, Maimonides thinks that no affection (אנפעאל, הפעלות) may be attributed to God (*Guide* I. 55). And so, as he explicitly says in *Guide* I. 54, God is only spoken of as angered because "actions similar to those that proceed from us from a certain aptitude of the soul – namely, jealousy, holding fast to vengeance, hatred, or anger – proceed from Him, may He be exalted, because of the deserts of those who are punished, and not because of any passion whatever, may He be exalted above every deficiency" (trans. Pines).

Now, the necessary function of traditional religion in Aristotle's view is quite different from its use for either social stability or moral habituation. It consists, as we have seen, in preparing future citizens for philosophical education culminating in the ability to contemplate the eternal truths of metaphysics. This use of religion and its unique significance is echoed in Maimonides' *Guide* by the status he affords to the commandments directed at the improvement of the soul, whose use he considers superior "in significance" (III. 27, 371:26 באלשרף, במעלה). Since Aristotle thinks the anthropomorphic content of traditional religion is false even when it is used for the purpose of philosophical education, we would expect Maimonides, in following him, to say something similar. His distinction between two types of religious content conveyed by the commandments directed at the improvement of the soul – explicitly stated opinions and parables (371:17–19) – would seem to get close to that idea of Aristotle's, since parables do contain fictitious or exaggerated elements to be interpreted away in order for truth to be uncovered.

However, in III. 27 Maimonides seems at first to exclude the possibility of using parables for attaining human perfection through philosophical knowledge. For he links there the use of parables to the education of "the multitude" (אלגמהור, ההמון), whose natural capabilities do not allow them to grasp the opinions that in the case of others can be conveyed explicitly (371:19–20). Maimonides would seem to think, *prima facie*, that those people who *do* have the natural capacity to acquire "divine knowledge" would go about acquiring it through direct communication of correct opinions. And indeed, in III. 28 he goes on to say that the belief in God's existence, unity, knowledge, power, will, and eternity are all conveyed by the Law directly in order to enable individuals to attain "final perfection." However, as he also says there, an individual can only be expected to attain such perfection after having learned many *other* opinions (373:10–11), including those constituting the various sciences (373:14–ff.). It is in this process of learning, as we shall presently see, that Maimonides' relation to Aristotle's view of religion is reinforced. For, like Aristotle, Maimonides thinks that philosophical knowledge (or "human perfection") can only be achieved on the basis of certain falsehoods supplied by traditional religion, as its necessary function, in order to get the individual interested in inquiring into the nature of divinity.

In *Guide* III. 29, Maimonides analyzes the story and character of Abraham – the first person to have reached the perfection of the soul described in the previous chapters. According to Maimonides, Abraham's original apprehension of God's existence, unity, and incorporeality, as well as his recognition of the creation of the cosmos in time, went against the grain of popular (indeed, universal) belief in his day. The Paganism dominant in that period countenanced the existence and worshipping of eternal star-gods, whose forces had such effects as making statues talk and prophesy, and enabling trees to communicate messages to people in dreams (376:19–28). Maimonides describes Abraham's intellectual development, after having been raised in such a culture, as follows:

> (. . .) when *the pillar of the world* [sc. Abraham] grew up and it became clear to him that there is a separate deity that is neither a body nor a force in a body and that all the stars and the spheres were made by Him, and he understood that the fables upon which he was brought up were absurd, he began to refute their doctrine and to show up their opinions as false; he publicly manifested his disagreement with them and called *in the name of the Lord, God of the world* – both the existence of the deity and the creation of the world in time by that deity being comprised in that call (trans. Pines).

This text makes it clear that Maimonides thinks Arbaham's original apprehension of truth concerning divine matters resulted from a process of responding to the beliefs of the Pagans of his day. In fact, Maimonides also thinks Abraham's learning of these truths was not guided by any instruction, since at the time all people, including Abraham himself, were under the spell of Paganism.

Maimonides provides this additional information in the *Mishneh Torah*, to which he explicitly refers the reader during his discussion of Abraham and the Pagans in *Guide* III. 29 (377:6):

ולא היה לו מלמד ולא מודיע דבר אלא מושקע באור כשדים בין עובדי כוכבים הטפשים ואביו ואמו וכל העם עובדי כוכבים והוא עובד עמהם ולבו משוטט ומבין עד שהשיג דרך האמת והבין קו הצדק מתבונתו הנכונה. וידע שיש שם אלוה אחד והוא מנהיג הגלגל והוא ברא הכל ואין בכל הנמצא אלוה חוץ ממנו. וידע שכל העולם טועים ודבר שגרם להם לטעות זה שעובדים את הכוכבים ואת הצורות עד שאבד האמת מדעתם.

> . . . and he had no teacher and no informant, but he was positioned in Ur Kaśdim among the foolish star-worshippers; and his father and mother, and the whole nation were star-worshippers, and he worshipped with them, and his heart was wandering and understanding until he attained the way of truth and understood the line of justice advancing from his correct reason. And he knew that there is one God, and He is the director of the sphere and He created everything and there is no deity in existence except for Him. And he knew the entire world is wrong, and what made them err was the fact that they were worshipping the stars and the images until the truth has gone away from their minds. (*Sefer Hamaddah*, Hilchot Avodat Kochavim, I. 3)

Abraham's intellectual development, as Maimonides understands it, proceeds from a refutation of erroneous opinions, such as the Pagans' belief in star-gods interacting with human beings through the mediation of speaking statues and trees. As we have seen, when Aristotle in *Met.* Λ. 8 discusses the "ancient and very old" philosophers who have concluded the existence of unmoved movers and their divinity, he is not clear on whether that recognition depended on the exposure of such people to previous erroneous depictions of divinity by traditional religion. Similarly, Maimonides does not tell us whether he thinks Abraham could have in principle arrived at his conclusion concerning the existence and nature of God without being previously exposed to the erroneous religion of the Pagans of his day.[4] However, since Maimonides explicitly says that Abraham had no external source of true information and no instructor, and that he himself held the false beliefs of the time until the age of forty, there is room for thinking that his process of discovering the truth depended at least in part on his previous exposure to (and acceptance of) the falsehoods of Paganism.

Of course, even if Abraham did reach his knowledge of God based on previous exposure to anthropomorphic false depictions of divinity, that would not indicate that such depictions play a necessary role in the attaining of such knowledge by people in general. Indeed, Maimonides might seem to reject such a possibility when he says, after describing Abraham's process of learning in the *Mishneh Torah*, that

ספרים רבים חברו עובדי כוכבים בעבודתה היאך עיקר עבודתה ומה מעשיה ומשפטיה. צונו הקב״ה שלא לקרות באותן הספרים כלל ולא נהרהר בה ולא בדבר מדבריה. ואפילו להסתכל בדמות הצורה אסור שנאמר אל תפנו אל האלילים.

> The star-worshippers composed many books concerning the principle of their worship and its practices and laws. God Almighty commanded us not to read those books at all, and we shall not ponder it [sc. that religion], nor any of its sayings. And it is even forbidden to look at the image of the form, for it has been said "do not turn to the idols." (Hilchot Avodat Kochavim II. 2)

The very same practices, sayings, and images that Abraham had been exposed to before he attained philosophical knowledge, then, are apparently prohibited and denied to all subsequent people aspiring to keep the Law and to attain human perfection, according to Maimonides. If it is indeed possible to do so, then it would seem unnecessary for people in

---

[4] Cf. *Mishneh Torah*, *Sefer Hamaddah*, Hilchot Avodat Kochavim, I. 3.

general to be exposed to any false depictions of divinity in order to learn the truth.

There are two points to consider in response to this concern, however. First, Maimonides himself disregards the prohibition mentioned in the *Mishneh Torah* when, in the *Guide*, he continuously analyzes parts of *The Nabatean Agriculture*, which he describes as "the most important book" concerning the opinions of the Sabians, and which he takes to be genuinely Sabian (III. 29, 378:13–14; trans. Pines).[5] He also mentions eight other works counting as "idolatrous books" (ספרי עבודה זרה), including Isḥāq al-Ṣābi's book "concerning the laws of the Sabians, the details of their religion, their festivals, their sacrifices, their prayers, and other matters belonging to their religion" (trans. Pines) (380:9–16). Clearly, the prohibition on reading such books and learning such facts in the *Mishneh Torah* applies neither to Maimonides himself, nor to the audience of the *Guide*. Most directly, Maimonides' student Joseph Ben-Judah is in his master's estimation educated enough in the sciences so as not to be susceptible to having his mind "attached to the fables of the Sabians and the ravings of the Casdeans and Chaldeans who are devoid of all science that is truly a science," unlike the "multitude" who "frequently incline to regarding fables as the truth" (380:4–9, trans. Pines).

Maimonides allows, indeed prescribes, the learning of the opinions and practices of Paganism for those who would not be negatively influenced by them because he believes that knowing such facts constitutes

> [A] very important chapter in the exposition of the reasons for the *com-mandments*. For the foundation of the whole of our Law and the pivot around which it turns, consists in the effacement of these opinions from the minds and of these monuments from existence. (380:26–8; trans. Pines)

The purpose of the Law, as we have seen (cf. III. 27), is to perfect both body and soul, culminating in enabling one to attain divine knowledge as far as humanly possible. So, in identifying the opposition to Paganism as the foundation and central point of the Law, and in saying that understanding the purpose of the Law requires familiarity with paganistic false depictions of divinity, Maimonides effectively says that gaining true knowledge concerning divinity crucially advances from exposure and a consequent reaction to such false depictions. This view is evidently akin to that of Aristotle, for whom it is the usefulness of false anthropomorphic

---

[5] As S. Pines notes, Ibn Waḥshiyya, whom Maimonides mentions as the translator of the work, was probably its author. See S. Pines (trans. and comm.), *Moses Maimonides: Guide* p. 518 n. 25.

depictions of divinity in motivating people to engage in philosophical inquiry that constitutes the naturally necessary political role of traditional religion.

Viewed thus, however, there would seem to be an obvious difference between Maimonides' and Aristotle's positions. For whereas Aristotle speaks of one and the same traditional religion, available to all, as being useful for social stability and moral habituation and necessary for philosophical education, Maimonides seems to distinguish between the content of the Scripture, which is available to everyone and is written in a way conducive to both social stability and moral habituation, and the false content of the "idolatrous books," which should only be absorbed by those capable of, and well on their way toward, attaining full philosophical knowledge. As we shall presently see, however, Maimonides views the Torah itself as useful for all of these purposes, so that this presumed difference is merely apparent.

Prior to stating that such people as Joseph Ben-Judah, but not the multitude, can benefit from the "idolatrous books" and should read them in order to understand the basis of the Law, Maimonides gives an example of one of the pernicious mistakes made in such books. In *The Nabatean Agriculture*, Maimonides relates, there is a Sabian version of the story of the Garden of Eden, in which Adam, the serpent, and the Tree of Knowledge of Good and Evil all appear, but whose conclusion is that the world is uncreated (III. 29, 379:27–ff.). Stories of this kind, according to Maimonides, result from the tendency of the Sabians to understand every story recounted in the Torah (here specifically the *Account of the Beginning*) "literally" (380:3, עלי טאהרה, לפי פשוטו). What concerns Maimonides in exposing the uneducated to Paganism is that they might form erroneous opinions by accepting the content of such a religion, a content based on the literal sense of the Torah taken at face value. But, if Pagans are able to misunderstand the Torah by taking it literally, and to construct erroneous and misleading stories on the basis of their misunderstanding, then there is no reason to assume that non-Pagans, e.g., the multitude of those adhering to the Law, would be unable to similarly misunderstand the Torah on their own and directly, i.e., without the mediation of Paganism. Indeed, in the introduction to *Guide* I, Maimonides states that the very reason for naming his work *The Guide of the Perplexed* is that one of its main purposes is to remove perplexity by clarifying "concealed" (כפיה, סתומים) parables (2:24–5). He then goes on to speak of the *Account of the Beginning* as containing particularly "concealed" (5:14, סתומות) matters, to be understood differently by "the multitude" and by "the perfect." The multitude, in their worst variety, are those to whom the truth always remains concealed (4:7–12).

It is not only some obscure, ancient, and banned false religions, then, that mislead their audience. The Torah itself, in Maimonides' view, is misleading in the same way, and is in fact itself responsible for serious occurrences of misleading stories generated in those other idolatrous traditions. The less capable and less educated, even if they spend their lives reading only the Torah (and not the "idolatrous books"), would still be quite unable to stir away from misinterpretations of Scripture on their own, let alone perfect their souls by apprehending truth. By contrast, we would expect the capable and educated to make use of those potentially misleading features of the Torah for perfecting their souls, similarly to the use we have seen they can make of the false content of Paganism. A hint toward this idea is again provided in the same discussion of the purposes of the *Guide* in the introduction to Book I. Maimonides raises the question concerning the original purpose of concealing the secrets of the Torah using parables. He gives two reasons for the concealment, which are also intended to explain why he himself sets out to uncover the secrets of the Torah in the *Guide*, and why he intends to do so only temporarily and partially (3:14–23). One reason, familiar to us through the emphasis laid on it by Straussian interpretations of the *Guide*, is that fully explaining these secrets in a book would be equivalent to communicating them to thousands, though they should be hidden from the "multitude of the people" (גמהור אלנאס, המון העם). But another reason for the concealment, more important for our purposes, is that, as Maimonides says, in the case of some principles of even natural science (not to mention those of metaphysics or "divine knowledge"), it is impossible (לא ימכן)[6] to teach or explain the science by conveying the principles simply or directly as what they are. The reason why this is impossible is explained most clearly in *Guide* I. 33, to which we now turn.

After discussing the scope and limitations of human knowledge in *Guide* I. 32, Maimonides goes on in I. 33 to discuss the proper mode of instruction for those individuals who are indeed capable of attaining as much knowledge as is humanly possible. He begins by noting that, even in the

---

[6] Note that Ibbn-Tibbon renders this phrase as "אין ראוי", implying that it is merely "improper," rather than "impossible," to explain (say) natural science by explaining some of its principles as what they simply are. His intention may be to equate the two reasons Maimonides gives for concealing the secrets of the Torah using parables, perhaps by pointing out that it is improper to convey them directly because that would make them accessible to the multitude. In any event, his translation is inadequate.

case of such (rare) individuals, instruction must be gradual. In particular, their education cannot begin with, but rather must culminate in, metaphysics or "divine wisdom" (אלעלם אלאלאהי, החכמה האלהית). An appropriate educational program must involve a curriculum that includes logic, mathematics, and natural science, in that order (I. 34, 50:23–4). It must also ensure that the student's initial exposure to metaphysical subjects would be suited to those who are not capable, or are not *yet* capable, of inculcating them "as they truly are" (I. 33, 48:12, כפי אמתתם, עלי חקיקתהא) or "in [their] true essence" (48:14, על אמתת מהותו, עלי חקיקّة מאהיתה). This remark clearly echoes the aforementioned statement of the purpose of the concealment of the secrets of the Torah in the introduction to *Guide* I, in which it is said that some principles of sciences, if they are ever to be grasped successfully, should not be initially taught directly as what they are (3:18, עלי מא הי עליה כפי מה שהם עליו בביאור). And in I. 33, too, Maimonides is concerned with explaining the purpose of parables and other literally false depictions in the Torah specifically with regard to the use of such devices in theoretical instruction. The Torah "speaks in the language of human beings," using images, parables, and anthropomorphisms, Maimonides says, so as to be readily tackled and learned by "children, women and all people" (48:9–10).

Very much like Aristotle, then, Maimonides thinks it is the same religious content, involving simplifications and even overt falsehoods (at least when interpreted literally), that functions both as the endpoint of the education of the intellectually incapable and as the commencement point for those who can potentially attain truth. Those who are incapable of advancing beyond the literal sense of that content are equivalent to children even in adulthood. Both should be addressed "according to their rational ability" (47:23–4), which is just to say that both should only be granted access to the literal sense of the Torah. This view is reminiscent of the one found in Strabo's *Geographica* 1.2.8, which as we have seen draws on Aristotelian materials and reflects Aristotle's view (see Section 2.3, pp. 61–ff.). There, Strabo says that "every ignorant and uneducated man is in a sense a child, and is likewise a lover of myths." He also says there that "it is impossible for a philosopher to lead a crowd of women, or any vulgar multitude, toward reverence, piety and belief by using reason (λόγῳ)" and that consequently "myth-creation and talking marvels" must be employed for that purpose. Maimonides agrees. It must, as he says, suffice to those who are incapable of full intellectual development to believe in the objects of the depiction (תצור, ציור) they have been acquainted with, on the authority of tradition proclaiming that it is preferable for them to do so (48:12–14).

As for those children who are capable of eventually attaining truth, Maimonides' view is again similar to that of Aristotle. Strabo, it will be remembered, joins two of Aristotle's statements in *Metaphysics* A, i.e., that human beings are naturally "lovers of knowledge" (1, 980a1) and that mythology is akin to philosophy in having "wonder" as its starting point (2, 982b12–19), and concludes on the basis of these that children must begin their intellectual development with myths, which provide for them a "new language" involving both wonder and pleasure:

> At the beginning, then, it is necessary to make use of such bait, and as [the children] come of age [one must] guide [them] toward learning of true facts, once the intelligence (τῆς διανοίας) develops and is no longer in need of flatterers. (1.2.8)

Maimonides, discussing the reasons why learning divine matters should be carried out gradually, lists as a third reason, after the difficulty of the topic and the unsuitability of minds at an early stage of their development, the "length of the preparations" (I. 34, 49:20, טול אלתותיאת, אורך ההצעות). As he immediately goes on to clarify, human beings have a natural desire to request "the ends" (אלגאיאת, התכליות), or as he calls it later on, more directly echoing Aristotle (in the opening sentence of the *Metaphysics*), a "natural desire to know these things [sc. e.g., the number and order of the heavenly spheres, the nature of angels, the manner of the creation of the world, the nature, creation, and separability of the soul] as they truly are" (50:1). Indeed, Maimonides continues, this natural desire is so great that it generally leaves people no patience for going through the preparatory stages of instruction crucial for attaining truth. For that reason, the tantalizing but literally inaccurate depictions of divinity in the Torah, e.g., by means of parables, are required, much as in Strabo's text, as "bait" for motivating people to inquire methodically and carefully into the questions that interest them. Without such bait, potential learners would be sure to grow disinterested in the topics they must learn in order to ultimately reach full knowledge, and they would consequently let themselves waste their own lives in the comfort of "misleading imaginations" (בכיאלאת כאדבה, בדמיונים מכזיבים 50:4).

In Maimonides' view, then, the literally false but nevertheless necessary features of the Torah, equivalent to the content of traditional religion in Aristotle's thought, ensure that potential philosophers neither expose themselves to truths they are not yet in a position to handle, nor abandon the line of inquiry gradually leading to such truths. They do so by providing a middle ground between sheer continued ignorance and full knowledge. For example, a question occurs to a potential philosopher concerning the duration of the cosmos. In order to satisfy her curiosity, the child might for instance adopt any chance idea, such as the doctrine of the eternity of the world, or simply give up on the inquiry altogether. Thus, she would be either wrong or clueless, but no longer actively perplexed. Alternatively, she could be taught the secrets of the Torah, expounding a detailed answer to that and many other questions, at a stage at which the learner is not yet capable of understanding them. In that case, the child would be "drowning in the sea of knowledge," so to speak (cf. I. 34, 49:7–11). By exposing her to anthropomorphisms, figures, and parables, the Torah enables the child to maintain her fascination with such topics as she advances in the process of properly obtaining answers to her questions.

This view of the usefulness of enticing depictions of divinity in motivating people to embark on the arduous process of learning metaphysics is clearly influenced by Aristotle. It remains to be seen whether this usefulness, for Maimonides, also amounts to a necessary role as it does for Aristotle. Is it, as a general rule, necessary for people to begin their philosophical education in divine matters by being confronted with simplified and literally false depictions of God? Let us revisit the passage quoted in Chapter 2,[7] which is arguably the clearest pronouncement of Maimonides' view concerning the role of such depictions in the process of philosophical instruction, this time focusing on the question at hand (attending to the parts of the text I emphasize here):

> When a person begins with "divine wisdom" (אלעלם אלאלאהי), there shall occur not only confusion with regard to belief but a complete annihilation thereof. Such a person would resemble an infant who is being fed wheaten bread, meat and wine. This would *surely* (or, undoubtedly: בלא שך, בלא ספק) kill that infant, not because these are unnatural foods for human beings, but because of the weakness of the child, precluding it from digesting and making use of them. This is why these true opinions [sc. the truths of metaphysics] are concealed, are only hinted at, and are deliberately taught by the wise in the most mysterious ways, not because they contain some evil content or are destructive of the principles of faith (as those fools believe, who only think themselves to be philosophers) but rather they are hidden *because of the incapability of the human mind* (לקצור אלעקול, לקצור השכל) to receive them at the beginning [of the educational process]. (I. 33, 47:27–48:8; trans. following Friedländer)

Maimonides here addresses the limitations of the human mind generally speaking and says that they involve the inability to imbibe metaphysical truths directly. The analogy he introduces, between attempting to gain knowledge of divine matters directly and feeding bread, meat, and wine to an infant, further emphasizes the universality of that limitation. Maimonides also clearly thinks that the indirect study of such topics must be carried out by means of anthropomorphism or parables. As he goes on to say, in attaining perfection a human being, through using the appropriate mode of argumentation, gets to know divine truths they were previously acquainted with only as "imaginations and parables" (48:14–19). This is so, furthermore, whether the person in question reaches their knowledge through instruction or on their own (48:15).

It follows that even the most qualified minds capable of attaining truth with no instruction – one is reminded of the aforementioned story of Abraham, who received no instruction in reaching his apprehension of God, though he had previously been exposed to the fables and practices of the Pagans of his day – must be exposed to metaphorical or figurative preambles prior to doing so. I. 34 reinforces this interpretation, at least according to one available reading. There, Maimonides says that if we were never instructed by traditional authority and parables, we would never have attained truth. Translations differ on the remark that follows at 51:3–4.[8] S. Pines' translation reads: "Nobody would ever be saved from this perdition except *one of a city or two of a family*," which indicates that a slight minority of people might be able to attain full wisdom without relying on either authority or parables. M. Friedländer's translation is closer to our interpretation: "From such a fate *not even* 'one of a city or two of a family' (Jer. iii. 14) would have escaped" (my emphasis).[9] On the first reading, Maimonides should be understood as following Aristotle quite closely on the role of traditional (aspects of) religion in initiating philosophical inquiry. But on the second reading, Maimonides follows Aristotle wholeheartedly, by fully accepting this use of the traditional content of religion as the thing (or one of the things) it is absolutely necessary for.

It is instructive that in the very last chapter of the *Guide* (III. 54), appropriately examining the ultimate purpose of human life, Maimonides

---

[8] The difference revolves around the understanding of the word אלא in Maimonides' text (Ibbn-Tibbon's Hebrew translation has אלא as in the original Judeo-Arabic).

[9] M. Friedländer (trans. and comm.), *The Guide of the Perplexed of Maimonides* (London, 1885), p. 121.

begins the discussion by distinguishing four senses of the Hebrew word
for wisdom (חכמה), followed by a sharp distinction between "wisdom
simply speaking" (467:7 אלחכמה באטלאק, החכמה הגמורה), through which
one demonstrates the true opinions one has previously obtained through
tradition, and knowledge of the Torah, each constituting a different "species" (ibid. נועא, מין). Based on Rabbinic authority, Maimonides proclaims
that a human being is required to obtain knowledge of the opinions of
the Torah, through tradition, prior to demonstrating them (which in turn
will set the ground for determining proper and noble action) (467:18–22).
The wisdom associated with the demonstration and full apprehension of
the highest truths of "divine science" is in Maimonides' final account the
ultimate end of both the traditional knowledge leading up to it and the
other, lower perfections he goes on to list in this chapter (i.e., possessions,
bodily perfection, and moral virtue). He concludes:

> The *Sages, may their memory be blessed,* apprehended from this *verse* <i.e.
> Jer. 9:22–3> the very notions we have mentioned and have explicitly stated
> that which I have explained to you in this chapter: namely, that the term
> wisdom <חכמה>, used in an unrestricted sense and regarded as the end,
> means in every place the apprehension of Him, may He be exalted; that
> the possession of the treasures acquired, and competed for, by man and
> thought to be perfection are not a perfection; and that similarly all the
> actions prescribed by the Law – I refer to the various species of worship
> and also the moral habits that are useful to all people in their mutual deal-
> ings – that all this is not to be compared with this ultimate end and does
> not equal it, being but preparation made for the sake of this end. (469:25–
> 470:3, trans. Pines)

As Maimonides clearly states here, fully fulfilling one's nature as a human
being consists of apprehending God. Moral perfection is secondary and,
more importantly for our purposes, both it and all modes of religious worship are by their nature instrumental and preparatory. For Maimonides, as
for Aristotle, the content of traditional religion, with its various anthropomorphic depictions of divinity, simplifications, parables, and rituals,
remains in the service of philosophical knowledge and is directed toward
it. And this service is needed, since, as we have seen, Maimonides, again
following Aristotle, thinks that human beings standardly, and quite possibly invariably, can only hope to attain such wisdom by first being confronted with such traditional ideas, which would motivate them toward
embarking on the type of inquiry relevant to achieving wisdom and keep
them interested as they go along.

5.2 Albertus Magnus

Maimonides' view extends well beyond his influence on subsequent Jewish thinkers. His writings play a key role in the development of medieval Christian philosophy and theology, for example. This is largely due to Albertus Magnus, whose own influence, most notably through his student Thomas Aquinas, has on many fronts determined the trajectory of subsequent Christian thought.[10] Albertus' writings are heavily influenced by Maimonides, mentioning him by name over a hundred times,[11] and relying on him implicitly on many other occasions.[12] As G. K. Hasselhoff puts it, Maimonides' influence on Albertus revolves mainly around their shared interest in finding a "synthesis between Aristotelianism and belief in the Bible" on such issues as the apprehension of God and the eternity of the universe.[13] As we shall now see, Albertus' interpretation of Aristotle on the usefulness of traditional religion and its content, devices, and practices also recognizably reacts to Maimonides' view. Albertus thinks that Aristotle views poetry and mythology as useful for initiating philosophical inquiry, similarly to Maimonides. But, unlike Maimonides, Albertus does not think traditional religion as such functions similarly.

In *Metaphysics* A. 2, 982b11–28, Aristotle seeks to establish the point that philosophy is not a productive science. To that end, he alludes to the fact that philosophy always has "wonder" (τὸ θαυμάζειν) as its starting point, and is hence directed toward escaping ignorance by gaining knowledge rather than toward any practical use. In this context, Aristotle establishes at 982b18–19 a kinship between the "philosopher" and the "mythologist," due to the fact that myth "is constructed out of wonders" (σύγκειται ἐκ θαυμασίων), by stating either that the philosopher is in a way a mythologist, or that the mythologist is in a way a philosopher (the sentence allows for both readings). In his commentary on the *Metaphysics*, Albertus draws the following conclusion concerning this part of Aristotle's discussion:

---

[10] G. K. Hasselhoff, "Zur Maimonidesrezeption in der christlich-lateinischen Literatur" in L. Muehlethaler (ed.), *Höre die Wahrheit, wer sie auch spricht: Stationen des Werkes von Moses Maimonides vom islamischen Spanien bis ins moderne Berlin* (Göttingen, 2014), pp. 64–9 at p. 66.

[11] Ibid.

[12] See, e.g., B. B. Price, "Interpreting Albert the Great on Astronomy," in I. M. Resnick (ed.), *A Companion to Albert the Great* (Leiden, 2013), pp. 397–436 at pp. 409–10.

[13] Hasselhoff, "Maimonidesrezeption," p. 66: "Insbesondere in Fragen des Gottesverständnisses und zur Frage der Ewigkeit der Welt, für die Maimonides eine Synthese von Aristotelismus und Bibelglauben angeboten hatte, wurde dem jüdischen Gelehrten vom Dominikaner hohe Autorität zuerkannt."

As Aristotle shows (. . .) the poet composes stories so that one is stimulated to wondering, and that wonder further stimulates one to inquiring, and this is what philosophy consists of. As is the case when Plato tells of Phaethon and of Deucalion in which story nothing is intended other than stimulating one to wondering at the causes of the two jets of water and fire which come from the wandering stars moving out of orbit, so that through wonder the cause might be sought and the truth known. And thus poetry provides a way of philosophizing, just as the other logical sciences. But the other sciences or parts of logic provide a way of proving a proposition by reason, using either a perfect or an imperfect argument. Poetry, on the other hand, provides a way of wondering (*admirandi*) through which [one] is excited [into] inquiring. Therefore, poetry may be [classified] under grammar as far as the measure of meter goes, but as far as the purpose (*intentio*) goes poetry is a certain part of logic.

Sicut (. . .) ostendit Aristoteles, poeta fingit fabulam ut excitet ad admirandum, et quod admiratio ulterius excitet ad inquirendum: et sic constet philosophia, sicut est de Phaetonte, et sicut de Deucalione monstrat Plato: in qua fabula non intenditur nisi excitatio ad mirandum causas duorum diluviorum aquae et ignis ex orbitatione stellarum erraticarum provenientium, ut per admirationem causa quaeratur, et sciatur veritas: et ideo poesis modum dat philosophandi sicut aliae scientiae logices: sed aliae scientiae vel partes logices modum dant probandi propositum a ratione vel argumentatione perfecta vel imperfecta: poesis autem non, sed modum dat admirandi per quem excitatur inquirens: licet ergo quoad mensuram metri poetria sit sub grammatica, tamen quoad intentionem logicae est poesis quaedam pars. (I. II. 6, p. 30, Borgnet) [14]

According to what Albertus says here, the comparison Aristotle draws between philosophy and mythology suggests that poetry is directed toward a philosophical goal. Whereas poetry cannot, and is not intended to, arrive at philosophical conclusions through reasoning, it can, and is in fact intended to, motivate people toward inquiring philosophically into a certain topic by getting them interested in it through poetic means.

As an example, Albertus brings up two myths mentioned in Plato's *Timaeus*. In that dialogue, in 21e–ff., Critias reports an exchange between Solon, the mythological lawgiver of Athens, and Egyptian priests, whereupon Solon discovers how ignorant he, as a Greek, is concerning such matters as ancient history by comparison to members of far older civilizations.

---

[14] Translations of this chapter of Albertus' commentary on Aristotle's *Metaphysics* A (i.e. I. II. 6, pp. 30–1, Borgnet) follow J. V. Cunningham, *Woe or Wonder: The Emotional Effect of Shakespearian Tragedy* (Denver, 1960), at 77–8.

Solon recounts to the priests three Greek myths, all relating to ancient history and intended to demonstrate how far back Greek knowledge of history goes. First, there is the myth of the allegedly first man – Phoroneus. The second myth, and the one mentioned first by Albertus, tells the story of Deucalion and Pyyrha's survival of the great deluge. The details of the myth, not given in Plato's text, resemble the biblical account of Noah's ark. Deucalion is told by his father, the clairvoyant Prometheus, to build a chest, upon predicting a great flood that thereafter turns out to have wiped out the whole of humanity with the single exception of Deucalion and his wife, Pyrrha (Apollodorus, *Lib.*, I. VII). The couple settles on Mount Parnassus in Delphi, or possibly Mount Etna in Sicily (Hyg., *Fab.*, 153), where they are given the task of repopulating the earth. They do so by throwing stones behind them, which consequently turn into human beings: those thrown by Deucalion into males, and those by Pyrrha, females. On Plato's Critias' report, upon hearing this exposition, an elder Egyptian priest rebukes Solon for thinking or implying that the Greeks have access to ancient wisdom (22b3–ff.). In truth, the priest says, "there is no old Greek" (22b5), and the genealogies Solon claims to have knowledge of are but "children's myths" (παίδων . . . μύθων) (23b3–5). Since the world is subject to repeated periodic cataclysms, it is only rare civilizations enjoying special geographic conditions (like the proximity to the Nile, lack of floods, and mild temperature) that manage to survive continuously and to impart their accumulated knowledge to future generations (22d1–23b3). The truth concerning the cyclical destruction of (e.g., Greek) civilization, the Egyptian priest says, is indicated by a story appearing in both Greek and Egyptian mythology, i.e., the myth of Phaethon, who borrowed his father's chariot and, driving it recklessly, crashed and caused the destruction of everything on earth including Phaethon himself (22c3–7). This myth is the second example Albertus mentions from Plato's *Timaeus* for the way in which poetry leads to philosophizing.

As Plato goes on to write, Solon, upon hearing the Egyptian priest, "says that he is in wonder" (ἔφη θαυμάσαι), and asks the priest to instruct him on ancient history in all its known details, which the priest proceeds to do (23d1–ff.). Though this feature of Critias' account is not explicitly mentioned in Albertus' text, it is clearly relevant to the point he is making. Albertus argues that poetry is useful for motivating people to inquire into a given topic, and he gives the myths mentioned in the *Timaeus* as examples. One of these, namely the myth of Phaethon, actually plays just this role in Plato's dialogue, for it gets a potential learner, in this case Solon – who turns out to be in need of instruction due to the insufficient resources of the civilization in which he was brought up – to wonder at a given topic or set of facts (in this case facts of ancient history) and to seek answers to related questions (in this case through learning directly from the priest). But it is important to note that it is also the second myth Albertus refers to, the myth of Deucalion and Pyrrha introduced in Critias' account by Solon himself, that he (Albertus) thinks should stimulate people to embark on an inquiry. Who are the potential learners in the case of such a myth, which according to the Egyptian priest in Critias' account amounts to no more than a "children's myth"? Such potential learners may well be actual children, who, upon hearing such myths, would wonder at and conse-quently inquire into the causes of such things as floods (or "the two jets of water," as Albertus puts it) or the facts of ancient history (the subject Solon is interested in clarifying by presenting the myth in question). Such potential learners could also be, or could include, Solon himself, who at an early stage of his intellectual development may have gained his origi-nal interest in ancient history by being exposed to myths of this kind, and may have gone on to inquire into ancient history as it was available to him in his homeland (which turned out not to be enough). Whichever option Albertus specifically has in mind, in presenting myths such as the myth of Deucalion and Pyrrha as useful and indeed intended for initiating inquiry he aligns himself with the view we have attributed to Aristotle, Strabo, and Maimonides.

Now, it has been argued that in presenting the preceding view Albertus, rather than consciously accepting Aristotle's view as interpreted, e.g., by Maimonides, is in fact relying on a faulty translation of Aristotle's remark on the affinity between the philosopher and the mythologist at *Metaphysics* A. 2, 982b18–19. For, prior to presenting his interpretation of Aristotle's view of poetry and its relation to philosophy as we have unpacked it here, Albertus introduces the remark in question as follows:

> But he who doubts and wonders seems ignorant. For wonder is a move-ment of the ignorant proceeding toward an inquiry, so that he would know the cause of that concerning which he wonders. A proof of that is that Philomithes himself according to that way of looking at things is a philos-opher. Because he composed his fable by himself from wonders. Indeed, I mention Philomithes as a poet loving to make fables. For *Mithes*, [with] the first [syllable] lengthened, signifies fable, and *Philomithes* signifies a lover of fables if the penultimate [syllable] is lengthened.

> Qui autem dubitat et admiratur, ignorans videtur: est enim admiratio motus ignorantis procedentis ad inquirendum, ut sciat causam ejus de quo miratur: cujus signum est, quia ipse Philomithes secundum hunc modum

Philosophus est: quia fabula sua construitur ab ipso ex mirandis. Dico autem Philomiton poetam amantem fingere fabulas. *Miton* enim, prima producta, fabulam sonat, et *Philomiton* sonat amatorem fabularum si penultima producatur. (I. II. 6, p. 30, Borgnet)

J. V. Cunningham says of this passages the following:[15]

The poet Philomithes, of course, is a character that grew from a misreading of the Greek text in the passage in which Aristotle states that "the lover of myth (*philomuthos*) is in a sense a lover of Wisdom, for the myth is composed of wonders" (*Metaphysics*, I. 2. 982b18–19). But he is a charming character, and he makes the point. The end of poetry is wonder, and the end of wonder is to excite inquiry . . .

If Cunningham is correct, then Albertus' point about the usefulness of poetry for philosophical instruction is contingent on a mistranslation of Aristotle's text, which gives one the impression, contrary to Aristotle's purposes, that an actual poet named Philomithes was apart from a maker of fables also a lover of wisdom. But, apart from the fact that not all interpreters translate Albertus' text as referring to that fictional character,[16] there is nothing about the figure Philomithes as such that specifically favors the interpretation of Aristotle as suggesting that poetry is designed in order to initiate inquiry. All that is said in Albertus' text about Philomithes is that he was both a lover of myths and a lover of wisdom. This character, then, simply embodies the affinity Aristotle himself draws between the mythologist and the philosopher, without adding further substantive content to it. In order to find the source of Albertus' interpretation, we must look elsewhere.

It is not unlikely that Albertus' interpretation has its source in his influence by Maimonides. Let us return to the myths Albertus appeals to from Plato's *Timaeus*. Albertus presents these as intended to stimulate one to inquire into the causes of "the two jets of water and fire which come from the wandering stars moving out of orbit." But as we have seen, what both of these phenomena have in common, in the context of the dialogue, is their relation to the ancient history of humankind, and it is this subject that those myths are most basically meant to get one to inquire into. Based on the myths of Phoroneus and of Deucalion and Pyrrha, Solon

---

[15] J. V. Cunningham, *Woe or Wonder: The Emotional Effect of Shakespearian Tragedy* (Denver, 1960), at pp. 78–9.

[16] M. I. George, "The Wonder of the Poet; the Wonder of the Philosopher," *Proceedings of the American Catholic Philosophical Association* 65 (1961), pp. 191–202 at p. 192.

presumes that the history of humankind is brief and that the world has only undergone one cataclysm. Though Solon is also familiar with the myth of Phaethon, he does not manage to derive from it the conclusion of his Egyptian interlocutor, namely that there have in fact been many cosmic catastrophes and consequently a whole host of apparently "first men," until it is directly communicated to him. As Albertus is no doubt aware, this view of repeated cataclysms extinguishing either whole civilizations or large portions of them is closely connected to Aristotle's view of the eternity of the cosmos. In fact, based on Philoponus' report, Aristotle may have himself mentioned Deucalion's myth in his *De philosophia* as evidence for the occurrence of multiple (and perhaps infinitely many) cataclysms (*in Nicom. Isagogen* I.1=Ross *De phil.* Fr. 8b).[17] In any event, Aristotle brings up the doctrine of cyclical catastrophes in several places, including the *Metaphysics* (Λ. 8, 1074b10–13; cf. *Pol.* II. 5, 1264a3–5; VII. 10, 1329b25–7).[18] And as Albertus also knows full well, Maimonides rejects Aristotle's doctrine of the world's eternity, and argues for its creation. In doing so, Maimonides first shows that, contrary to later interpretations, Aristotle himself realized, correctly, that his own arguments for the eternity of the world cannot be demonstrative (*Guide* II. 15). He then goes on to offer his own arguments for the creation of the world in time, taking into consideration the fact that no demonstration concerning such matters could be given (II. 16–20). In fact, Albertus is not only aware of these discussions in Maimonides. In his commentary on Aristotle's *Physics* (Book VIII), he actively follows Maimonides in stating that the controversy concerning the eternity of the universe cannot be settled through demonstration, explicitly presenting arguments from Maimonides in the course of the discussion.[19]

In bringing up as examples of poetry as inducing inquiry the myths of Phoroneus, Deucalion and Pyrrha, and Phaethon from the *Timaeus*, then, Albertus may well have them in mind as prototypes of the dialectical exchanges between Aristotelianism/Platonism and Jewish Law as Maimonides portrays them in *Guide* II. 13 (indeed, in presenting Plato's position there as equivalent to Aristotle's view of the eternity of the cosmos Maimonides consciously and explicitly relies on the *Timaeus*; cf. *Guide*

---

[17] See Bodéüs, *Aristotle and the Theology of the Living Immortals*, p. 89.

[18] I discuss Aristotle's view of the eternity of the cosmos as discussed by Maimonides, and the connection between that view and the doctrine of repeated cataclysms, elsewhere.

[19] See S. Baldner, "III. Eternity and the Prime Mover in Albert's *Physica* 7–8," in D. Twetten, S. Baldner, and S. C. Snyder, "Albert's Physics" in I. M. Resnick (ed.), *A Companion to Albert the Great* (Leiden, 2013), pp. 173–220 at pp. 204–8. Cf. Albertus, *Phys.* VIII.1.12–14; *Summa de mir. scient. dei.* 2, q. 4, quaest. incid. 2.

II. 13, 198:2–5). His point in bringing up the examples would then be to emphasize the role of poetry and myth in the beginning points of inquiry into such difficult topics. Maimonides, as we have seen, warns us against misinterpreting the parables of the Torah, as the Sabians did when they took the story of the Garden of Eden to signify the eternity of the cosmos. But he also thinks that secure knowledge of the truth of the matter, in this case the creation of the world in time, necessitates first being exposed to such stories, and embarking on an inquiry as a result. Similarly, we might say, Albertus appeals to Solon, who according to Critias' account in the *Timaeus* misinterprets the story of Phaethon when he fails to see that it signifies a continuous succession of world catastrophes. But the very same myth nevertheless later on intrigues Solon, leading him to seek an explanation of the world's history from his interlocutor. Insofar as the view Solon ultimately hears from his interlocutor approximates or resembles Aristotle's view of the eternity of the cosmos, Albertus would of course reject it (along with Maimonides). But where he agrees with both Aristotle and Maimonides is on the point of the role of poetic devices in commencing the inquiry at the end of which truth concerning such matters may be discovered.

However, one basic difference between Maimonides' and Albertus' views still remains. Whereas Maimonides speaks of the fables of Pagan religions and the parables, anthropomorphisms, and rituals of the Torah as conducive to philosophical inquiry, Albertus, in the texts we have been considering, speaks only of poetry as being useful in that way, and incidentally not even exclusively religious poetry (even though the examples he mentions in his discussion are all taken from the myths of Greek religion). Albertus, unlike Maimonides, does not seem to be concerned with interpreting Aristotle's view of the usefulness of religion, as such. But there is more to be said on that point as well. For, once Albertus gets around to interpreting the key passage from *Metaphysics* Λ. 8 in which Aristotle discusses the "ancient and very old" philosophers and the truths they have discovered, which were subsequently supplemented with mythical additions (1074a38–b14), he relates his interpretation of *Met.* Λ. 2 to that discussion, and says:

> But all these philosophers thus coming in succession through the generations [sc. the philosophers who have appeared in succession after the "ancient and very old ones" mentioned in Λ. 8] have supposed in agreement, as we have said, that there are divine substances, and that their movers are separable substances, and are themselves the principles of generation. And for that reason the number of the movers and immovable

substances is to be accepted according to those who have passed on philosophy mythically (*fabulose*), according to the way mentioned above. For a myth (*fabula*) is some philosophy, and from the wonders by which philosophy has begun it constructs philosophy. But although [their] myth wraps up the divine objects with the likeness of human beings and of other animals, they nevertheless have not intended that [to mean that] they are humans and animals, but rather from certain similarities through certain dissimilar properties they make some natural science publicly (*vulgariter*) known.

Omnes autem isti Philosophi sic succedentes per saecula concorditer posuerunt, ut diximus, has esse substantias divinas, et motores earum esse substantias separatas, et esse ipsa principia generationis: et ideo etiam secundum eos qui fabulose philosophiam tradiderunt, secundum superius inductum modum accipiendus est numerus motorum, et substantiarum immobilium: fabula enim aliquid philosophiae est, et ex miris quibus philosophari inceptum est, contexit philosophiam. Quamvis autem fabula ad hominum similitudinem et aliorum animalium retorqueat coelestia, tamen hoc non intenderunt quod homines essent et animalia, sed potius ex similitudinibus quibusdam per proprietates quasdam dissimiles faciunt vulgariter innostescere quaedam physica. (*Metaph.* XI, II. 29; p. 658 Borgnet)

Here, Albertus clearly draws on Aristotle's idea of the affinity between philosophy and mythology in *Met.* A. 2. Poetry in general "provides a way of philosophizing" (I. II. 6, p. 30, Borgnet), and so the myths of (or those subsequent to) the ancient philosophers brought up in Λ. 8 also make for "some philosophy." In both cases, the common denominator between philosophy and mythology is the "wonder" at the basis of both, just as Aristotle states in A. 2. But, specifically with regard to Λ. 8, Albertus links the myths functioning there as "some philosophy" with the religious practices accompanying them. He says:

And the rest concerning these things have been said by the ancients, and have been transmitted to posterity for persuasion of the vulgar multitude, and have been directed toward laws by which their religions are practiced, and toward the benefit to the life of human beings, thus insofar as they worship those things by means of public prayers and sacrifices, they lead to appeasing and pacifying.

Et reliqua quae de his dicta sunt ab Antiquis, jam a posteris sunt adducta ad persuasionem multorum vulgarium, et conversa sunt ad leges quibus coluntur religiones eorum, et ad conferens ad vitam hominum, ita quod colunt ea supplicationibus et sacrificiis, ut ad propitiationem et placationem inducant. (*Metaph.* XI, II. 29; Borgnet, p. 657)

The myths accompanying the truths discovered by Aristotle's ancient philosophers form the basis of traditional religions through instilling certain laws.

These religions, in turn, are useful for reaching various political goals, such as the amelioration of human life by adding to social tranquility and stability.

It is the same myths that constitute "some philosophy," reliably indicating certain cosmological and metaphysical truths, that also form the basis of traditional religion. The obvious next step, which both Strabo and Maimonides take, as we have seen, is to say that traditional religion in general is useful for, and perhaps even (as we have suggested) has its necessary function in, its role in philosophical inquiry. Albertus, however, does not take this further step. Rather, he seems to think that traditional religion is inherently directed exclusively toward the "vulgar multitude": it is meant either to make natural science known publicly (or "vulgarly": *vulgariter*) or else to persuade the vulgar multitude (*multorum vulgarium*) to behave correctly and peacefully. Poetry and mythology are used to initiate philosophical inquiry, as we see for instance in Plato, but they certainly do not necessarily do so as part of a religious system, and may not even necessarily involve religious themes or content. Indeed, even when Albertus links *Met.* Λ. 8 to A. 2 on the point that poetry or myth is a "kind of philosophy," he does not say of the myths added to the truths of the ancients in Λ. 8 that they constitute "some philosophy" by enticing people to inquire. Rather, he uses the affinity between poetry and philosophy in that discussion in order to argue that the myths of the ancients might reliably supply true information (in that case, concerning the number of the unmoved movers of the heavens). Though Albertus agrees that poetry is used both as the foundation of traditional religion and as a tool for initiating philosophical activity, he seems to vehemently separate these two uses so as to free religion and religious poetry from its role in philosophy.

Albertus quite clearly has reasons for thus deviating from Maimonides' view. He explicitly contrasts philosophy or theoretical science with theology throughout his writings. He thinks that, though they may share some of the same objects, they nevertheless differ radically in their point of focus, their purpose, the kind of science they constitute, their methodology, and their level of certainty – in theology's favor. Given his commitment to this kind of superiority of theology over philosophy, Albertus cannot accept any view that assigns to theology and to its various methods and devices, including parables and metaphors, an instrumental role in arriving at truth philosophically.

First, then, Albertus' view in his commentary on the *Ethics* is that though we may contemplate God both philosophically and theologically, philosophical contemplation differs from theological contemplation in that "the philosopher contemplates God according as he or she possesses God as a demonstrative conclusion, whereas the theologian contemplates him as existing beyond reason and understanding."[20] As Albertus explains further in the *Summa Theologiae*, philosophy (i.e., metaphysics) is concerned with its objects (specifically, with God) as "being and parts of being," whereas theology is concerned with the same objects (again, specifically with God) "in relation to the 'enjoyable' (*fruibile*) and as underlying properties attributed to them as such."[21] Philosophy and theology study, or may study, the same object, but in doing so they are examining entirely different aspects of it.

This difference in focus helps to explain Albertus' decision to classify theology in the *Summa Theologiae* I. 3 as a "practical science," to be distinguished from the theoretical sciences. As M. Olszewski puts it, Albertus' view is that[22]

> (. . .) when Scripture considers the truth of an object of eternal *fruitio* (that is, enjoyment), it relates truth to affect. For example, the affective intellect enjoys the highest truth in faith, the salutary element in hope, and goodness in charity. Moreover, the truth about God is discovered in the Bible primarily not as truth in general but as salutary truth.

Whereas theoretical science deals with truth as such, theology is concerned with truth insofar as it pertains to a resulting action, and especially to "enjoyment" (or "fruition": *fruitio*) of truth,[23] understood in the *Summa* as "an act of charity, performed through the power of 'affective intellect,' fortified by faith and hope, to which the cardinal virtues are dispositive."[24]

It is partly because of its being a practical science that theology also differs from philosophy methodologically. Whereas science uses demonstrations, theology uses metaphors or parables, and it does so at least in part because such devices are especially useful for initiating action and for reaching all audiences, including the least intellectually capable.[25] In saying such things, Aristotle could not have been far from Albertus' mind. In

---

[20] H. Anzulewicz, "2. Metaphysics and Its Relation to Theology in Albert's Thought," in F. J. Romero Carrasquillo, D. Twetten, B. Tremblay, T. Noone, and H. Anzulewicz, "Albert the Great on Metaphysics" (pp. 541–94), in I. M. Resnick (ed.), *A Companion to Albert the Great* (Leiden, 2013), pp. 553–61 at pp. 557–8; cf. *Super Ethica* X).

[21] H. Anzulewicz, "2. Metaphysics," p. 561; cf. *Summa de mir. scient. dei.* 1, q. 4, Ed. Colon. 34/1, 15, ll. 55–62.

[22] M. Olszewski, "The Nature of Theology According to Albert the Great," in I. M. Resnick (ed.), *A Companion to Albert the Great* (Leiden, 2013), pp. 69–104 at p. 89, cf. *ST* I. 3.3.1–3, Ed. Colon. 34/1, 13.

[23] See Olszewski, "Nature of Theology," p. 96; Cf. *ST* I. 6, Ed. Colon. 34/1, 23, lns. 77–90.

[24] M. J. Tracey, "The Moral Thought of Albert the Great," in I. M Resnick (ed.), *A Companion to Albert the Great* (Leiden, 2013), pp. 347–80 at p. 378.

[25] See Olszewski, "Nature of Theology," p. 92; cf. *ST* I. 4.1.1, Ed. Colon. 34/1, 16.

his analysis of *Metaph.* Λ. 8, it will be remembered, Albertus emphasizes the role of religion-founding myths in prompting people to correct and proper action and in persuading the "vulgar multitude." In the *Summa*, Albertus zeroes in on one particular action to be prompted and aimed at by theological devices, i.e., the enjoyment of ultimate truth, and bestows upon that action the status of the highest goal achievable. Indeed, the nature and end of theology so far surpass those of philosophy, as far as Albertus is concerned, that it is in fact absurd in his view to entertain the possibility that theology, or its methodology and devices, would be used as preparatory stages for attaining philosophical knowledge. If anything, Albertus would say, it should be the other way around. It is theology that provides us with the highest degree of certainty, and so the poetic devices characterizing it cannot be conceived of as being in the service of philosophy: furthermore, it is *dangerous* for philosophy to use such devices *since it* cannot reach theological certainty.[26]

Rather than leading us toward philosophical inquiry and thereby to truth, through theology we directly engage with the highest truth actively and directly, in Albertus' view. Through the metaphors and parables used in Scripture, for instance, we gain access to truths in a way over and beyond the standard operation of our intellect (i.e., in philosophical or theoretical activity), comparably to a bat becoming accustomed to seeing the sunlight.[27] Here we may return to Aristotle's statement concerning the affinity between poetry and philosophy, and to Albertus' interpretation of it. Even though in his commentary on *Met.* A. 2 Albertus thinks Aristotle views poetry as providing a way of philosophizing and as constructing philosophy by getting one to wonder at a certain subject, he also reserves a special and radically different role for the poetic devices used by (Christian) theology, which he announces in his other writings (but which he also hints at already in his comment on *Met.* Λ. 8). That role consists of enabling one to apprehend ultimate truths directly, and in that way to maintain the wonder that vanishes once philosophical inquiry arrives at a satisfactory answer. As Anzulewicz puts it, for Albertus "even if philosophy begins in wonder, it ends in knowledge, so that only the theologian as such marvels (*miratur*)."[28]

---

[26] Ibid., pp. 92–3; cf. *ST* I. 4.2.1–5, Ed. Colon. 34/1, 17; I. 4.2 ad 1–4, Ed. Colon. 34/1, 18.

[27] Ibid., p. 92; cf. *ST* I. 4.1.1, Ed. Colon. 34/1, 16–17.

[28] Anzulewicz, "2. Metaphysics," p. 558; cf. *Super Ethica* X. 16.927c, Ed. Colon. 14/2, 774, ll. 73–9. Anzulewicz also refers the reader to Aristotle's *Met.* A. 2, 982b17–21 and to Albertus' commentary on that text in *Met.* I. 2.6 (and a related discussion in I. 2.10).

This makes for quite a significant deviation from the Maimonidean view. Though, following Maimonides, Albertus recognizes the usefulness Aristotle attributes to poetry and mythology for generating wonder and thereby initiating philosophical inquiry, he is unwilling to take Maimonides' next step – he refuses to view *all* traditional aspects of all religion, including the parables and practices found in the Bible, as functioning or as useful in the same way. Theological poetry, for Albertus, is privileged, since it is a part of theology, which in itself is a privileged science, and which cannot in any way serve the theoretical sciences subordinate to it in rank. By arguing so, Albertus quite likely intends to bypass objections concerning the possible arbitrariness of religious content (why should it matter which parable one chooses, or indeed which religion, as long as it is useful toward attaining philosophical knowledge, assuming this is what religion is essentially directed toward and necessary for?) The cost of Albertus' move, on the other hand, is that it compromises his reliance on Aristotle. Albertus' own account of theological poetry (and of theology) falls outside the scope of anything Aristotle wishes to say concerning poetry (and religion). Moreover, since Albertus himself *accepts* Aristotle's account of poetry with regard to some forms of it (say, Greek mythology), but supplants it with another view with regard to its specifically Christian form, his overall view of the phenomenon seems to lack unity.

5.3 Conclusion

Maimonides, like Aristotle, views traditional religion (including the traditional aspects of the Torah, such as its parables and commandments) as useful for social stability through persuading the multitude and for prescribing correct and proper behavior. He also thinks of it, again along Aristotelian lines, as useful, indeed as necessary, for motivating people to inquire philosophically into the nature of the divine and ultimately to arrive at philosophical knowledge. Albertus agrees with Aristotle and Maimonides on the uses of religion for persuasion and behavior guidance, but disagrees on the last use. Though he agrees that poetry and myths are generally useful for motivating people toward philosophical inquiry, he also thinks that the type of poetry used in theology has a purpose higher than anything achievable through philosophy. Unlike Aristotle (as well as Strabo) and Maimonides, then, Albertus thinks that religion and its devices and methods are not directed toward philosophical knowledge, but rather toward the active and direct enjoyment of ultimate truth through theological, rather than theoretical, contemplation.

The difference between Maimonides and Albertus reflects a long-standing controversy concerning the relation between scientific or philosophical knowledge and the knowledge aimed at by religion. I have argued that Maimonides, by viewing "divine knowledge" – the highest type of knowledge obtainable by human beings – as knowledge of (Aristotelian) metaphysics, and by regarding religion and its various devices as directed toward that knowledge, is more faithfully Aristotelian than Albertus. But it is important to note one basic point at which Maimonides' and Albertus' views converge and stand in opposition to other prominent conceptions of religion. Whether religion aims at philosophical knowledge, as Maimonides thinks, or at some knowledge surpassing philosophy, as Albertus thinks, both would agree that it necessarily does so using certain devices, such as parables, metaphors, anthropomorphisms, and similar kinds of representation of divinity, and that these are not intended to and ought not to be interpreted literally. The employment by religion of depictions of divinity that are literally false, but are nevertheless useful for arriving at knowledge, is noticed by both Maimonides and Albertus and is, as we have seen, traceable back to Aristotle, who has influenced them both.

CHAPTER 6

Conclusion

6.1 Aristotle's View of Religion

Aristotle seems to be in two minds about traditional religion. On the one hand, he invariably criticizes the anthropomorphism underlying the traditional depictions of divinity. On the other hand, he deems traditional religion, depicting the gods in just this way, crucially important for political organization, and wishes to retain it even in his ideal *polis*, in an unrevised form. One might be tempted to ascribe this apparent tension to an internal conflict between Aristotle's rationalism and his personal belief in the truth of the religion of his day. However, Aristotle's conservatism about traditional religion is perfectly compatible with his uncompromising rejection of the truth of its main tenets and ideas, such as the existence of gods who are interested in, and meddle with, human affairs. This compatibility is made possible by Aristotle's recognition of the crucial sociopolitical role traditional religion plays in human society. In this book I have provided an account of this role, based on an examination of various texts.

In order to discover the role Aristotle ascribes to traditional religion, one must first appreciate the scope of his criticism of it. In particular, I have argued that Aristotle, in various places in his extant *corpus*, rejects the existence of anthropomorphic gods out of hand. No gods exist, he thinks, who resemble us either in external appearance or in intentional action. Consequently, we should not rely on divine providence or intervention. Traditional religion, insofar as it introduces such ideas, is useless as a source of information or knowledge. In his lost work, *De philosophia*, furthermore, Aristotle exposed the considerable weakness of a major piece of reasoning leading to the belief in divine providence, i.e., the "teleological argument." Importantly, however, Aristotle's view of traditional religion as unable to provide reliable information still leaves room for that religion to have some additional benefits.

In the *Politics*, Aristotle commits himself to a stronger view. There, he argues that traditional religion, along with its institutions and the people maintaining them, are in fact necessary for any correctly organized political constitution to exist as such. Though he acknowledges the use of religion for persuading the "masses" to obey the law, as well as (possibly) for moral habituation, a thorough examination makes it clear that what he thinks traditional religion is *necessary* for is its role in enabling citizens to attain the top human good – the active knowing or understanding of the true gods of Aristotelian metaphysics – which any *polis* is by nature aimed toward. Religion does this by exposing citizens to traditional, anthropomorphic depictions of gods, which generate in them a sense of "wonder" at gods. The citizens consequently turn to a philosophical inquiry into the gods whereby, if everything proceeds in the right way, they would eventually gain knowledge of ultimate metaphysical truth and be able to practice "first philosophy" – the science dealing with, and deserving to be dealt with by, the true gods, primarily the first unmoved mover of the heavenly bodies and spheres. By doing so, the citizens in question would in fact approximate the very condition of the beings they have inquired into, since true gods, in Aristotle's system, consist just in active knowing or understanding of their own nature.

It is therefore not simply knowing the nature of gods that is relevant to one's attaining ultimate philosophical knowledge, and hence the top human good. It is also relevant to come to know the relation between one's own nature as a human being and the nature of the divine, in order to understand in what way one might approximate the activity of the true gods. Traditional religion is useful for both of the inquiries just mentioned, namely the inquiry into the nature of the divine and the inquiry into the relation between that nature and the nature of human beings. Its anthropomorphic, fictional gods are easy for humans, who are naturally hardwired to take pleasure in what is akin to themselves, to identify with, and thus have the propensity to get people interested in, and to motivate them to inquire into, divinity in general. And it is appropriate for these gods to initiate such an inquiry, since they also share in the same definition of god (namely "immortal/eternal living thing") as the true gods, the full knowledge of whose nature the inquiry in question ultimately yields.

Part of the reason why the traditional gods are easy to identify with is that they lead social and political lives and engage in moral action. They are subject, in other words, to limitations that human beings are closely familiar with, but of which true gods are completely free. Upon recognizing these human aspects of the traditional gods, one may use them as a point of reference for learning about the connections between humans and the true gods, who otherwise seem to be worlds apart. As we can infer from the relevant discussions in the *MM* and the *EE*, this process, which importantly also requires friendship, would advance from the awareness and perception of one's own character traits to an apprehension of one's true nature as an intellectual being, whose best activity is comparable to the activity of which god consists eternally. The role of traditional religion in enabling this full realization of human nature, through which human flourishing in its most complete form is attained, constitutes its necessary political role, as we have conjectured based on the *Politics*.

This account of the role of traditional religion in Aristotle shows clearly that his endorsement of traditional religion does not stem from a belief in the truth of its content, but rather from a belief in its usefulness for *obtaining* truth. It is true that Aristotle thinks some religious myths, for instance those transmitted by the wise sages of old, are *based* on philosophical truths. But this only goes to show that philosophers prior to Aristotle's day recognized the role of traditional religion in *getting* people to philosophize. It does not mean that religion *itself* (or its content) should be compared to philosophy (or philosophical truth). In *Metaphysics* Λ. 8, 1074a38–b14, Aristotle tells us that, to some extent, the idea that there are unmoved movers of the heavenly bodies, which deserve to be called gods, is prefigured by traditional religion, though it is veiled by its mythological and anthropomorphic modes of expression.[1] Similarly, in *De motu animalium*, Aristotle famously traces his own idea of the prime mover to Homer's description of Zeus as immovable ("You will not drag Zeus, the highest of all, from the heavens down to earth, not even if you wear yourselves out: hang on [to your chains], all you gods and all you goddesses": IV. 699b32–700a6; cf. *Il.* VIII. 20–22). These anthropomorphic depictions of divinity, constituting the content of traditional religion, are entirely false, and they are equally and often used to depict stories that are *not* grounded in anything true, in which case, as we have seen in Chapter 4, they may still be shown to have been introduced for some other purpose. However, they are useful, indeed crucial, for motivating us to study philosophy, whereby we may gain true knowledge of the gods, and it is this fact that is represented by

---

[1] See Sections 1.1, 2.3, and 4.1. For *criticisms* of the doctrines underlying (or appearing to underlie) certain myths about the gods cf. e.g., *Met.* Λ. 6, 1071b26–9; N. 4, 1091a29-b8. In addition, Aristotle draws on myths about the gods in explaining facts unrelated to his views on divinity, cf. e.g., *De motu* III, 699a27–ff., *NE* VIII. 10, 1160b24–7, *Pol.* II. 9, 1269b27–31. See Chapter 4 for further discussion.

the attribution of such modes of expression to ancient people who have already attained philosophical wisdom.

In conclusion, we may allude to the document that concludes Aristotle's life, as has been traditionally done by scholars writing on Aristotle's view of religion.[2] Aristotle is said to have concluded his will with the following requests:

> And [my executors shall] set up my mother's [statue] as a votive gift to Demeter at Nemea or wherever else would seem appropriate. And wherever they may bury [me], there they shall also place Pythias' bones, just as she dictated. And they shall also set up as votive gifts, upon Nicanor's safe return, as I have prayed for him to have, four-cubits long stone statues for Zeus Sōtēr and Athena Sōteira in Stagira. (*Diog. Laert.* V. 16)

We need not interpret these words as "showing between the lines" an "adherence to a religious faith which [Aristotle] never renounced,"[3] or as a "proof of his fidelity to the gods of his ancestors."[4] Given the account expounded in this book, it makes all the sense in the world for Aristotle to adhere to the practices of traditional religion and to aspire for them to be preserved even after he is gone. Aristotle does not believe, of course, that Demeter, Zeus Sōtēr, or Athena Sōteira exist, let alone that they would care whether or not statues are erected in their honor. He does believe, however, that erecting such statues for these gods, and maintaining traditional religion in general, would have a positive impact on society: it would advance the chances of the *polis* to flourish, by motivating its citizens to inquire philosophically into the nature of divinity. Rather than contrasting with his theory, then, Aristotle's will demonstrates it.

Aristotle's own adherence to the practices and conventions of the same traditional religion whose content he pronounces false, albeit useful, is also useful for understanding his influence on subsequent religious thinkers, as we have discussed it in Chapter 5. When someone like Maimonides accepts Aristotle's critical outlook on anthropomorphism in religion and applies it to his own religion, while still adhering to Judaism and remaining the highest authority on its Law and commandments, some of which explicitly involve an appeal to just such an anthropomorphic content, he is doing nothing sinister. For, in doing so, Maimonides again follows Aristotle, according to whose theory traditional religion should be

---

[2] Bodéüs, *Living Immortals*, p. 220; Rowland, *Religion of Aristotle*, pp. 198–9.
[3] Rowland, *Religion of Aristotle*, p. 199.
[4] Bodéüs, *Living Immortals*, p. 220.

practiced and maintained even – indeed especially – by those who recognize the falsity of its overt content, since it is these people who would be in a position to appreciate the usefulness of religion remaining intact, along with its traditional aspects.

6.2 Traditional Religion and Contemplation in Aristotle's Ideal *Polis*

As we have pointed out at the outset, correctly interpreting Aristotle's view of traditional religion and its necessary political function also has ramifications for understanding the rest of his views, and for resolving certain controversies surrounding them. Of particular importance for our understanding of Aristotle's projects in the *Politics*, *Ethics*, and *Metaphysics* is the question concerning the status of theoretical contemplation in Aristotle's envisaged ideal *polis*, and the extent to which it is pursued as a goal by the constitution of that *polis*. The emphasis put on theoretical contemplation as the highest goal of human life in both the *Ethics* and the *Metaphysics* would seem to suggest that that activity should be actively pursued and furthered as much as possible in ideal political circumstances. Nevertheless, scholars have also pointed out reasons for thinking that the "*polis* of our prayers" of *Politics* VII–VIII would not include that activity as one of its goals. As we shall see, perhaps unexpectedly, Aristotle's view of traditional religion holds the potential for solving this long-standing controversy in Aristotle scholarship.

In *Nicomachean Ethics* X, Aristotle commits himself to the view that human flourishing or happiness (*eudaimonia*) consists primarily of a life of theoretical contemplation based on knowledge or understanding of the first principles of being as such (7, 1177a16–18; 8, 1178b7–23). He retains his view that a life dominated by theoretical activity is preferable over a life of political virtue in *Politics* VII–VIII (e.g., VII. 3, 1325b14–30). In these books, in which Aristotle sketches his envisaged best *polis*, he also states that the *eudaimonia* of individual human beings is the same as that of the *polis* (VII. 2, 1324a5–8; 3, 1325b30–2).

The conclusion to draw based on this evidence is that, as J. M. Cooper puts it, "[Aristotle's] account of how the people of a *polis* that is completely self-sufficient for human life will live must include the provision that among them will be a group of citizens who live the contemplative life (and so are provided an education that will enable them to live that way)."[5] This is *a fortiori* true of the *ideal polis* of *Politics* VII–VIII. Since this *polis*

5 J. M. Cooper, "Political Community and the Highest Good," in *Being, Nature and Life in Aristotle* (eds. J. G. Lennox and R. Bolton) (Cambridge, 2010), pp. 212–64 at p. 241 n. 40.

is the one most capable of affording its citizens the opportunity of leading the most flourishing lives possible for them, that is, it must be designed so as to enable its citizens, or those of them who are capable of it, to live as flourishingly as humanly possible, by leading a life dominated by theoretical activity.

And yet, the place of theoretical contemplation in Aristotle's ideal *polis* is far from clear, and is indeed a subject of much controversy. Aristotle thinks the education in such a city must be the same for all citizens (VIII. 1, 1337a21–3), and he provides a detailed account of what the educational program in question would look like. But there is no explicit reference in that description to any expectations of that educational program to contain, culminate in, or lead to theoretical activity. It is true that Aristotle puts the emphasis on "philosophy" as being particularly required for leisure, in which the happiness of the citizens lies (VII. 15, 1334a22–34). But it is not clear that by "philosophy" in this context he has in mind theoretical activity *à la NE* X. 7–8, rather than a broader set of leisurely activities. Indeed, the discussion in the rest of the *Politics* (book VIII) focuses on just such a non-theoretical leisurely activity – music.

This fact has led some to believe that Aristotle views theoretical contemplation, the activity most constitutive of *eudaimonia* according to his theory, as "politically inaccessible," and that he posits music as an "analogue of and substitute for" theoretical activity in his ideal *polis.*[6] Against this view, it has been suggested that in Aristotle's ideal *polis*, theoretical activity, though practicable only by a select few, will necessarily be recognized by the entire citizenry as the highest goal of the city as a whole, and "will be continuous with, and to some extent will emerge naturally from, musical pursuits."[7]

Part of the difficulty in explaining the place of contemplation in Aristotle's account of the city based on his discussion of music education in *Politics* VIII is that this discussion is confined to the ideal *polis*. Aristotle says that in that city music should be used for amusement, the development of

---

[6] D. J. Depew, "Politics, Music and Education in Aristotle's Best State," *A Companion to Aristotle's Politics*, edited by D. Keyt and F. Miller (London, 1991), pp. 346–80 at p. 347 and n. 2. DePew in his paper argues against this position, which he attributes to the following: F. Solmsen, "Leisure and Play in Aristotle's Ideal State," *Rheinisches Museum* 107 (1964), pp. 193–220, repr. in Solmsen, *Kleine Schriften* II (Hildesheim, 1968), pp. 1–28; C. Lord, "Politics and Philosophy in Aristotle's *Politics*," *Hermes* 106 (1978), pp. 336–57, and *Education and Culture in the Political Thought of Aristotle* (Ithaca, 1982); P. A. Vander Waerdt, "Kingship and Philosophy in Aristotle's Best Regime," *Phronesis* 30 (1985), pp. 249–73. See also Kraut (2002), pp. 201–2.

[7] Depew, "Politics, Music, Education," p. 347.

moral virtue, leisurely pursuits, practical wisdom (*phronēsis*), and *katharsis* (VIII. 5, 1339b11–15; 3, 1337b27–32; 7, 1341b36–40). But it is not clear which of these uses, if any, he considers a necessary function of music in *every* naturally existing *polis*. Thus, we cannot expect any of these uses of music to determine the main goal of natural *poleis*, and whether or not that goal consists of or includes theoretical activity. And, unless we show that the main goal of the ideal city is unique in kind (not just in degree of success), we cannot expect music to determine the main objective of the *ideal polis* either. But if some other phenomenon were necessary in order for *any polis* to reach its natural end (e.g., by enabling theoretical activity in it), then that *would* help to determine the main aim of any natural *polis*, including the ideal one (e.g., as consisting of or including theoretical activity).

And, in fact, according to Aristotle's view of religion as we have unpacked it thus far, traditional religion constitutes a political phenomenon that *does* count as a necessary part of any natural *polis* and whose necessary role *does* help to determine the status of theoretical activity as the top goal aimed at directly by the *polis*. Since Aristotle views traditional religion as a necessary and natural part of any *polis*, and does so *on the basis of* the role of traditional religion in enabling theoretical activity, he must maintain that this type of activity is necessarily promoted directly by any (naturally and correctly constituted) *polis*. Hence, even if certain social and cultural phenomena, such as music, are to function in Aristotle's best *polis* as ways of approximating theoretical activity by those citizens who would be incapable of engaging in such an activity, as some scholars have suggested,[8] this datum cannot successfully be used to argue that that *polis* would not directly pursue theoretical contemplation in its own right, as part of its main objective. Indeed, since, as our account of Aristotle's view of traditional religion has shown, theoretical contemplation *is* sought after by Aristotle's best *polis* (in fact, by any correctly organized *polis*), and since Aristotle views the life dominated by such an activity as the highest and most choice-worthy one for human beings, Aristotle must think that theoretical contemplation amounts to the *top* political goal.

---

[8] See p. 172, n. 6.

Bibliography

Annas, J., "Aristotle's *Politics*: A Symposium: Aristotle on Human Nature and Political Virtue," *Review of Metaphysics* 49.4 (1996), pp. 731–53.

Anzulewicz, H., "2. Metaphysics and Its Relation to Theology in Albert's Thought," in F. J. Romero Carrasquillo, D. Twetten, B. Tremblay, T. Noone, and H. Anzulewicz, "Albert the Great on Metaphysics" (541–94), in I. M. Resnick (ed.), *A Companion to Albert the Great* (Leiden, 2013), pp. 553–61.

Arnim, H. von, "Die Entstehung der Gotteslehre des Aristoteles," *SB. Akad. W. Wien*, 212.5 (1931), pp. 3–80; repr. as "Die Entwicklung der Aristotelischen Gotteslehre," in F. P. Hager (ed.), *Metaphysik und Theologie des Aristoteles* (Darmstadt, 1969), pp. 1–74.

Baldner, S., "III. Eternity and the Prime Mover in Albert's *Physica* 7–8," in D. Twetten, S. Baldner, and S. C. Snyder, "Albert's Physics" in I. M. Resnick (ed.), *A Companion to Albert the Great* (Leiden, 2013), pp. 173–220 at pp. 204–8.

Barnes, J. (ed.), *The Complete Works of Aristotle: The Revised Oxford Translation* (Princeton, 1984).

   "Property in Aristotle's *Topics*," *Archiv für Geschichte der Philosophie* 52 (2009), pp. 136–55.

Beere, J., "Thinking Thinking Thinking: On God's Self-Thinking in Aristotle's," (2010), pp. 1–31. Available at https://ancient-philosophy.hu-berlin.de/en/ancient-philosophy/hpold/fac/jonathanbeere

Benor, E. Z., "Meaning of Reference in Maimonides' Negative Theology," *The Harvard Theological Review* 88 (1995), pp. 339–60.

Berman, L. V., "Maimonides, the Disciple of Alfarabi," *I.Q.S.* 4 (1974), pp. 154–78.

Blass, F., "Aristotelisches," *Rheinisches Museum* 30 (1875), pp. 481–505.

Blum, W., *Höhlengleichnisse: Thema mit Variationen* (Bielefeld, 2004).

Blyth, D., "Heavenly Soul in Aristotle," *Apeiron* 48.4 (2015), pp. 427–65.

   "The Role of Aristotle's *Metaphysics* 12.9," *Methexis* 28 (2016), pp. 76–92.

Bodéüs, R., *Aristotle and the Theology of the Living Immortals*, trans. J. E. Garrett (Albany, 2000).

   The Political Dimensions of Aristotle's Ethics, trans. J. E. Garrett (Albany, 1993).

Bonitz, H., *Observationes Criticae in Aristotelis Libros Metaphysicos* (Berlin, 1842).
  Observationes Criticae in Aristotelis quae feruntur Magna Moralia et Ethica Eudemia (Berlin, 1844).
Bos, A. P., *Cosmic and Meta-Cosmic Theology in Aristotle's Lost Dialogues* (Leiden, 2003).
Boys-Stones, G., "Introduction," in *The History of Western Philosophy of Religion* v. 1, ed. G. Oppy and N. Trakakis (Oxon, 2014), pp. 1–22.
Bremmer, J. N., *Greek Religion* (Cambridge, 1999).
Broadie, S., "Aristotelian Piety," *Phronesis* 48.1 (2003), pp. 54–70.
  "Aristotle," in *The History of Western Philosophy of Religion* v. 1, ed. G. Oppy and N. Trakakis (Durham, 2009), pp. 79–92.
Brunschwig, J., "*Metaphysics* Λ. 9: A Short Lived Thought-Experiment?" in M. Frede and D. Charles (eds.), *Aristotle's Metaphysics Lambda* (Oxford, 1997), pp. 275–306.
Burnet, J. (ed. and comm.), *The Ethics of Aristotle* (London, 1900).
Burnyeat, M. F., "Aristotle on Learning to Be Good," in *Essays on Aristotle's Ethics*, ed. A. O. Rorty (Berkeley, 1980), pp. 69–92.
  A Map of Metaphysics Zeta (Pittsburgh, 2001).
  "Platonism and Mathematics: A Prelude to Discussion," in A. Graeser (ed.), *Mathematics and Metaphysics in Aristotle* (Berne, 1987), pp. 213–41.
  "Plato on Why Mathematics Is Good for the Soul," *Proceedings – British Academy* 103 (Oxford, 2000), pp. 1–82.
Bywater, I., "Aristotle's Dialogue on Philosophy," *Journal of Philology* 7.13 (1876), pp. 64–87.
Calhoun, G. M., "Zeus the Father in Homer," *Transactions and Proceedings of the American Philological Association* 66 (1935), pp. 1–17.
Caston, V., "Aristotle's Two Intellects: A Modest Proposal," *Phronesis* 44.3 (1999), 199–227.
Cherniss, H., *Aristotle's Criticism of Plato and the Academy* (Baltimore, 1944).
Chroust, A. H., "Eudemus or on the Soul: A Lost Dialogue of Aristotle on the Immortality of the Soul," *Mnemosyne* (1966), pp. 17–30.
  "Aristotle's *on Philosophy*," *Laval Théologique et Philosophique* 29 (1973), pp. 19–22.
  "Aristotle's *Protrepticus* versus Aristotle's *On Philosophy*: A Controversy Over the Nature of Dreams," *Theta-Pi* (1974), pp. 169–78.
Chuska, J., *Aristotle's Best Regime: A Reading of Aristotle's Politics VII. 1–10* (Lanham, 2000).
Cooper, J. M., "Friendship and the Good in Aristotle," in *Reason and Emotion* (Princeton, 1998), pp. 336–56.
  "The *Magna Moralia* and Aristotle's Moral Philosophy," in *Reason and Emotion* (Princeton, 1998), pp. 195–211.
  "Political Community and the Highest Good," in J. G. Lennox and R. Bolton (eds.), *Being, Nature and Life in Aristotle* (Cambridge, 2010), pp. 212–64.
Crisp, R. (trans. and ed.), *Aristotle: Nicomachean Ethics* (Cambridge, 2000).

Cunningham, J. V., *Woe or Wonder: The Emotional Effect of Shakespearian Tragedy* (Denver, 1960).

De Graff, T. B., "Plato in Cicero," *Classical Philology* 35.2 (1940), pp. 143–53.

DeFilippo, J., "Aristotle's Identification of the Prime Mover as God," *The Classical Quarterly* 44.2 (1994), pp. 393–409.

DePew, D. J., "Politics, Music and Education in Aristotle's Best State," in D. Keyt and F. D. Miller (eds.), *A Companion to Aristotle's* Politics (London, 1991), pp. 346–80.

Dirlmeier, F., *Aristoteles Nikomachische Ethik* (Berlin, 1999).

Dumoulin, B., *Recherches sur le premier Aristote* (Eudème, de la Philosophie, Protreptique) (Paris, 1981).

Effe, B., *Studien zur Kosmologie und Theologie der Aristotelischen Schrift* "Über die Philosophie" (Munich, 1970).

Elders, L., *Aristotle's Theology* (Assen, 1972).

Feibleman, J. K., "Aristotle's Religion," in H. Cairns (ed.), *The Two-Story World* (New York, 1966), pp. 126–34.

Flashar, H., "Aristoteles, *Über die Philosophie*," in A. Bierl, A. Schmitt, and A. Willie (eds.), *Antike Literatur in neuer Deutung* (Munich/Leipzig, 2004), pp. 257–73.

Flashar, H. and Grumach, E. (ed.), *Aristoteles Werke* Bd. 20, 1: *Fragmente I* (Berlin, 2004).

Friedländer, M. (trans. and comm.), *The Guide of the Perplexed of Maimonides* (London, 1885).

Gartner, C. A., *Aristotle's Eudemian Account of Friendship* (PhD Dissertation, Princeton University, 2011).

Geiger, R., "Aristoteles über Politik und Religion," in S. Herzbeg and R. Geiger (eds.), *Philosophie, Politik und Religion* (Berlin, 2013).

George, M. I., "The Wonder of the Poet; the Wonder of the Philosopher," *Proceedings of the American Catholic Philosophical Association* 65 (1961), 191–202.

Gildenhard, I., "Of Cicero's Plato: fictions, Forms, foundations," in M. Schofield (ed.), *Plato, Aristotle and Pythagoreanism in the First Century BC: New Directions for Philosophy* (Cambridge, 2013), pp. 225–75.

Guthrie, S. E., *Faces in the Clouds* (Oxford, 1993).

Guthrie, W. K. C. (trans.), *Aristotle* on the Heavens (*Loeb Classical Library*) (Cambridge, 1939).

"The Development of Aristotle's Theology," *The Classical Quarterly* 27 (1933), pp. 162–71.

Hahm, D. E., "The Fifth Element in Aristotle's *De Philosophia*: A Critical Examination," *Journal of Hellenic Studies* 102 (1982), pp. 60–74.

Hankinson, R. J., *Cause and Explanation in Ancient Greek Thought* (New York, 1998).

Hansen, W., *Handbook of Classical Mythology* (Santa Barbara, 2004).

Hard, R., *The Routledge Handbook of Greek Mythology* (London, 2004).

Hasselhoff, G. K., "Zur Maimonidesrezeption in der christlich-lateinischen Literatur" in L. Muehlethaler (ed.), *Höre die Wahrheit, wer sie auch spricht: Stationen des Werkes von Moses Maimonides vom islamischen Spanien bis ins moderne Berlin* (Göttingen, 2014), pp. 64–9.

Hitz, Z., "Aristotle on Self-Knowledge and Friendship," *Philosopher's Imprint* 11 (2011), pp. 1–28.

Hollerich, M. J., "Myth and History in Eusebius's '*De Vita Constantini*': '*Vit. Const.* 1.12' in Its Contemporary Setting," *The Harvard Theological Review* 82 (1989), pp. 421–45.

Hutchinson, D. S. and Johnson, M. R., *Protrepticus: A Reconstruction of Aristotle's Lost Dialogue*, <http://protrepticus.info/evidence.html>.

Irwin, T. (trans. and comm.), *Aristotle: Nicomachean Ethics* (Indianapolis, 1999).

Jaeger, W. J., *Aristotle: Fundamentals of the History of His Philosophy*, trans. R. Robinson (Oxford, 1948).

Joel, I., דלאלה אלחאירין (Jerusalem, 1930/1).

Johansen, T. K., "Myth and Logos in Aristotle," in R. Buxton (ed.), *From Myth to Reason? Studies in the Development of Greek Thought* (Oxford, 1999), pp. 279–94.

Johnson, M. R., *Aristotle on Teleology* (New York, 2005).

Kahn, C. H., "Aristotle and Altruism," *Mind* 90 (1981), pp. 20–40.

Kosman, A., "Aristotle on the Desirability of Friends," *Ancient Philosophy* 24 (2004), pp. 135–54.

Kraemer, H. J., "Grundfrgagen der Aristotelischen Theologie," *Theologie und Philosophie* 44 (1969), pp. 363–82 and 481–505.

Kraut, R., *Aristotle: Political Philosophy* (Oxford, 2002).

(trans. comm.), *Aristotle: Politics Books VII and VIII* (Oxford, 1997).

Lear, G. R., *Happy Lives and the Highest Good: An Essay on Aristotle's* Nicomachean Ethics (Princeton, 2004).

Lesher, J., "Xenophanes," in *The History of Western Philosophy of Religion* v. 1 ed. G. Oppy and N. Trakakis (Oxon, 2014), pp. 41–52.

Lindsay, T. K., "The 'God-Like Man' versus the 'Best Laws': Politics and Religion in Aristotle's *Politics*," *The Review of Politics* 53 (1991), 488–509.

Lord, C., *Education and Culture in the Political Thought of Aristotle* (Ithaca, 1982).

"Politics and Philosophy in Aristotle's Politics," *Hermes* 106 (1978), pp. 336–57.

Mayhew, R., "Aristotle on Prayer," *Rhizai. A Journal for Ancient Philosophy and Science* 2 (2007), pp. 295–309.

"Impiety and Political Unity: Aristotle, *Politics* 1262a25–32," *Classical Philology* 9.1 (1996), pp. 54–9.

McCabe, M. M., "Self-Perception in *Eudemian Ethics* VII. 12," in F. Leigh (ed.), *The Eudemian Ethics on the Voluntary, Friendship and Luck* (Leiden, 2012), pp. 43–76.

Meikle, S., "Aristotle on Money," *Phronesis* 39.1 (1994), pp. 26–44.

Melamed, A., "Aristotle's *Politics* in Medieval and Renaissance Jewish Philosophy (Hebrew)," *Pe'amim* 51 (1991), pp. 27–69.

Menn, S., *The Aim and the Argument of Aristotle's* Metaphysics (a work in progress: <www.philosophie.hu-berlin.de/institut/lehrbereiche/antike/mitarbeiter/menn/contents/>

"Aristotle's Theology," in C. Shields (ed.), *The Oxford Handbook of Aristotle* (Oxford, 2012), 422–64.

"On Dennis De Chene's *Physiologia*," *Perspectives on Science* 8.2 (2000), pp. 119–43.

Mikalson, J. D., *Greek Popular Religion in Greek Philosophy* (Oxford, 2010).

Honor Thy Gods: Popular Religion in Greek Tragedy (Chapel-Hill/London, 1991).

Miller, F. D., *Nature, Justice and Rights in Aristotle's* Politics (Oxford, 1995).

Moreau, J., *L'âme du monde de Platon aux Stoïciens* (Paris, 1939; repr. Hildesheim, 1965).

Nehamas, A., "Aristotelian *Philia*: Modern Friendship?," *Oxford Studies in Ancient Philosophy* 39 (2010), pp. 213–48.

Nelson, A., *Marx' Concept of Money* (New York, 1999).

Norman, R., "Aristotle's Philosopher-God," *Phronesis* 14 (1969), pp. 63–74.

Oehler, K., "Aristotle on Self-Knowledge," *Proceedings of the American Philosophical Society* 118 (1974), pp. 493–506.

Olszewski, M., "The Nature of Theology According to Albert the Great," in I. M. Resnick (ed.), *A Companion to Albert the Great* (Leiden, 2013), pp. 69–104.

Osborne, C., "Selves and Other Selves in Aristotle's *Eudemian Ethics* vii 12," *Ancient Philosophy* 23 (2009), pp. 349–71.

Owens, J., "The Relation of God to World in the *Metaphysics*," *Études sur la Métaphysique d'Aristote (Symposium Aristotelicum VI)* (Paris, 1979), pp. 207–22.

Palmer, J., "Aristotle on the Ancient Theologians," *Apeiron: A Journal for Ancient Philosophy and Science* 33.3 (2000), pp. 181–205.

Pangle, L. S., *Aristotle and the Philosophy of Friendship* (Cambridge, 2003).

Parker, R., "Gods Cruel and Kind: Tragic and Civic Theology" in C. Pelling (ed.), *Greek Tragedy and the Historian* (Oxford, 1997).

"The Origins of Pronoia: A Mystery," in *Apodosis: Essays Presented to Dr. W. W. Cruickshank to Mark His Eightieth Birthday* (London, 1992), pp. 84–94.

"Pleasing Thighs: Reciprocity in Greek Religion" in Gill C., Postlethwaite N., and Seaford R., *Reciprocity in Ancient Greece* (Oxford, 1998), pp. 105–25.

Pépin, J., *Théologie cosmique et théologie chrétienne* (Paris, 1964).

Pines. S. "Aristotle's *Politics* in Arabic Philosophy," *Israel Oriental Studies* 5 (1975), pp. 150–60.

(trans. and comm.), *Moses Maimonides The Guide of the Perplexed* (Chicago, 1963).

Polansky, R., *Aristotle's* De anima (Cambridge, 2007).

Price, B. B., "Interpreting Albert the Great on Astronomy," in I. M. Resnick (ed.), *A Companion to Albert the Great* (Leiden, 2013), pp. 397–436.

Price, H. S., *The Philosophies of Religion of Plato and Aristotle* (PhD Dissertation, Swansea University, 1962).

Putnam, H., "On Negative Theology," *Faith and Philosophy* 14 (1997), pp. 407–22.

Quinn, D., "*Me audiendi . . . stupentem*: The Restoration of Wonder in Boethius's *Consolation*," *University of Toronto Quarterly* 57 (1988), pp. 447–70.

Rackham H. (trans.), *Aristotle: Nicomachean Ethics* (Cambridge Mass., 1934).

Radovic, F., "Aristotle on Prevision through Dreams," *Ancient Philosophy* 36 (2016), pp. 383–407.

Reeve, C. D. C. (trans. ed. comm.), *Aristotle: Politics* (Indianapolis/Cambridge, 1998).

Rorty, A. O., "The Place of Contemplation in Aristotle's *Nicomachean Ethics*," *Mind* 87 (1978), pp. 343–58.

Ross, W. D., *Aristotle's* Metaphysics: *A Revised Text with Introduction and Commentary. Volume II* (Oxford, 1924).

    Aristotle's Physics (Oxford, 1936).

    (trans.), *Nicomachean Ethics* in J. Barnes (ed.), *The Complete Works of Aristotle* (Princeton, 1991).

Rowland, J. B., *The Religion of Aristotle* (PhD Dissertation, Temple University, 1953).

Salkever, S., "Whose Prayer? The Best Regime of Book 7 and the Lessons of Aristotle's *Politics*," *Political Theory* 35.1 (2007), pp. 29–46.

Sedley, D., "Cicero and the *Timaeus*," in M. Schofield (ed.), *Plato, Aristotle and Pythagoreanism in the First Century BC: New Directions for Philosophy* (Cambridge, 2013), pp. 187–205.

    "Philosophy, the Forms, and the Art of Ruling," in G. R. F. Ferrari (ed.), *The Cambridge Companion to Plato's* Republic (Cambridge, 2007), pp. 256–283.

Segev, M., "The Teleological Significance of Dreaming in Aristotle," *Oxford Studies in Ancient Philosophy* 43 (2012), pp. 107–41.

Sharples, R. W., "Aristotelian Theology after Aristotle," in D. Frede and A. Laks (eds.), *Traditions of Theology: Studies in Hellenistic Theology, Its Background and Its Aftermath* (Leiden, 2002), pp. 1–40.

Slomkowski, S., *Aristotle's* Topics (Leiden, 1997).

Smith, W., *A Dictionary of Greek and Roman Biography and Mythology* (London, 1880).

Solmsen, F., "Leisure and Play in Aristotle's Ideal State," *Rheinisches Museum* 107 (1964), pp. 193–220, repr. in Solmsen, *Kleine Schriften* II (Hildesheim, 1968), pp. 1–28.

Sorabji, R., *Self* (Chicago, 2006).

Sourvinou-Inwood, C., "Tragedy and Religion: Constructs and Readings," in C. B. R. Pelling (ed.), *Greek Tragedy and the Historian* (Oxford, 1997).

Stern-Gillet, S., *Aristotle's Philosophy of Friendship* (Albany, 1995).

Struck, P. T., *Divination and Human Nature* (Princeton, 2016).

Tracey, M. J., "The Moral Thought of Albert the Great," in I. M. Resnick (ed.), *A Companion to Albert the Great* (Leiden, 2013), pp. 347–79.

Van der Eijk, P., "Divine Movement and Human Nature in *Eudemian Ethics* 8, 2," *Hermes* 117 (1989), pp. 24–42.

Vander Waerdt, P. A., "Kingship and Philosophy in Aristotle's Best Regime," *Phronesis* 30 (1985), pp. 249–73.

Verdenius, W. J., "Traditional and Personal Elements in Aristotle's Religion," *Phronesis* 5.1 (1960), pp. 56–70.

Walker, M. D., "Contemplation and Self-Awareness in the *Nicomachean Ethics*," *Rhizai* VII (2010), pp. 221–38.

Whiting, J., "The Pleasure of Thinking Together: Prolegomenon to a Complete Reading of *EE* VII. 12," in F. Leigh (ed.), *The* Eudemian Ethics *on the Voluntary, Friendship and Luck* (Leiden, 2012), pp. 77–154.

Winthrop, D., "Aristotle's *Politics*, Book I: A Reconsideration," *Perspectives on Political Science* 37 (2008), 189–99.

Wolfson, H. A., "The Problem of the Souls of the Spheres from the Byzantine Commentaries on Aristotle," *Dumbarton Oaks Papers* 16 (1962), pp. 65–93.

Zeller, E., *Die Philosophie der Griechen in ihrer geschichtlichen Entwicklung* (Leipzig, 1921).

Index Locorum

General Index

For EU product safety concerns, contact us at Calle de José Abascal, 56–1°, 28003 Madrid, Spain or eugpsr@cambridge.org.

www.ingramcontent.com/pod-product-compliance
Ingram Content Group UK Ltd.
Pitfield, Milton Keynes, MK11 3LW, UK
UKHW020351140625
459647UK00020B/2404